CULTURE after the HURRICANES

CULTURE
after the
HURRICANES

Rhetoric and Reinvention on the Gulf Coast

Edited by M. B. Hackler

UNIVERSITY PRESS OF MISSISSIPPI / JACKSON

www.upress.state.ms.us

The University Press of Mississippi is a member of
the Association of American University Presses.

Copyright © 2010 by University Press of Mississippi
All rights reserved
Manufactured in the United States of America

First printing 2010

∞

Library of Congress Cataloging-in-Publication Data

Culture after the hurricanes : rhetoric and reinvention on the Gulf Coast /
edited by M. B. Hackler.
p. cm.
Includes bibliographical references and index.
ISBN 978-1-60473-490-4 (cloth : alk. paper) — ISBN 978-1-60473-491-1 (ebook)
1. Cultural industries—Louisiana. 2. Cultural industries—Gulf States. 3. Hurricane Katrina, 2005—Social aspects. 4. Hurricane Rita, 2005—Social aspects. I. Hackler, M. B.
HD9999.C9473U63 2010
306.0976—dc22   2010007043

British Library Cataloging-in-Publication Data available

CONTENTS

ACKNOWLEDGMENTS
- vii -

INTRODUCTION
"Louisiana's New Oil"
Planning for Culture on the New Gulf Coast
M. B. HACKLER
- 3 -

CHAPTER 1
Civic Culture and the Politics of Planning for Neighborhoods and Housing in Post-Katrina New Orleans
ADELAIDE H. VILLMOARE AND PETER G. STILLMAN
- 17 -

CHAPTER 2
New Orleans Shotgun
A Historic Cultural Geography
JAY D. EDWARDS
- 44 -

CHAPTER 3
Soul Food
Katrina and the Culinary Arts
BENJAMIN MORRIS
- 91 -

CHAPTER 4
Making Groceries
Food, Neighborhood Markets, and Neighborhood Recovery in Post-Katrina New Orleans
JEFFREY SCHWARTZ
- 107 -

CONTENTS

CHAPTER 5
Losing Ground
The Cultural Politics of Cultural Landscapes in Plaquemines Parish
W. D. WILKERSON
- 139 -

CHAPTER 6
Hurricane Rita and the New Normal
Modified Communication and New Traditions in Calcasieu and Cameron Parishes
KEAGAN LEJEUNE
- 166 -

CONTRIBUTORS
- 187 -

INDEX
- 189 -

ACKNOWLEDGMENTS

This collection would not have been possible without the time, advice, and expertise of a number of people. I am indebted to Marcia Gaudet and John Laudun for their instruction and support during my time at the University of Louisiana at Lafayette. Craig Gill has been instrumental in bringing this project to fruition, and I am deeply grateful for his kind and generous stewardship. Christine DeVine has proved an invaluable friend and mentor in this, as in all things. Finally, I thank my parents, Jerry and Darlene Hackler, for their patience and enthusiasm, each at just the right moments.

CULTURE after the HURRICANES

Introduction

"LOUISIANA'S NEW OIL"
Planning for Culture on the New Gulf Coast

M. B. HACKLER

Several years after the devastating Gulf Coast storms of 2005, Hurricanes Katrina and Rita have left a discursive legacy that may prove more pervasive and longer lasting than their imprint of mud and water on the communities they ravaged. Indeed, for stakeholders along the Gulf Coast, navigating the books, articles, reports, and declarations may prove as disorienting and overwhelming as navigating the bureaucracies of rebuilding. Journalists, academics, pundits, and planners recognized in the early days of the disaster an event of historic proportions, as evidenced by the sheer volume of their output on the subject to date. Their responses run the ideological gamut, drawing from the events beginning with Katrina's 29 August 2005 landfall stories of survival and resilience, of bureaucratic collapse, of cronyism and political infighting, and of tremendous gaps in wealth and enfranchisement. The books, articles, blogs, and editorials that have come out of the hurricanes and their aftermath respond to sometimes drastically different visions of highly contested histories. In many of these documents—from the first personal narratives rushed to press in the storms' wake to the analyses of race relations and government response that followed—the events of August and September 2005 are revealed as the culmination of powerful historical forces operating not only on the Gulf Coast but across the United States and even abroad.

There is now little doubt that the destructive force of Katrina and Rita cannot be entirely explained by the failure of levees and the relentless tug of winds and storm surge on Gulf Coast communities. As geographer Cindi Katz has noted, "Katrina churned through historical geographies of extraordinary multiculturalism but extreme racial segregation, of amazing environmental wealth exploited rapaciously, of mythic significance in the American and even global imaginary whose celebrations masked the enduring legacies of poverty and discrimination that they fed off and opposed" (2008: 16). Katz's characterization of the social conditions of the Gulf Coast at the time of the hurricanes' landfall has become common. What remains very much in debate, however, are sometimes strikingly different articulations of what has been lost in the wake of the storms and how it might be—indeed, *if* it might be—regained, rebuilt, or reconstituted. As is clear from even the most cursory review of the documents born out of the storms' immediate aftermath, what was lost includes far more than the bricks and mortar of houses, businesses, and public facilities.

The Gulf Coast is home to some of the most distinctive U.S. regional cultures, and perhaps more than any other American city, New Orleans holds a privileged place in the national imagination. If not quite as celebrated, the communities stretching east of New Orleans through Mississippi and Alabama and west to southeast Texas are no less diverse and culturally rich, containing as they do a mélange of Native Americans, African Americans, Creoles, Cajuns, Isleños with roots in the Canary Islands, and the descendants of Italian, Irish, English, Croatian, and German immigrants and other transplants to the region's port cities and coastal towns. The unique cultural constructions and performances that grew out of their several centuries of contact—from New Orleans's urban Mardi Gras to the *courir* of southwest Louisiana's Cajun Prairie, from the Asian-inspired paintings of Mississippian Walter Anderson to the ubiquitous blue dog of Louisiana's George Rodrigue—have been the subject of more than a few documentary films, coffee table books, and scholarly treatises. Critical and popular interest combined with a well-developed tourist industry to connect this region with people from around the globe. Thus, when the first articles after the hurricanes appeared, asking, in the phrasing of a classic jazz tune, "Do You Know What It Means to Miss New Orleans?" a surprising number of readers answered in the affirmative.

This collection concerns that loss. More than that, however, it concerns the ways in which the culture of the affected region has been described, quantified, and understood by a wide variety of stakeholders, from community activists to elected officials, artists to policy wonks. It interrogates the process of cultural planning in the region by analyzing the language employed in cultural discourse and examining the implications for those who call the Gulf Coast and its cultures home. By focusing on a particular cultural form or genre that has been the subject of considerable public discourse in the wake of the hurricanes, the authors navigate between rhetoric and the lived experience of culture. Much has changed for the people of the Gulf Coast since Katrina made landfall, and much more stands to change as governments, national and international nonprofit organizations, churches, and community groups determine how and even where life will go on. This collection helps elucidate some of the ways in which this process occurs as well as the understandings of culture that underlie that process.

Taken together, all that has been said and done to re-create, revitalize, or reinvent the cultural life of Gulf Coast communities post-Katrina constitutes a discourse of cultural policy. Although commonly understood as the sole province of governments and official bodies, the definition of cultural policy may be extended to include all ideas, beliefs, schemes, and other assertions that influence the experience of culture in a particular place at a particular time. The broadening of this definition benefits cultural analysis in several ways. First, it recognizes that just as individual cultures are complex and cultural systems diffuse, so too are the forces operating on them. While such a recognition complicates the easy assignment of cause and effect favored by some traditional cultural policy researchers, it opens the door for more nuanced, culturally specific models to enter into the field. Furthermore, by identifying cultural policy, with Toby Miller and George Yúdice, as "a synergistic complex of government programs, media representations, and market lures" (2002: 14), we move it beyond the confines of individual localities and into the global arena in which many of its most influential practitioners—international nongovernmental organizations, the United Nations Educational, Scientific, and Cultural Organization, cultural consulting firms—conduct business. Finally, this more comprehensive definition allows for the possibility of resistance by individuals and groups unsatisfied with accounts that utilize and affirm a top-down, authority-oriented approach to cultural policy studies and that fail to take into account fundamental differences in how culture and policy operate. For Miller and Yúdice, the pairing of culture and policy produces conflict between what is essentially organic on the one hand and bureaucratic on the other. They explain that through the exercise of a broad and diverse set of cultural policies, "governments, trade unions, colleges, social movements, community groups, foundations and businesses aid, fund, control, promote, teach and evaluate creative persons; in fact, they often decide and implement the very criteria that make possible the use of the word 'creative'" (1). If we accept the claim that "over time, a policy construct acquires a normative quality in that it embodies a belief or preference about how things should be" (Cherbo and Wyszomirski 2000b: 9) and recognize that cultural policies wield significant power in organizing the experience of culture, then the sheer volume of cultural policy discourse regarding the posthurricane Gulf Coast demands that careful attention be paid to the role of policy in shaping the region's (re)emerging culture.

A brief history of cultural policy studies aids in understanding the policy landscape into which Katrina entered. The cultural policy statements born out of the hurricane experience are as much the results of historical, cultural, and political forces as are the storms' toll in lives and property. This history of cultural policy studies benefits from research focused more narrowly on the arts. While I do not suggest that the terms *culture* and *the arts* are interchangeable—each has its own complex history as well as myriad contemporary connotations—many scholars in the field of policy studies have found cultural policy statements most easily discernible in their application to visual and performing arts activity. As a result, much of the current research available in the field imagines cultural policy as arts policy. While this idea may appear too reductive in assessing the cultural life of a region after a disaster, the research nevertheless proves instructive.

Although the history of discourse on the value of culture stretches at least back to antiquity, the foundations of cultural policy as a field of inquiry were laid in the years following the end of World War II. In the wake of the dismantling of Western empire, newly independent nations and their former colonizers alike became interested in the ways in which cultural activity could be harnessed for national and international goals. The establishment of ministries of culture, cultural exchange programs, and arts councils was backed by the dominant Keynesian economic program, which supported heavy investments in social initiatives, and a pervading belief in the power of local cultural activities to shape citizens and combat the homogenizing threat posed by mass media. Culture was generally viewed at this time as a deserving charity that with a little help from the government and philanthropic foundations could play the democratic role of extending the high arts to those who might not otherwise have access to them. While the United States chose not to set up a cultural ministry as such, it participated in the global trend toward cultural support through a host of official bodies before establishing national endowments in both the arts and humanities in 1965.

For cultural administrators and arts and cultural advocates, the years following the birth of the National Endowment for the Arts (NEA) and National Endowment for the Humanities (NEH) are remembered as a golden age for national investment in culture in the United States. Although never totally without opposition, this period saw the doubling of the endowments' budgets and a dramatic increase in new cultural organizations

(Strom with Cook 2004: 513–14). This same period saw the emergence of "cultural policy studies" as a legitimate field through the formation of the Association of Cultural Economics and the Center for Urban Studies at the University of Akron (Miller and Yúdice 2002: 29). By the late 1980s, however, the cultural landscape began to change in ways that forced those working in the arts and culture to rethink the means through which they sought support for their work. Cultural policy researcher Elizabeth Strom describes this shift in terms of three challenges that emerged for cultural advocates. She explains that as cultural organizations founded in the 1960s and 1970s grew and institutionalized, they began to include on their staffs administrators more adept at public policy who broke with the less sophisticated approach of an earlier generation of administrators to "promote the sorts of claims most likely to win over reelection-minded, tax-averse politicians" (Strom with Cook 2004: 506). At the same time, those at the helms of cultural organizations became influenced by those in urban economic development who saw cultural forms and activity as potential magnets for increased investment. Finally, in the "culture wars" and beyond, those in the cultural sector increasingly found themselves the targets of fiscal and cultural conservatives who questioned the necessity of government support of the arts and culture. Together, these factors reinforced the idea in the cultural sector that "claims about the concrete, place-based benefits of public arts investment appear[ed] to be the most likely to win legislative support" (Strom with Cook 2004: 506).

The arguments that eventually won the most legislative support were those that most convincingly linked cultural activity with economic development goals. What may at first have seemed an unlikely partnership between culture and economics grew out of the same decade in which American arts funding seemed most unassailable. The year 1979 saw the publication of "the ur-text of cultural assistance" (Miller and Yúdice 2002: 14), C. D. Throsby and G. A. Withers's *The Economics of the Performing Arts*. Cultural administrators and researchers subsequently became increasingly interested in investigating this connection between cultural activities and the economy. This process reached a turning point in 1988 with the publication of John Myerscough's *The Economic Importance of the Arts in Britain* and the series of city-based studies that followed. Myerscough's project was simple: "to demonstrate that investment in the arts had a knock-on effect in stimulating economic activity generally, and urban regeneration particularly, in a period of deindustrialization" (McGuigan 2004: 94). For Myerscough and those who began to take up his ideas as justification for their support of the arts and culture, "public subsidy to the arts was not a luxury, a wealthy extravagance, a waste of taxpayers' money, but had an instrumental value beyond the arts themselves" (McGuigan 2004: 94). What followed was a sectorwide shift in discourse as cultural advocates abandoned their former strategy of emphasizing "the intangible, individual benefits of cultural participation" in favor of "instrumental arguments—those claiming that the arts are useful in achieving unrelated goals" (Strom with Cook 2004: 509). Miller and Yúdice describe this shift as the birth of a new "legitimizing narrative" for those in the arts, called for by the demise of the cultural certainties of the Cold War and the rise of neoliberalism at all levels of government (2002: 20). Jim McGuigan describes this formulation, in which "cultural policy has been rethought in such a way that it no longer requires a specifically cultural rationale," as "a manifestation of the perverse dominance of economic reason today: to put it bluntly, naked capitalism" (2004: 1).

In the past two decades, the turn toward economic justifications for government support of and intervention in culture has been buoyed by a host of studies by academics and cultural consulting firms. Typically framed by the assumption that those in power undervalue cultural activities, these research projects tend to follow a similar pattern. First, they seek to demonstrate that cultural activity operates as a valuable economic sphere that "constitute[s] a significant sector or industry" and "make[s] noteworthy contributions to the GNP, employment, and the tax base" (Cherbo and Wyszomirski 2000a: viii). Second, they assert that cultural advocates have begun to see the advantages of emphasizing the economic potential of the arts and cultural activities over other potential benefits (Cherbo and Wyszomirski 2000b: 8). Finally, adherents of this view claim that this sector remains largely untapped and when harnessed effectively will "contribute significantly to local and regional economies, fueling other sectors of the economy in unique ways" (DeNatale and Wassall 2008: 3). To achieve their objectives, the cultural advocates and policy researchers involved in this project have relied on frameworks for cultural analysis that, when examined closely, prove questionable. Adapting cultural analysis to the language of economic development can result in problematic conclusions, as in one study asserting that "ninety-six percent of the U.S. population is engaged in some aspect of the arts" (Cherbo and Wyszomirski 2000b: 6). Are we then to assume that the other 4 percent of the population lives without artistic or cultural activity altogether? Or is it simply too difficult to quantify all of those artistic forms that operate outside or on the periphery of "the economy"? While it is less problematic to consider some of the reports' other findings, such as the claim that "America's combined cultural industries . . . are 5.6% of GDP, generating $443.5 billion in revenues" (Cherbo and Wyszomirski 2000b: 6), these claims demand careful inquiry into what is and is not included in the definition of "cultural industries" and, more important, how that determination was made.

The concept of the "cultural" or "creative industries" has provided the framework for much of the research on the connection between culture and the economy, but like the related concept of the "cultural economy," the idea remains problematic. Both terms appear throughout the cultural planning discourse on the Gulf Coast and promise to shape cultural rebuilding efforts in the region. The term *the culture industry* first appeared in the title of Max Horkheimer and Theodor Adorno's midcentury essay criticizing the influence of the mass media in lowering cultural standards, but the "achievement of standardization and mass production," which the authors decried as "mass deception" (1993: 120), is entirely absent in the term's current usage.

McGuigan defines the creative industries as "a catch-all for the production and circulation of 'knowledge' generally that is driven by the post-industrial economy" (2004: 96). David Hesmondhaugh is a bit more specific, defining the cultural industries as "those institutions (mainly profit-making companies but also state organisations and non-profit organizations) that are most directly involved in the production of meaning"—that is, he explains, those "the primary aim of which is to communicate to an audience, to create texts" (2007: 12). Hesmondhaugh identifies broadcasting, the film industry, the content aspect of the Internet industry, the music industry, print and electronic publishing, advertising, and marketing as the most common economic enterprises covered in this definition (12) but recognizes that to truly delineate a "cultural" sector within the overall economy presents difficulties, as "commodities are always cultural, and cultural products are always commodities" (73). Proponents of the cultural industries/creative economy approach to cultural research and advocacy tend to ignore this issue, however, focusing instead on cultural goods and services and intellectual property. In economic terms, the focus on production makes sense, as it allows for more easy quantification of the sector's impact on the overall economy, but its ability to account for all of an area's cultural life is questionable.

Cultural economy possesses yet another meaning in contemporary discourse, however. For a growing number of academics, economists, and policy experts, the use of the term reflects a collapsing of boundaries between our traditional understandings of what constitute cultural and economic activities, respectively. The complexity of the interaction between culture and the economy has led to the realization that "the pursuit of prosperity is a hybrid process of aggregation and ordering that cannot be reduced to either of these terms, and, as such, requires the use of a unitary term such as cultural economy" (Amin and Thrift 2004: xii). At the core of this field of inquiry lie questions concerning the meaning of economic well-being and thus the pursuit of comfort, security, and even self-fulfillment. Advocates of the "cultural industries" model fail to address this last definition in the documents they produce, an understandable omission considering its orientation toward critical inquiry and not easily identifiable policy recommendations. This more complex area of research may, however, suggest ways forward in conducting a different kind of cultural policy research that bridges cultural and economic processes in a way that reflects our innate need to be more than purveyors and consumers of cultural products but rather to make meaning out of what it is that we do and experience.

By the time Katrina's storm surge pushed over coastal seawalls and overtopped urban levees, an entire cultural planning industry was in place, and its dominant model emphasized the economic and social benefits of a focus on cultural economies and creative industries. The timing of the introduction of this discourse into Louisiana was auspicious. Just one month prior to Katrina's landfall, the Office of the Lieutenant Governor's Department of Culture, Recreation, and Tourism and the Office of Cultural Development of the Louisiana Division of the Arts announced a "creative economy initiative" with the publication of an official cultural planning document, *Louisiana: Where Culture Means Business*. Prepared by the consultants at Mt. Auburn Associates, the document, in the words of Lieutenant Governor Mitch Landrieu, "defines and evaluates Louisiana's cultural economy" and "recommends strategic objectives and action for developing our arts and culture" (Mt. Auburn 2005: i). Landrieu's administration used this document to rehearse much of the language that would inform the public debate about arts and culture on the Gulf Coast immediately following the hurricanes. This report introduces, for example, the idea of the region's cultural life as an unexploited resource. Its value is described in economic terms, suggesting that Louisiana, a state "that has long relied on oil, gas, and timber to fuel its economy, . . . is now realizing that, in culture, it may have a new source of largely untapped economic energy" (4). The authors go on to argue that "if culture—abundant, renewable, and clean—is Louisiana's metaphorical new oil then it requires the industrial equivalent of the skilled workers, refineries, pipelines, and business entities to bring it to the global marketplace" (4). By linking cultural activities with the oil and natural gas industry, the writers may cast the language of cultural economy in distinctly local terms, but the underlying ideology remains intact. Just as countless similar documents provide assurances that the pairing of cultural life with the economy is natural and inevitable, the authors insist "that connection between a healthy culture and a healthy economy is now beginning to be made" in Louisiana (4).

In the weeks following the disaster, government bodies focused on cultural policy issues were convened in at the state and local levels in Louisiana. New Orleans mayor Ray Nagin established the Bring New Orleans Back Commission, one committee of which was devoted to cultural affairs, and Lieutenant Governor Landrieu established New Orleans Rebirth, sponsored by the Louisiana Department of Culture, Recreation, and Tourism. The reports eventually released by both bodies are structured by the dominant language of the cultural planning industry. Landrieu's commission, returning to the language of the cultural economy document, links regional economic recovery with the expansion of local cultural enterprise. It describes Katrina's devastation as an opportunity to capitalize on "the creative and cultural economy we now have a chance to truly develop" (*Louisiana Rebirth*: 1). While the report includes promises to address poverty, racism, and disparities in quality of life in the rebuilt city, its preoccupation with narrowly economic goals is unmistakable. The four-point plan it outlines begins with a pledge not to restore the neighborhoods, churches, and cultural venues crucial to the city's creative spirit but to "rebuild Louisiana to worldwide preeminence as a top tourist destination," while its second pledge is to "make Louisiana's Cultural Economy the engine of economic and social rebirth" (ii).

The cultural committee of the mayor's commission, consisting of artists and cultural advocates, adopts similar language in its assessment of the city's cultural situation, declaring that "culture is business in New Orleans" (Bring New Orleans Back Commission 2006: 12) and providing an impressive set of figures to support that claim. Out of a governmental expenditure of only two million dollars in 2003, the report claims, the city's cultural industries provided a return of upward of six hundred million dollars (10). Despite asserting that the "culture of New Orleans *is* its identity" (14) and that "the culture of the city is essential to its well-being—something the city will die without" (13), the report does not hesitate to fix a dollar amount for unique cultural traditions. The authors suggest that just as cultural benefits are quantifiable, so are cultural losses, with "financial losses for social aid and pleasure clubs, Mardi Gras Indian tribes, [and] second line companies . . . conservatively estimated at over $3 million" (9). Framed as a calculation of losses of cultural artifacts, a fiscal estimate such as this one is only practical. There can be no denying either that financial considerations play a role in even the most traditional cultural practice or that tradition bearers such as those who take part in Mardi Gras Indian tribes and second-line companies are often acutely aware of the financial demands of their groups. In this instance, however, contextualized within a larger report on losses to the city's economy, the writers seem to be suggesting that the three million dollars is a loss of potential tourist revenue rather than of meaningful and historic cultural materials. The assignment of an economic value to neighborhood cultural traditions may at first seem surprising, but on closer inspection, it simply provides evidence of the pervasiveness of the cultural economy paradigm in the discourse of cultural planning.

Reviewing these policy statements, cultural policy researcher Ruth Bereson argues, "It will come as no surprise to students of the language of 'policy-making' that debate about the physical rebuilding of New Orleans should have become intermingled with debate about how its own distinctive 'culture' might be reconstituted" (2006: 1). Bereson criticizes the trend toward justifying support of culture in economic terms and insists that cultural policymakers and advocates reexamine what she sees as a fundamentally flawed proposition. She argues that "the semantics of 'cultural policy-making' have at best only a marginal effect upon the ways cultures develop," with policy statements often amounting to "little more than an empty piety" (2), accusing cultural policymakers in the wake of Katrina of "willed ignorance of the nature of culture, and cultural renewal" (3). Bereson concludes that what in cultural policy statements "is being 'sold' as the future of New Orleans is no more than a cleverly veiled propagandist scam" (8).

While I agree with Bereson that the cultural policy statements that have come out of the hurricane experience present a very limited understanding of how culture operates and that such narrow thinking about culture can result in a range of negative unintended consequences, it is equally unassailable that proponents and critics of cultural planning often have the same goals. We need not question Landrieu's sincerity when he said that the "culture we seek to preserve in Louisiana is rooted in our people and our neighborhoods" or his earnestness that "our rich heritage and cultural advantages will serve as our guides to rebirth" (2005: 7, 10) to question his assertion that "art and the business of art and music and historic preservation are no different than the business of the port, or no different than the business of natural gas, or no different than the business of oil or tourism" (Rawls 2007). Questioning the validity of such an assertion does more than cast light on a problematic statement: it calls into question the underlying definition of *culture*.

At the center of debates about cultural investment, revitalization, and rebirth are conflicting understandings of what culture is, how it works, and what it is good for. At their core, cultural policy statements are always statements about what qualifies as culture and what does not. And for every cultural form that is included in a definition, many more are necessarily excluded. Culture, as Raymond Williams reminds us, "is one of the two or three most complicated words in the English language" (1976: 76), its denotative and connotative meanings a product of the interplay between their histories and contemporary circumstances. For Matthew Arnold, culture was restricted to what are now commonly referred to as the high arts. Arnold defined culture as "the study of perfection," of "sweetness and light" (2006: 2, 17) and argued that a strong cultural education promised to elevate a nation's moral standards. While Arnold's formulation is a product of a particular cultural moment—the late nineteenth century—his definition continues to resonate in contemporary culture through statements that conflate the notion of worthwhile culture with classical art forms. Writing just after World War II, T. S. Eliot took a more anthropological approach—and one more in line with the definition proposed by this collection—by identifying culture as "all the characteristic activities and interests of a people" (1949: 30). But theorizing about culture is not the sole province of poets and critics. In the days following Hurricane Katrina, famed musician and New Orleans native Wynton Marsalis posited that "culture is the metamorphosis of a community's personality into a way of life. It unites us and distinguishes us. It gives us confidence and provides the barometer of who we are. It provides solutions to problems of living in a specific time and place distilled through generations" (Landrieu 2005: 13). In connecting the concept of culture with the sense of group identity and lived experience of a people, Marsalis's definition is well suited to approaches taken in this volume but does not go quite far enough. For that, we can turn to the work of Raymond Williams, who argued that culture is essentially "ordinary," encompassing "common meanings, the product of a whole people" as well as "offered individual meanings, the product of a man's whole committed personal and social experience" (1989: 9). Williams's definition, though abstract, offers a broader understanding of culture that in its situation both *at* and *between* the individual and the community provides the space essential for meaningful inquiries into culture. Because culture is ordinary, Williams seems to suggest, it can be found everywhere. This notion seems particularly prescient in the wake of 2005's hurricanes. As communities struggle to rebuild and individuals struggle to make sense of what has happened and what may yet come, reminders of the culture that was and manifestations of the culture to come are likewise everywhere. For this reason, this collection's authors adopt Williams's definition of culture as their own. For the residents of the Gulf Coast, however, personal and community definitions will continue to evolve.

In countless articles after the storms, the people of the Gulf Coast have described the value of their cultures in terms that challenge the language of policy documents. They remind us that whereas cultural economy approaches emphasize products and services, culture as it is lived resists commodification if for no other reason than because it is constantly in motion. Asa Briggs notes that through its diverse history, the concept of culture "has retained within it the sense of process" (1992: 3). Michael White reveals an understanding of the centrality of process in his claim that New Orleans's culture is much like jazz, reflecting as it does "a way of life that's improvisational" (Gundersen 2006: 3D). This definition of culture does not place it outside economic forces but suggests that culture operates not only in the marketplace but also in economies of a different sort, in arenas of exchange within families and neighborhoods, between generations, and across both time and space.

People along the hurricanes' paths have their definitions of culture, of course, and they will also guide rebuilding efforts. In analyzing cultural policy statements in the wake of such a disaster, one of Williams's ideas seems especially poignant: "It is stupid and arrogant to suppose that any of these meanings can in any way be prescribed; they are made by living, made and remade, in ways we cannot know in advance" (1989: 9).

The chapters that follow take Williams's assertion as points of departure. Through careful attention to not only what has been said about Gulf Coast culture in the wake of the hurricanes but to the ways in which Gulf Coast culture is being made and remade by the people who live it, the authors here provide an interface between culture and cultural planning while taking to heart Andrei Codrescu's assertion that "culture is never wholly destroyed, but sometimes what remains is so small it calls for redefinition, transcription, or, god forbid, reinvention" (2008).

In chapter 1, Adelaide H. Villmoare and Peter G. Stillman examine the ongoing story of residents' return to the places they called home before 29 August 2005. The authors explore the complex set of forces that have created the patchwork city as it currently exists, where some neighborhoods have experienced almost total recovery while others continue to languish sparsely inhabited and disconnected from the rest of the city. Chapter 2 also focuses on housing in the posthurricane city, but Jay D. Edwards's research takes a historical look at what stands—and what stands to be lost—in many of New Orleans's flooded neighborhoods. Edwards's cultural geography of the city's ubiquitous shotgun houses poses a challenge to accepted histories and connects the city's identity with its architectural heritage.

Chapters 3 and 4 address another essential cultural concept and one very much entwined with the culture of New Orleans: its food. In chapter 3, Benjamin Morris uses the city's two most revered culinary components, its restaurants and its recipes, as a means of exploring how culinary culture has been harnessed to aid in recovery while the experience of recovery has affected culinary culture. In chapter 4, Jeffrey Schwartz uses a historical approach to analyze the role of neighborhood farmers' markets in the rebuilding city. He reveals not only a story of community development but also a legacy of food access whose repercussions continue to be felt.

Chapters 5 and 6 move outside of the city of New Orleans to examine cultural issues elsewhere in the Gulf Coast region. W. D. Wilkerson's analysis in chapter 5 focuses on the cultural implications of land loss in one of Louisiana's most environmentally fragile regions. By examining several decades of governmental activity on Plaquemines Parish's cultural landscapes, she discovers a strong connection between official cultural priorities and coastal residents' loss of homes, occupations, and ways of life. In chapter 6, Keagan LeJeune addresses the tremendous changes in lifestyle and communication Hurricane Rita brought to the people of southwest Louisiana. His research explores the cultural resilience of communities as revealed by their ability to renegotiate cultural circumstances without relinquishing the ability to make meaning on their own terms.

A small gesture in the wake of all that has come and will no doubt continue to come in the wake of the hurricanes, these chapters seek to engage cultural planning and policy discourse at its most elemental level, by calling into question what counts as culture and by suggesting some of the implications of that determination.

REFERENCES

Amin, Ash, and Nigel Thrift. 2004. Introduction to *The Blackwell Cultural Economy Reader*, ed. Ash Amin and Nigel Thrift, x–xxx. Malden, Mass.: Blackwell.

Arnold, Matthew. 2006. *Culture and Anarchy: An Essay in Political and Social Criticism*. 1869. McLean, Va.: IndyPublish.

Bereson, Ruth. 2006. "Fats Domino Is Missing: An Analysis of Arts and Cultural Policy Making in the Wake of Hurricane Katrina." Presentation to the Baldy Center for Law and Social Policy, University at Buffalo Law School, 3 May. http://www.law.buffalo.edu/baldycenter/pdfs/BeresonPaper06.pdf. Accessed 30 April 2006.

Briggs, Asa. 1992. "Culture." In *Folklore, Cultural Performances, and Popular Entertainments*, ed. Richard Bauman, 3–11. New York: Oxford University Press.

Bring New Orleans Back Commission. 2006. *Report of the Cultural Committee*. 10 January. http://www.aeaconsulting.com/site/bnob/BNOB%20EXECUTIVE%20SUMMARY%20 20060202.pdf. Accessed 3 March 2006.

Cherbo, Joni M., and Margaret Wyszomirski. 2000a. Introduction to *The Public Life of the Arts in America*, ed. Joni M. Cherbo and Margaret J. Wyszomirski, vii–x. New Brunswick: Rutgers University Press.

———. 2000b. "Mapping the Public Life of the Arts in America." In *The Public Life of the Arts in America*, ed. Joni M. Cherbo and Margaret J. Wyszomirski, 3–21. New Brunswick: Rutgers University Press.

Codrescu, Andrei. 2008. "Reinventing New Orleans (Again)." Keynote address, Cultures of Rebuilding in Post-Katrina New Orleans Conference, New Orleans, 6 November.

DeNatale, Douglas, and Gregory H. Wassall. 2008. "The Creative Economy: A New Definition" Study produced for the New England Foundation of the Arts. http://www.nefa.org/pubs/documents/CEReport_2007.000.pdf. Accessed 30 March 2008.

Eliot, T. S. 1949. *Notes towards the Definition of Culture*. New York: Harcourt, Brace.

Gundersen, Edna. 2006. "'So Much of My Life, Well, Drowned'": New Orleans' Music Culture Lost Far More Than Lives and Homes." *USA Today*, 4 May, final ed., 3D+

Hesmondhaugh, David. 2007. *The Culture Industries*. London: Sage.

Horkheimer, Max, and Theodor Adorno. 1993. "The Culture Industry: Enlightenment as Mass Deception." In *The Dialectic of Enlightenment*, 120–67. New York: Continuum.

Katz, Cindi. 2008. "Bad Elements: Katrina and the Scoured Landscape of Social Reproduction." *Gender, Place and Culture* 15.1 (February): 15–29.

Landrieu, Mitch. 2005. Speech given at the Louisiana Recovery and Rebuilding Conference presented by the American Institute of Architects, New Orleans, 10 November. http://lrrc.aia.org/Site Objects/files/Mitch_Landrieu.pdf. Accessed 15 January 2007.

Louisiana Rebirth: Restoring the Soul of America. 2005. Baton Rouge: Louisiana Department of Culture, Recreation and Tourism. http://www.crt.state.la.us/LouisianaRebirth/Plan/LouisianaRebirthplan.pdf. Accessed 2 November 2009.

McGuigan, Jim. 2004. *Rethinking Cultural Policy*. London: Open University Press.

Miller, Toby, and George Yúdice. 2002. *Cultural Policy*. London: Sage.

Mt. Auburn Associates. 2005. *Louisiana: Where Culture Means Business*. Baton Rouge: State of Louisiana, Office of the Lieutenant Governor, Department of Culture, Recreation and Tourism, Office of Cultural Development, Louisiana Division of the Arts, 31 July.

Myerscough, John, with Alec Bruce. *The Economic Importance of the Arts in Britain*. London: Policy Studies Institute, 1988.

Rawls, Alex. 2007. "BackTalk with Lieutenant-Governor Mitch Landrieu." *Offbeat Louisiana Music and Culture Magazine* 20.7 (July). www.offbeat.com. Accessed 3 August 2007.

Strom, Elizabeth, with Angela Cook. 2004. "Old Pictures in New Frames: Issue Definition and Federal Arts Policy." *Review of Policy Research* 21.4 (July): 505–22.

Throsby, C. D., and G. A. Withers, *The Economics of the Performing Arts*. New York: St. Martin's, 1979.

Williams, Raymond. 1976. *Keywords*. Glasgow: Fontana.

———. 1989. "Culture Is Ordinary." In *Resources of Hope: Culture, Democracy, Socialism*, 5–14. London: Verso.

CIVIC CULTURE AND THE POLITICS OF PLANNING FOR NEIGHBORHOODS AND HOUSING IN POST-KATRINA NEW ORLEANS

ADELAIDE H. VILLMOARE AND PETER G. STILLMAN

The United States is enamored of the culture of opportunity, usually cast as the chance for individuals to improve their economic lots in life. In this culture, individuals can always remake themselves. And in rare circumstances, cities can, too. While the opportunity to remake implies betterment, it can involve erasure of things people take to be central to their lives. When openly debated, the meanings of opportunity and the role of government in creating opportunities are not a given; they may be highly contentious because individuals and groups have differing, even conflicting, interests and visions about courses of action if not the meanings of opportunity.

To some observers, the human catastrophe following Hurricane Katrina forced a moment of "opportunity" to remake New Orleans. So much of the city had been damaged or destroyed that it was if not a blank slate, certainly a space where much reimagining and redoing of the city's infrastructure, neighborhoods, and housing could take place. Proposals for New Orleans ranged from Dennis Hastert's (2005) notorious comment that perhaps it should not be rebuilt at all to plans for a smaller footprint for the city (Meitrodt and Donze 2005) to more inclusive ideas for most neighborhoods to be largely reconstituted. But one person's opportunity may be another's catastrophe; one New Orleans Katrina survivor, for example, remarked, "This isn't an opportunity. It's a goddamned tragedy" (Klein 2007: 4).

Responding to the tragedy or opportunity, the many plans for the future New Orleans expressed distinct interests, values, and visions. Because a planning process frequently begins with a willingness to think outside the box or to reject the usual socioeconomic and cultural constraints, a plan often embodies the dreams and aspirations of those undertaking it; it may be an expression of hope, a statement of how the city can be not marginally but drastically improved. In this time of environmental concerns, for example, many plans proposed green ideas—open spaces, new types of housing, non-automobile-based transportation.

One plan, however, may negate others' aspirations. As two observers write, "But the vision of New Orleans' poorest neighborhoods being remade as mixed-income meccas, with tree-lined streets and bustling parks, has run smack up against another imperative of the post-Katrina era: building back low- income housing so that poor New Orleanians can return home and land jobs in the recovery economy" (Maggi and Filosa 2006). Eradicating the "blight" of public housing and building mixed-income housing runs against the "right of return," asserted in different forums and derived in part from the United Nations statement on displaced persons (Inniss 2007).[1] The earliest plan, Bring New Orleans Back (BNOB), drawn up by a group appointed by Mayor Ray Nagin in the weeks after Katrina, advocated more green spaces for the city, particularly in low-lying areas. Residents rejected the idea since those spaces would have eliminated their neighborhoods.[3] One door opens only to close another; opportunities create and erase.

Planning for a new New Orleans has suffered from many constraints that intensify this dynamic of creation and erasure and raise questions about government's contributions to this effort. The hurricane devastated the city and destroyed or severely damaged neighborhoods and the physical, economic, social, and governmental infrastructure. The city was and is poor, the tax base low, and the school system and criminal justice systems dysfunctional; residents struggle with day-to-day survival. Neither New Orleans nor Louisiana is noted for efficient or effective government, and since Katrina, the federal government has seemed to pay little constructive attention to the state or city. Some think that the George W. Bush White House was convinced that government cannot govern well and so did not try to make federal agencies competent (Wolfe 2006). Blunders by the Federal Emergency Management Agency (FEMA) during and after the storm are the federal government's best-known failures, but such failures continued after the storm. Another "deadly blow" was "Treasury Secretary [John W.] Snow's refusal to guarantee New Orleans municipal bonds, forcing Mayor Nagin to lay off 3,000 city employees" (Davis 2006). Mike Davis wrote that by April 2006, "saving New Orleans was no longer high on the Bush agenda," if it ever had been.

The stakes for rebuilding a post-Katrina New Orleans are high. The future of one of the most deeply rooted African American cities is at risk, as is the role of government in supporting its citizens in times of crisis. Indeed, the politics of planning for this city casts serious doubt on government's ability and willingness to play a major part in reconstructing New Orleans in any kind of equitable fashion. With white flight from the 1950s on, New Orleans became a black-majority city in the 1960s and began to experience population loss.[3] The city has long struggled with economic and political adversity but nevertheless has a history of vital neighborhoods across classes and deep connections of people to place.[4] Until Katrina, New Orleans was a vibrant African American community. And post-Katrina, residents' reactions and activism, rooted in this community, have enlivened democratic culture and civil society and tested their role and government's in the ways in which democracy works in the United States.

Contestation of visions enriched the civic culture of the city. The planning processes prompted energetic political engagement, especially around issues of neighborhoods and housing. Broad, impassioned political debate took place among those who lost the most as well as among those who thought they could profit the most in the rebuilding. The assemblies, actions, plans, and hopes of those participating brought people out to face one another in struggle over whose plans should prevail. Democratic engagement, even among the most marginalized, was notable as all kinds of different people entered civic space to have a role in rebuilding homes and communities.

Democracy in its grandest visions requires a participatory public sphere in all its dimensions, and even a minimal level of democracy requires a functioning, vocal, and organized public sphere. *Public* here encompasses both government and civil society and speaks to the relationships among government and residents. In a democratic public sphere, people across class, race, and other hierarchies are actively involved with government and with one another in determining visions, opportunities, and outcomes. Some visions may prevail, some may be modified, and others may fail to win support, but everyone's voice can be expressed and should be respected. Silencing or erasure—where people's voices are widely excluded from the development and implementation of plans—does not occur in a vibrant public sphere. Further, a lively and open public sphere means that major decisions about social investment and rebuilding are not left solely or primarily to the market, where inequalities continually reinforce themselves. Those without property or the ability to invest funds in redevelopment are just as much a part of a genuinely public planning process as the more privileged members of society. In a fully functioning democracy, the public sphere offers protections against erasure of visions, communities, and neighborhoods through open debate, consideration of policy alternatives, and adoption of broadly representative policies.

ADELAIDE H. VILLMOARE AND PETER G. STILLMAN

In post-Katrina New Orleans, government failures and rejections energized civil society. Intense community organization among Katrina survivors and nongovernmental organizations (NGOs) assured that their visions for their neighborhoods and homes have had a public airing and that they have been part of political action on the ground. Residents and NGOs have moved ahead with rebuilding, sometimes with governmental assistance, like the Road Home program,[5] sometimes independently of or in opposition to government.[6] Advocates of public housing determinedly acted through protest and litigation to resist its demolition. Continual pulling and hauling has occurred over visions of opportunity and realities of responses. Government actions and inactions roiled residents, who organized to start rebuilding and to resist making New Orleans anew when doing so meant erasure of their neighborhoods or homes. The failures of one segment of the public sphere, government, have spurred action in another, civil society.

While the civic culture of post-Katrina New Orleans has been greatly enriched, it has yet to produce the policy effects desired by many of those involved. Visions for housing have encountered other visions. And in some instances, government officials have directly thwarted goals for rebuilding. For example, federal and local public housing officials, including the city council, have decided to tear down the four major remaining public housing communities. Although New Orleanians have moved well beyond their initial shock from the devastation into action and sought a substantial role in rebuilding the city, the city, state, and federal governments have either failed to act on or have rejected many of the residents' visions.[7]

A democratic culture should but does not necessarily result in broad government responsiveness to the aspirations expressed by those actively involved. Democracy may work at one level but not at another. The civic culture may run up against government's limited resources, entrenched interest groups, bureaucracy, and lack of experience with an engaged citizenry. All of these factors have influenced the planning process in post-Katrina New Orleans and resulted in great disappointments for many of the participants.

INITIAL APPROACH: BRING NEW ORLEANS BACK

Speaking in Jackson Square about two weeks after Katrina, President Bush promised the reconstruction and improvement of New Orleans, proclaiming, "Throughout the area hit by the hurricane, we will do what it takes, we will stay as long as it takes, to help citizens rebuild their communities and their lives. And all who question the future of the Crescent City need to know there is no way to imagine America without New Orleans, and this great city will rise again" (2005). Shortly after Bush left, an outpouring of NGO money and private-sector volunteers began planning to rebuild New Orleans.[8] At the early stage of imagining what changes might result from the destruction, a report by the Rockefeller Foundation candidly stated, "Reconstructing such a city would mean accepting profound changes to its identity. . . . It would mean acknowledging that the new city would be a different place, with possibly fewer residents, a different economic base, perhaps a somewhat different sense of itself. At the same time, the reconstruction process held out the prospect of a better city—one that would be more open and collaborative, and that would extend more opportunities to its residents for self-determination" (2006: 3). Planners clearly sensed from the outset that New Orleans would be a different city and could be better.

Mayor Nagin moved quickly to begin planning. In September 2005, he formed BNOB, which bypassed the underfunded and understaffed City Planning Commission, the local body officially charged with city planning. Supported with donations and the pro bono work of private individuals and assisted by the American Planning Association and the Urban Land Institute, a real estate NGO, the commission presented the first official government plan after a few town hall meetings run by those two groups. The BNOB plan espoused the rhetoric of a better city: "In rebuilding New Orleans the goal must be more than recovery, it must be transformation—a reconstruction that takes the city of New Orleans to a new level" (BNOB Urban Planning Committee 2006c: 21). The commission's work was an "opportunity to create the best city New Orleans can be" (BNOB Urban Planning Committee 2006a: introduction), "the best city in the world" (BNOB Urban Planning Committee 2006b: 20). The vision was articulated with some detail by BNOB's Urban Planning Committee, chaired by local real estate developer Joseph Canizaro: "New Orleans will be a sustainable, environmentally safe, socially equitable community with a vibrant economy. Its neighborhoods will be planned with its citizens, and connect to jobs and the region. Each will preserve and celebrate its heritage of culture, landscape, and architecture" (BNOB Urban Planning Committee 2006c: 1). To attain these goals, the plan called for neighborhood planning that included citizen involvement, insisted that neighborhoods be 50 percent inhabited before infrastructure would be rebuilt, and looked to increase green spaces throughout the city. It drew up a wish list that included an extensive light rail system, better schools, parks and open spaces in every neighborhood, rapid residential rebuilding on higher ground, and a series of flood prevention and control measures, including improved levees. On the one hand, it articulated a vision for the city; on the other, it only perfunctorily included citizen participation in the process and supported erasure of parts of neighborhoods.[9]

Members of the BNOB's Urban Planning Committee acknowledged that certain low-lying areas should not be repopulated, that the city would have fewer poor people, and that green spaces could replace some previously populated areas.[10] Heavily flooded areas would face a four-month moratorium on building permits to see if enough residents had returned to create a viable neighborhood. The committee worried that the levees were not yet reconstructed, that the city's services remained fragile and its budget weak, and that another hurricane could easily destroy newly built houses, making New Orleans, its plans, and its planners look foolish, improvident, and imprudent.

The work of the BNOB Urban Planning Committee provoked sharp community reactions.[11] Although the BNOB process included some popular participation and called for citizen involvement in neighborhood planning, some people saw the committee's final plan as threatening the future of their neighborhoods and housing. Early in January 2006, the committee presented its proposals at a public meeting. A resident of Lakeview, a predominantly white, middle-class area near Lake Pontchartrain where the floodwaters topped ten feet deep, told the committee, "Our neighborhood is ready to come home. Don't get in our way and prevent us from doing that. Help us cut the red tape" (Burdeau 2006). A more personal response came from Harvey Bender, a resident of the Lower Ninth Ward, which is predominantly African American, relatively poor, and working class but has a homeownership rate of more than 50 percent and where the floodwaters ranged from a few inches to about eight feet deep. Bender told the head of the Urban Planning Committee, "I don't know you, but Mr. Canizaro, I hate you. You've been in the background scheming to take our land." Another resident, Carolyn Parker, insisted, "I don't think it's right that you take our properties. Over my dead body." Their reactions reflected the heat in the room, and police were asked to secure the microphones (Shulte 2006).[12] The Holy Cross Neighborhood Association, established before Katrina, stepped up to reject the plan to turn some of its neighborhood into green space and worked to establish the "right to rebuild" regardless of what percentage of a neighborhood's residents had returned (Institute for Southern Studies 2007: 22).

In envisioning a new New Orleans, the Urban Planning Committee produced a reasonably thought-out plan that nonetheless failed to take into account the values and interests of significant portions of New Orleans's population. The plan did not reckon with the willingness—indeed, eagerness—of those who wanted to return to their neighborhoods or with the suspicion of others that the new New Orleans of Canizaro and his committee was not to their liking and was probably a well-packaged front for plans that would dispossess many people of their property and eject them from their neighborhoods. Those who were suspicious of Canizaro's motives noted that when the plan specifically addressed the Lower Ninth Ward's development, it suggested that high-density housing be built on higher ground (the Holy Cross section of the Lower Ninth did not flood). So one likely result of the plan would be to facilitate development, enrich developers (among them Canizaro), and most likely gentrify a predominantly black, working-class, poor area. Bender and Parker were joined in their opposition to the committee's plan by some city council members, the New Orleans chapter of the National Association for the Advancement of Colored People, and Marc Morial, New Orleans's first African American mayor and current president of the National Urban League. Such strong and widespread community opposition led Nagin, who had appointed the commission but was up for reelection, to oppose BNOB's moratorium on rebuilding and its vision of a smaller New Orleans. Lacking further funds, BNOB slipped slowly and silently out of the realm of the politically possible.

The BNOB plan and the community's reaction to it set in motion a political dynamic that revealed shifting relationships among segments of the public sphere and between government and civil society. Nongovernmental actors pushed into a process where government lacked funds, political understanding, or the will to act in the interests of a wide range of New Orleans residents. And the failure of the BNOB plans meant that there was, in effect, no official guidance structure with the force of law to assist individuals in their decisions to return. As *New Orleans Times-Picayune* writer Gordon Russell commented almost a year after the storm, the lack of planning "has forced homeowners to make up their minds about what to do without any clear direction from the government" (2006). In other words, people were forced to make their private decisions about rebuilding in a realm absent the public guidance of government.

LAMBERT PLAN

One response to the BNOB's failure was that the city council hired Miami-based planning consultant Paul Lambert and Sheila Danzey of New Orleans to create a neighborhood planning project, doing so on 7 April 2006, less than three weeks after the final BNOB report was issued. Nagin had bypassed the city council and the City Planning Commission in appointing the BNOB commission, so when that plan fell flat, the council turned to a planning team that had worked for the council before Katrina.

Lambert and Danzey tried to respond to problems in the BNOB plan. They avoided the issue that had most publicly torpedoed the BNOB, the question of neighborhood viability; they worked with all flooded neighborhoods to have each neighborhood create its own plan. Lambert also tried to engage in more extensive citizen participation than the BNOB commission; more than eighty public meetings were held in New Orleans, and one each took place in Houston, Atlanta, and Baton Rouge, with about seventy-five hundred residents participating (Horne and Nee 2006a; *Lambert Plan* 2006: 12–13).

But the Lambert Plan too was mired in controversy from the start. Critics objected to Lambert's hiring on a no-bid contract (Warner 2006b; Bureau of Governmental Research 2006). And the Lambert Plan ultimately clashed with a requirement by the Louisiana Recovery Authority (LRA) that every parish's recovery plan include the entire parish (New Orleans and Orleans Parish are coterminous) to receive LRA money: The Lambert Plan included about forty-nine of the seventy-six official New Orleans neighborhoods, ignoring those areas with minimal or no flooding (Warner 2006b). And the consultants' attempt to involve more citizens met with mixed success. Lambert and Danzey picked local architects and planners and assigned them to neighborhoods; according to Jedidiah Horne and Brendan Nee, "Hiring decisions were made with little public input, and neighborhood boundaries used often did not line up with informal boundaries understood by active neighborhood associations, causing public skepticism from the start" (2006b: 7). The quality of the (many) architects and planners varied considerably, as did their receptiveness to local suggestions.

Conflicts continued. The mayor and city council were patently at odds over how to proceed. Disagreement about open bidding for planning contracts aggravated discord within government. The project drew "mixed reviews" from neighborhoods (Warner 2006d). Some communities were highly organized. For example, the Broadmoor Improvement Association, founded in 1930, had undertaken its own planning, in part because of the BNOB's proposal to make the neighborhood into green space, and energetically encouraged people and resources to return. Broadmoor's plan, developed independently of Lambert and with help from students from the Kennedy School of Government at Harvard, was not formally incorporated into the final Lambert Plan (Warner and Eggler 2006).

Residents and neighborhoods asserted their own visions of rebuilding. Through Lambert and Danzey, government worked with the neighborhoods most devastated by Katrina flooding, even though not all neighborhoods or residents were fully included in the process and even though several key neighborhoods were so vacant that they could muster only a few residents for a sustained process of deliberation. The Lambert Plan did reach out to evacuees in other cities to get their input. The participatory part of the planning process fed residents' expectations, since neighborhoods and old and new civic groups concentrated on drawing up plans. Civic culture was coming to life, people were speaking up, and government was facing demands to respond.

UNIFIED NEW ORLEANS PLAN

Shortly after Lambert started to work in April, Governor Kathleen Blanco and the LRA approached the Rockefeller Foundation to ask for planning funds for New Orleans; the foundation offered $3.5 million to assist in the planning process. Over the next few months, the offer was examined, and in late July, the mayor and the city council, along with Blanco and the LRA, agreed to a new planning structure, the United New Orleans Plan (UNOP), to be drafted by the newly created New Orleans Community Support Foundation. This foundation would incorporate the neighborhood Lambert plan reports but would have plans for all city neighborhoods, not only the ones that flooded, and would unify the local plans into a single, comprehensive, citywide plan to be submitted to the relevant New Orleans governmental bodies—the City Planning Commission, the mayor, and the city council—and then to the LRA. The Community Support Foundation obtained additional funding from other NGOs (Warner 2006a; Horne and Nee 2006b).

The UNOP enhanced resident and neighborhood groups' participation. Some Lambert planning groups continued to meet, and some neighborhood groups sought different experts for advice, choosing among a range of local and national planners and architects. Indeed, all previous planning attempts were to be incorporated into UNOP's unified plan. The UNOP divided the city into thirteen planning districts and organized meetings within those districts. Even in the Lower Ninth, where fewer than three hundred of the twenty thousand pre-Katrina residents had returned, the four public meetings garnered an average attendance of about one hundred, and each of the six stakeholders' meetings was attended by about thirty participants (UNOP

2007b: 23). A few citywide meetings were held to discuss the drafts of the entire plan. Thus, serious efforts at civic engagement in the planning process took place.

But the UNOP's scope and attempted inclusiveness raised problems because it was unclear exactly how all the ideas of many different planning bodies and community groups could be melded into one coherent scheme, and those at both the top and at the bottom of the process felt this uncertainty. Disagreements about Lambert's relation to the UNOP and Lambert supporters' concerns that UNOP would further slow the planning process permeated the city council. And community groups were unsure about what would happen to their ideas when they entered the "maze of public and private decision makers, all controlling a substantial piece of a so-called 'unified' planning process—but none with ultimate authority to make the vital but politically volatile decisions that lay ahead" (Warner 2006c). The uncertainty about inclusion became apparent at the end of the process, when the city council approved the UNOP plan without the input of the Broadmoor Improvement Association. At a meeting seven days later, association representatives insisted that their plans be included in the final UNOP framework sent to the LRA (Warner and Eggler 2006).

The final April 2007 citywide plan was an extensive document, with about 180 pages of text and more than 200 pages of appendixes. The UNOP attempted to bring together the work of many different agencies, groups, and neighborhood associations in a way that would be acceptable to both City Hall and Baton Rouge (UNOP 2007a). The overall "recovery framework" involved a series of "recovery projects," such as infrastructure and utilities, transportation, housing, and economic development.[13] But the framework was just that; it did not establish how projects were to be accomplished. Most important, money was a serious problem. Full implementation of the UNOP would cost $14 billion, and even a scaled-back version would total $1.1 billion, but there was no real sense of how to obtain such funding, except for $117 million immediately available in federal block grants funneled through the LRA. Allocating the scarce funds was also difficult, because the high-priority projects alone were likely to cost more than would be forthcoming from the state and federal governments (Krupa 2007; Warner 2007).[14]

As a result, many people saw the UNOP plan as a kind of wish list: if all the projects could be implemented as proposed and funded, the result would be an ideal city. Echoing BNOB's promise, the UNOP asserted that "all citizens, businesses and investors in our Great City have a right to a Safer, Smarter, Stronger City that enables a substantially higher quality of life, greater economic opportunity, and greater security against hurricanes than New Orleans had prior to Katrina" (2007a: 51–52). It was a statement of vision in which New Orleanians had shared. Most of the neighborhood plans, for example, emphasized the importance of flood protection, security, and schools, and many had imaginative proposals. The Lower Ninth Ward (UNOP 2007b), for example, focused on flood protection, a manned police substation, improved bus routes, and good schools; and it also proposed light rail transit, a tropical garden in abandoned or bought-out low-lying blocks, and the restoration of parks and playgrounds. Indeed, almost all of the district plans, taken as a whole, included a vision of a good city, including the most mundane and practical features (jobs, infrastructure, flood protection) along with those that addressed the quality of individual and neighborhood life.

But too many of those proposals were to be unfunded dreams. As Tom Farley lamented in a *Times-Picayune* op-ed piece, despite the rhetoric of reconstruction since Bush's promise, the funding had been so low that "we can forget about 'visionary' items, including bike paths, playgrounds and beautification." He closed with a rhetorical question: "In the long line of petitioners for the federal dollars, why should neighborhoods be dead last?" (2007: 5). For many residents, what started out as encouragement to dream large in rebuilding and envisioning a new, inclusive, and better city ended up thwarted by the lack of funding. Residents had taken part in civic discussion and imagining futures only to have their public dreams come up against government inaction. Two sides of the public arena were ultimately at odds. Government was either unresponsive or resistant to many, if not most, citizens' visions.

The civil society also was at odds with the government on the issue of the right of return. The UNOP tried to avoid one problem that had sunk BNOB by not suggesting that the city's footprint be shrunk and by insisting "that every citizen, regardless of current residence, has the right to return to New Orleans" (2007a: 51). But the UNOP failed to produce a policy that would make that right real. Moreover, when Mayor Nagin articulated his interpretation of the right of return, he expressed that right in neoliberal terms—as the right of individuals to do what they could as individuals, with little or no government support. Shortly after the outcry over BNOB, the mayor had advocated a laissez-faire approach and said that anyone could return and the market would decide which neighborhoods were viable. According to Steven Bingler, a UNOP architect, planner, and coordinator, the mayor's idea was that "the commitment is that individual decisions made by individual citizens will determine which neighborhoods come back and which neighborhoods don't come back—and if they do, how they come back" (Warner 2006c). The mayor professed satisfaction: "The market is reacting properly. ... If you get the information out there, the marketplace is going to make a good decision" (Russell 2006).

After saying that everyone could come back, the mayor soon warned those who might return to the Lower Ninth and New Orleans East that some neighborhoods in those areas would struggle to recover. After his reelection, he went further: "I've been saying this publicly, and people are starting to hear it: low-lying areas of New Orleans East, stay away from. . . . Move closer to the river" (Russell 2006). The mayor also threatened that the city was going to focus most of its rebuilding resources upriver of the Industrial Canal, not on the downriver Lower Ninth Ward and New Orleans East. In effect, therefore, the mayor as authority figure was saying both that people could come back (and even had a right to do so) and that it would be better if they did not (and that the city would not be investing in them, providing city services for them, or reintegrating their neighborhoods into the city as a whole).

The commitment to individual rights, individual decisions, and the market, however, diminishes governmental responsibilities and means that a right of return is not much more than an abstraction for those lacking personal resources.[15] The mayor's articulation of the UNOP with its individualistic, market approach states that people can choose to come back—but it will be at their own peril, subject to forces that they cannot control, and without the information they need to make informed decisions. As a member of the LRA who believed in the marketplace stated, "The market needs information. Otherwise the market won't work" (Russell 2006). Without government guidance about the government's planned actions, people's rights could not be intelligently exercised. This approach results in erasure of significant parts of the Lower Ninth Ward and New Orleans East not by overt words in a planning document but by a rhetoric of free choice that does not divulge necessary information.

PUBLIC HOUSING

The governmental response to UNOP, then, involved a more subtle and indirect erasure than did BNOB; planning groups' dreams would go unrealized for lack of government funds, and the right to return would remain abstract, dependent on individual resources. Alongside the UNOP, which stated its support for reopening public housing in the city, the Housing Authority of New Orleans (HANO), controlled by the federal Department of Housing and Urban Development (HUD) since well before Katrina, was planning to close all of the city's public housing.[16] While the closings spoke to the vision of a new New Orleans with mixed-use and mixed-income housing as a replacement, there was no widespread dedication to one-to-one replacement for the units of public housing and for the right of return of the poor, who, lacking significant economic resources, were likely the least able to exercise a right of return because they had few places to live.[17]

When Katrina struck, more than five thousand families were living in public housing, with a waiting list of more than eight thousand; perhaps three thousand units were vacant or uninhabitable, many slated for demolition (Levy 2005). During Katrina, most public housing units sustained some damage from flooding, although the sturdy brick buildings from the 1930s and 1940s remained structurally sound. Indeed, of the "big four" slated for demolition before Katrina—St. Bernard, C. J. Peete, B. W. Cooper, and Lafitte—C. J. Peete did not flood, and the water was only two or three feet deep around much of Lafitte. When tenants attempted to return to their apartments throughout New Orleans, only about one thousand units were made available, and HUD fenced and locked the four largest projects. In June 2006, HUD reiterated its plans to demolish them—about five thousand units in all (Saulny 2006). Tenant groups almost immediately organized in response. One large group was Survivors' Village, established on 3 June 2006 by residents of St. Bernard and other public housing as a tent city outside the St. Bernard complex. The tent city was both a symbol of many public housing residents' desire to return to New Orleans and a location where the displaced could live, meet, and organize.

Members of Survivors' Village and other former residents of public housing engaged in a number of public activities. On Martin Luther King Day 2007, the residents, in a deal with local and HANO police, had the fences opened so that they could go in and clean their apartments (Hamilton 2007). At the same time, some residents occupied the St. Bernard Community Center and refused to leave; two weeks later, a 2:30 A.M. visit from a SWAT team cleared them out, with two people arrested. A week later, some residents of C. J. Peete returned to their apartments, with a "generator on the fire escape" and some supplies and "without the government's help or permission" (Filosa 2007a). Survivors' Village and other organizations sprang up in response to HANO's refusal to open (or in some cases even allow residents into) their homes and its renewed threat to raze public housing. Public housing residents were trying to create an open, participatory organization and to act publicly to change the direction of the city and federal government. They were not going to be invisible in the remaking of housing in New Orleans.

Survivors' Village and those supporting that group had five central demands. They argued for a right of return, for no demolition of public housing, and for the reopening of all units that were open before Katrina. They also insisted that "safe, decent, and sanitary housing is a right, not a privilege" and that "residents have a right to social, political, and economic SELF-DETERMINATION" (*Survivors' Village* 2007). While aspects of these demands go deep into problems of public housing beyond New Orleans, some of them speak directly to the vision of a post-Katrina city. One is the right of return, presented as legal arguments based in international law as well as social justice. Displaced residents insisted that they be able to return to their hometown and to the places where some of them had lived for years, where they had made friendships and connections, and that they called home. And they advocated for places to live in New Orleans, especially in their old neighborhoods. The desire to return home and the lack of affordable rental units resulted in a "No Demolition" demand. Signs sprang up around public housing as the issue became very visible.

As HANO faced off with the residents at required public hearings, mistrust on both sides was evident. Residents gave numbers different from the official ones provided by HANO/HUD about the income distribution of the new units planned for construction and for currently available units (Justice for New Orleans 2007: nos. 1, 6).[18] Residents voiced suspicion of the developers, seeing them as unfairly profiting from redevelopment (Filosa 2007c). The hearings involved passionate residents and stone-faced HANO representatives, who listened without responding before producing written responses about a month later in which their position remained unchanged (Filosa 2007c). Despite the intense civic activities by residents of public housing and their supporters, HANO/HUD appeared unmovable and implacable.[19]

To some observers, the problem of post-Katrina public housing demanded compromise. Residents' groups had formed on their own and had considerable staying power (especially considering the difficulty in organizing dispersed residents who had no homes in New Orleans). They had solid reasons for their demands, even if they remained needlessly intransigent. But HANO/HUD officials hardly listened and worked at every turn against the lawsuit filed on behalf of public housing residents (*Anderson v. Jackson* 2008). The city council claimed that its agreement was necessary for demolition, but in December 2007, it unanimously voted to demolish. The only compromises the council extracted were that HUD needed to report periodically to the council and that "if practicable," HUD make available no more than three hundred interim housing units at Lafitte and St. Bernard (Filosa 2007b; Nagin 2007; Grahamad 2007). Nonetheless, protests continued: the Coalition against Demolition dedicated itself to continued action against the destruction of public housing, and other protesters built a tent city for the homeless across from City Hall (Justice for New Orleans 2007; *Homeless Camp*).

VISIONS, NEIGHBORHOOD, AND PUBLIC HOUSING

Both Lambert and UNOP emphasized that local groups in conjunction with professional planners and architects should come up with organized and coherent plans for the future of their areas. Central to this process were neighborhood rebuilding plans. The plans, which tended to run between about twenty-five and thirty-five pages, focused on what different neighborhood groups regarded as the most central for the rebuilding of their neighborhoods. The document for the Sixth Ward/Tremé/Lafitte Neighborhood was typical in many ways. It noted that the May–September 2006 "planning process consisted of significant research combined with multiple meetings in the Tremé neighborhood, with both small and large groups" as well as outreach meetings with displaced residents in Baton Rouge, Atlanta, and Houston and resident survey forms that identified needs and prioritized projects (Tremé/Lafitte Neighborhood 2006: 6). As its name suggests, the neighborhood included the Lafitte Housing Project, one of those slated for demolition.

The area's plan stated that although a "significant number of voices" wished little change, "a greater majority suggested that changes were needed" (Tremé/Lafitte Neighborhood 2006: 23). In light of the HANO/HUD decision to raze public housing, the neighborhood plan put forth a creative alternative. It addressed density reduction by decreasing the area's 900 units to approximately 550 by tearing down 668 units, building 290 new units (as townhouses with direct street access) on the site, and by adding other new housing within the neighborhood. The plan spelled out the utility, community and memory, and aesthetic reasons for this proposal: (1) although the buildings needed significant work, they were structurally salvageable and could be reconfigured internally; (2) the buildings had some historic meaning within the evolving Tremé neighborhood story; and (3) the buildings selected to remain created desirable spaces in relationship with the mature oak trees.[20] In addition, some demolition would provide open spaces for "active and passive recreation" as well as other community facilities. The plan for Lafitte was not conceived in the abstract but was tied into other elements of the neighborhood's plan, such as the redevelopment of a nearby closed Winn-Dixie supermarket area and other commercial and housing development. The planners insisted that their proposal was "not a compromise plan between the extremes of either total removal or total return to before-Katrina conditions" because they were trying to take into account modern rather than 1940s ideas regarding public housing and to "synergize" the current realities. In other words, the plan had been drafted with care and forethought. On this issue as on many others, the citizens of Tremé mobilized, met, canvassed, and prioritized using a variety of criteria. They were concerned about erasure of people, housing, and memory.

But the planners for Tremé lamented in a passive voice what may have hidden a foreboding: "During the planning process, we were not provided access to . . . HANO, who was considering what direction to take." Nonetheless, they concluded, "HANO is now planning the redevelopment of Lafitte; this report suggests that the full involvement of Tremé/Sixth Ward and Lafitte residents and community groups will be critical in achieving a successful plan" (Tremé/Lafitte Neighborhood 2006: 23). They hoped that HANO officials would communicate with neighborhood representatives because they had canvassed the neighborhood extensively and thought intensely about what the area needed. Their vision took into account all neighborhood residents, even if it did not fully satisfy all.

But HANO/HUD showed little concern for the extensive planning process, the thoughtfulness, and the public participation and activities undertaken by the citizens of Tremé.[21] HUD single-mindedly pushed its pre-Katrina plans to raze Lafitte. When the city council insisted that it have the final vote on Lafitte, that vote supported demolition, even though the council had voted to accept the Tremé plan as part of UNOP and knew the political backlash that would follow the vote to demolish.[22]

By January 2008, it was apparent that government was thoroughly disregarding the visions of the Tremé neighborhood and of the residents of public housing. All the civic involvement, protest, and litigation had not prevented HANO/HUD from acting on its own ideas, which had been developed before Katrina, ignored the changed housing market after Katrina, and disregarded post-Katrina proposals that ran counter to the determination to demolish public housing in New Orleans.

CONCLUSION: CIVIC CULTURE, DEMOCRACY, AND THE POLITICS OF PLANNING

The catastrophe of Katrina plunged New Orleans into a political world of planning and attempts at recovery. BNOB prompted activist responses by residents and evacuees who feared that the new New Orleans would erase their neighborhoods and homes. These reactions led the government to include many more voices in the later planning processes, as in the Lambert Plan. While speaking up certainly did not guarantee that residents' voices would be heard, the processes meant that many people became organized, watching and constructing their own visions for their neighborhoods. At the same time, individuals were acting on their own and with others in their neighborhoods to rebuild and come home and to prove to any commission that they lived in a viable neighborhood.

Enormous political energy was expended during the often contentious planning processes. In their Lambert Plan reports, neighborhoods such as Tremé detailed the extensive meetings, subcommittees, surveys, and interviews conducted to produce the plan and indicated areas in which disagreements remained ongoing. In other neighborhoods, such as Broadmoor, with long-established improvement associations, the activities have been just as extensive and if anything took place over longer periods of time. A dedicated civic culture surrounded the planning process and showed the willingness, ability, and seriousness of people working together to propose what was best for their neighborhoods.

Similarly, despite being excluded from their homes, residents of public housing complexes returned to New Orleans and organized to stand up for their rights and needs in the face of a rental housing crisis. They established tent cities near their apartments, engaged in protest, and supported legal challenges to their banning from their homes and to the plans to tear down the remaining public housing complexes. Many public housing residents showed by their actions that they wished to return; some argued that they had a right to return. Indeed both the BNOB and Mayor Nagin acknowledged that all who wished to return to New Orleans should be able to do so.

People came together to work on the future of their homes and neighborhoods and their place in the city. It may be, as Charles C. Mann of *Fortune Magazine* (2006) writes, that "New Orleans' best chance for recovery may lie in its reawakened sense of community, born of shared disaster—because government, it is now clear, will not act unless pushed hard." Community has certainly been shored up in some neighborhoods where people have returned or worked with NGOs on reconstruction projects. Community has also been furthered by government inaction and adverse action. But the civic action of residents, evacuees, and NGOs has brought few results for those involved.

Government often ignored the visions and rights claims of organized and active residents. HANO/HUD stuck to its pre-Katrina plans to raze public housing complexes, and the New Orleans City Council concurred, claiming only marginal oversight. Similarly, the mayor and city council ignored most of the well-thought-out and dedicated plans created by neighborhood associations and other planning groups (Office of Recovery Management 2007; Warner 2007).

Events in New Orleans after Katrina showed that people can build associations and organizations in the face of disaster and threats of erasure. Across class and race, neighborhoods and residents banded together to imagine and work for a future. Sometimes in conjunction with NGOs, they injected democratic voices into the politics of planning, and their groups often articulated intelligent, imaginative, and insistent ideas. For Tocqueville, one of the major roots and manifestations of American democratic culture was this creation of public associations or groups that act to better their condition either on their own or by influencing government. A civic culture requires that citizens act with other citizens. What has happened in New Orleans is in many ways a contemporary real-world example of what Tocqueville reported as central to American civic culture as far back as the 1830s.

This vibrant civic public, however, has had little effect on government or on rebuilding and redevelopment. The plans for the neighborhoods and the overarching UNOP were accepted by government, but neither the political will nor governmental funds exists to act on almost all the hopes, ideas, and needs embodied in the plan. New Orleans is a poor city, and the federal government has not come up with anywhere near the resources needed to restore it, much less the funds to re-create it as a better city despite the promises implicit in Bush's post-Katrina speech. Even the $1.1 billion estimated to be needed for the first seventeen "target development areas" will have to be raised from the private sector (DuBos 2007). That there is a national public responsibility to assist victims of a catastrophe and to respond to democratic participation of citizens seems to have been an idea with an extraordinarily short political half-life in New Orleans.

Lacking the ability or willingness to fund almost any of the proposals under the full UNOP, one response, articulated most clearly by Nagin about resettlement but implicit also in the BNOB plan, has been for government to abjure responsibility for who settles where and claim that such decisions remain the free choice of individuals. If enough individuals resettle a neighborhood so that it is viable, then the city will provide city services and ask Entergy, the local utility, to turn on the power. If not enough come home, then people are on their own, an island in a sea of slabs where houses once were, with no police, fire, or health services—indeed, with no electricity, streetlights, or even navigable streets. Of course, this neoliberal or neoconservative "free choice" is rigged: it favors some and hurts others.

Mayor Nagin said that he would concentrate redevelopment in certain areas (for example, not downriver of the Industrial Canal).[23] The Army Corps of Engineers has gone to work first on shoring up the levees and the pumps along Lake Pontchartrain, not downriver. Further, Louisiana's Road Home project requires much paperwork and many meetings between applicants and administrators; anticorruption safeguards have been taken to extremes. As a result, those for whom filling out forms comes easily and those accustomed to the ways of bureaucrats (and who from experience see the bureaucrats as eventually convincible) have had a distinct advantage over those for whom forms constitute a challenge and to whom bureaucrats have historically appeared uncooperative, inaccessible, or unaccommodating. While all residents have been told that they are free to choose, choices have been extraordinarily constrained, frequently by overt governmental action and inaction.

Even where funds exist, the government need not respect the citizens, as is evident in the case of public housing.[24] HANO/HUD officials did not consider why residents of public housing wished to have their housing restored or what compromises were possible. Equally distressing was the unwillingness of the mayor and the city council to offer substantive responses to the residents of public housing, whose ideas about rebuilding were dismissed.

As with the residents of public housing, so too with many of the plans drawn up by the neighborhoods and UNOP, particularly the Tremé plan. One dimension of the public (government) disregarded another (citizens). Housing authorities decided what should happen without giving any consideration to the self-organized activity and opinions of the public housing residents or to the plans of New Orleans's neighborhoods, although HANO and HUD did ask for a kind of political cover from the city council. Similarly, the representative authorities—the mayor and the city council—showed no respect for the hard work of the Tremé citizens.

Residents' extensive political participation in drawing up plans has come to very little in New Orleans. Government and private developers are moving ahead with their own visions.[25] The democratic desires of citizens are being cast aside as New Orleans's public sphere shrinks.[26] Erasures—of ideas, of neighborhood, of communities—are integral to this diminishment as those lacking private economic resources and political clout are ignored.

Civic life, associational diversity, political participation—all considered critical elements of democracy—have not yielded results that instill continued respect for or hope in government. While these qualities have enlivened the political culture of post-Katrina New Orleans, their failure to effect results for participants could well lead to further disenchantment with government and democracy altogether.

NOTES

Residents of New Orleans were very generous in sharing their insights and time with us. Everyone with whom we spoke wanted people to understand the city's challenges, especially for the people displaced by the storm and its aftermath. We particularly thank the following individuals for their valuable insights. Coleman Warner, journalist for the *New Orleans Times-Picayune*, drove us around the city, shared with us the trials of his community, and helped us grasp not only the bureaucratic hurdles of the individual decision about whether to rebuild a home but the day-to-day lives of those struggling to rebuild. Rose Scott told us stories about the hurricane, its immediate aftermath, and its effects on her and her family, friends, and community. Elizabeth Cook and Jay Arena explained their perspectives on the politics of New Orleans and public housing. At ACORN, Wade Rathke and Beth Butler added views about difficulties of getting houses rebuilt and facilitated our attendance at a meeting on housing in the Lower Ninth Ward. Sharon Jasper spoke about her determination to see the right of return realized for tenants of public housing. We deeply appreciate the thoughtfulness of everyone who so graciously helped to educate us about the large and small issues of rebuilding New Orleans.

We also acknowledge generous support from the Lucy Maynard Salmon Research Fund of Vassar College.

1. Perhaps the most vocal and best-attended forum advocating the right of return was held in New Orleans over Labor Day Weekend 2007 and was attended by, among others, Representative Maxine Waters. It was sponsored by the People's Hurricane Relief Fund.
2. Various planning maps from the Urban Land Institute and the BNOB's Urban Planning Committee proposed "open space" or "green space" in significant areas of Broadmoor, Lakeview, Gentilly, the Lower Ninth, and New Orleans East (see, e.g., BNOB Urban Planning Committee 2006a: figure 30).
3. Cashin states that "academic studies show that the two primary motives for the formation of new suburban communities in the 1950s and 1960s were the desire to escape redistributive taxes of the central cities and to escape black people" (2007: 97). For a compelling analysis of how white flight unfolded in Atlanta, see Kruse 2005.
4. In New Orleans, African Americans have evinced a profound connection to their homes, including in public housing (see, e.g., Nine Times Social Club 2007). Dawn Logsdon and Lolis Eric Elie's 2007 documentary, *Faubourg Tremé: The Untold Story of Black New Orleans*, movingly demonstrates that connection. At a viewing in New Orleans on 14 October 2007 at the Canal Place Cinema, many more people showed up than could be admitted. Much of

Civic Culture and the Politics of Planning

the casual conversation had to do with place in New Orleans and individuals' connections to Faubourg Tremé.

5. The Road Home program was instituted by the state to buy back houses of people not planning to return after the flooding and to help returning homeowners cover the financial gap between what insurance would pay and what it cost to rebuild a house.
6. NGOs include ACORN, Habitat for Humanity, Global Green, and many churches that set up shop to assist residents of Lakeview and other neighborhoods in rebuilding their houses.
7. Klein's "shock doctrine" of "disaster capitalism" may well play out fully in New Orleans. She analyzes the ways in which disasters are treated as "exciting market opportunities" (2007: 6) where the public sphere is raided not directly to help people and communities but to help businesses.
8. This outpouring arose in part from a desire to help the wounded city and in part from the recognition that little government money for planning would be forthcoming. FEMA had made clear to Nagin that it would not provide funds for planning (Warner 2006e). A 2006 report from the Rockefeller Foundation notes that "within days of Katrina, the Rockefeller Foundation made more than $3 million in commitments aimed at the rebuilding of New Orleans. . . . Nearly all other leading foundations collectively pledged hundreds of millions of dollars as well, and money and other resources flowed in from a wide range of donors to support immediate relief efforts" (2).
9. An 18 June 2006 *Times-Picayune* editorial ("Not Coming Together") observed, "The BNOB map infamously showed green dots over Broadmoor and certain low-lying areas—which residents took to mean their neighborhood was being targeted for conversion into parkland. So Broadmoor residents enlisted multiple Harvard University graduate schools to help them envision their neighborhood's future. Andres Duany, a Miami planner whose New Urbanist movement seeks to recreate the feel of walkable towns, led an effort to come up with a blueprint for Gentilly." Plans begat counterplans.
10. Canizaro said, "At least 50 percent of those people are going to have to be committed to coming back before we have a neighborhood to design. . . . We will be the same diverse city. We are going to make doggone sure that our African-American population is as strong as ever. But I will tell you we will not have as many poor people." And the president of Tulane University, Scott Cowen, commented, "If, in fact, we know that there are certain parts of the city that will never be safe from flooding, no matter what the levee system is, then I think we have an obligation to tell people that and probably to say we should not repopulate those areas" (PBS Online News Hour 2006).
11. According to Tim Jackson of the New Orleans Planning Commission, "One recommendation that caused a giant stir was that City and other government resources should only go to those neighborhoods that could demonstrate that a majority of its residents would return and rebuild. The resulting storm, pardon the pun, of neighborhood grass roots planning was and is incredible" (2007).
12. The charges against Canizaro partly reflected his personal history: he has been a leading real estate developer since he moved to New Orleans in 1963; he owns one of the most elegant private houses in the area; and he had close ties to the Bush White House, having raised enough money (two hundred thousand dollars) for the president's reelection campaign to become a Ranger (Rivlin 2005; Fleming 2006). Canizaro is, in short, a leading member of the local business elite who makes his money buying and developing land. Many other members of the commission were similarly situated (if not quite so well off), although the

commission also included a few religious and cultural leaders (PBS Online News Hour 2006).
13. Within each project area, the UNOP ranked projects (high, medium, or low priority or "community interest"), suggested their costs, and allocated those costs into the short, medium, or long term. But that apparent specificity masked significant issues regarding how visions were to be realized. (By contrast, the economic meltdown of 2008 has shown what sums the federal government will allocate when it perceives a crisis.)
14. Ed Blakely, hired in December 2006 as chief of the city's Office of Recovery Management, proposed in March 2007 seventeen "target areas" with expenditures of the $117 million available and further reconstruction totaling $1.1 billion, little of which was on hand (Office of Recovery Management 2007: 18; Nossiter 2007).
15. Even without the mayor's warnings and threats, free choice and the market lift some and erase others. When the BNOB was still potentially viable, many relatively well-off residents of Lakeview decided that they would return to rebuild their houses on their own, thereby creating houses and neighborhoods that the BNOB could not turn into green space. The Broadmoor Improvement Association too responded by organizing, reaching out to those who had left, and trying to make sure that Broadmoor would meet the 50 percent returnee requirement to qualify as a viable neighborhood. Individuals who had their own or group resources thus could exercise the right to come back, but many of those who had owned homes or rented in the Lower Ninth or public housing, for example, had much more difficult choices or no choice at all. Unlike Lakeview residents, people who lived in the Lower Ninth and in public housing were poor; unlike Broadmoor, which had a long-standing civic association whose members were active and had returned, the Lower Ninth's residents were still dispersed, and residents of public housing were only beginning to organize. Moreover, regardless of the mayor's threat to withhold recovery funds from the Lower Ninth, even basic city services like streets, health care, fire and police protection, and water hardly existed. The market was at work, but the market for returnees was far from a level playing field; it was and is tilted and bumpy, favoring those who are better off, those who are in place (or whose neighbors have returned), and those on whom the government looks favorably. The UNOP may have formally supported the return of all residents, but government actions and inactions and the market made returning exceedingly difficult, if not impossible, for many people. And the market worked its erasure by a kind of silent and invisible hand, although residents were determined to prevent such erasures from happening.
16. Political action was taking place concerning HUD's plans to demolish public housing prior to Katrina; see Arena 2007.
17. Part of the problem with U.S. public housing is that funds for maintenance and repairs were cut sharply in the 1980s, with the result that the quality of the units declined sharply (Ouroussoff 2006; 2007). Lack of a public commitment to decent housing and developers' desire to acquire property on which such housing sits also contributed to HUD's policies. In New Orleans, private developers have had their eyes on the Iberville Housing Project since 2001 because it sits very near the French Quarter (Long 2007). The redevelopment of the St. Thomas projects reduced public housing units on the site from 1,500 to as few as 120 units (Bates 2006: 25).
18. The residents were familiar with precedents that fueled their distrust; they were very aware of the controversies that had surrounded the pre-Katrina razing and redevelopment of the St. Thomas housing project, which resulted in gentrification and fewer units available for those who lived in the St. Thomas buildings (Filosa 2007b, c).

19. HUD had been tearing down public housing across the country, and New Orleans seemed to present no unusual circumstances. Residents, however, saw major differences: New Orleans public housing was low-rise, and so had less crime, at least potentially, than did high-rises. New Orleans features many extended families whose members have lived in the city for generations and who have connections and memories of place; and New Orleans public housing, despite its problems, also had an active culture of community and cooperation. Moreover, Katrina's devastation made the case for keeping public housing even more compelling because the hurricane wiped out many possible alternatives. Public housing provided the only place in the short (and possibly long) term to which low-income renters could return (Ouroussoff 2006, 2007; Filosa 2007b).

20. Tremé suffered a great sense of loss when Claiborne Avenue, the four-lane divided boulevard with magnificent oaks that was the district's commercial center, was reengineered, the oaks uprooted, and the commerce destroyed by the construction of the elevated I-10 highway over the street.

21. HANO/HUD also ignored the expert opinions of architectural writers (Ouroussoff 2006) and preservationists (see the letters posted at http://www.hano.org/news.htm).

22. The day of the city council vote, extra New Orleans police were on hand to control reactions (Filosa 2007b). For videos, go to YouTube 2007. The city council did make two gestures to the residents, neither of which was enforceable: it insisted that HANO/HUD promise yet again to open the 94 interim units that were supposed to have been available the preceding September, and it asked that an additional 102 interim units "potentially" be opened.

23. Blakely announced one project in New Orleans East and one in the Lower Ninth Ward (DuBos 2007; Office of Recovery Management 2007), but most projects are slated for the areas favored by Nagin for investment.

24. Residents were not unanimous about preserving the housing; some testified before the city council in favor of demolition. But a significant number of residents not only voiced support for public housing but also took the time and trouble—including, in many cases, serious sacrifices—to act on their political convictions and to try to solve the problem of a lack of decent places to live after Katrina.

25. NGOs such as ACORN, Global Green USA, and Make It Right NOLA have assisted and continue to assist residents in rebuilding homes.

26. Other aspects of public life have also diminished: for example, all the public school teachers were fired as charter schools assumed a larger role, and Charity Hospital remains closed (see Klein 2007). Bill Quigley (2007), counsel for residents of public housing in their litigation to prevent demolition, writes about "How to Destroy an African-American City in Thirty-three Steps": many of these steps involve government action or inaction that ultimately reduces not just the footprint of the city but the footprint of the public sphere of life.

REFERENCES

In general, articles in the *New Orleans Times-Picayune* are currently available electronically through the newspaper's archives, Lexis-Nexis, and Proquest; we accessed many originally during the two-week window they are available at the paper's Web site, and those URLs are no longer valid. *New York Times* articles are also available from the newspaper's Web site and other sources. Planning documents, including those for the major governmental planning bodies (BNOB, the Lambert Plan, and UNOP) and many other groups, are available at http://www.nolaplans.com.

American Planning Association. 2005. *Charting the Course for Rebuilding a Great American City: An Assessment of the Planning Function in Post-Katrina New Orleans*. www.planning.org/katrina/pdf/rebuildingreport.pdf. Accessed 3 December 2007.

Anderson v. Jackson. 2008. 06-3298, Section B(5) (E.D. La.) 6 February. WL 10395.

Arena, John D. 2007. "Whose City Is It? Public Housing, Public Sociology, and the Struggle for Social Justice in New Orleans before and after Katrina." In *Through the Eye of Katrina*, ed. Kristin A. Bates and Richelle S. Swan, 367–86. Durham: Carolina Academic.

Bates, Lisa K. 2006. "Post-Katrina Housing: Problems, Policies, and Prospects for African-Americans in New Orleans." *Black Scholar* 36.4 (Winter): 13–31.

Bring New Orleans Back Commission, Urban Planning Committee. 2006a. *Action Plan for New Orleans: The New American City* (final report). 11 January. www.bringneworleansback.org/. Accessed 7 March 2008. The map alone is also available at www.nola.com/katrina/pdf/planmap.pdf. Accessed 7 March 2008.

———. 2006b. *Action Plan for New Orleans* (executive summary). 30 January. http://www.bringneworleansback.org/. Accessed 4 November 2007).

———. 2006c. *Mayor's Rebuilding Plan: Final*. http://www.bringneworleansback.org/. Accessed 4 November 2007.

Broadmoor Improvement Association. n.d. http://broadmoorimprovement.com/node/21. Accessed 4 November 2007.

Burdeau, Cain. 2006. "Fearing Land Takeover, Angry New Orleanians Blast Plan for Rebuilding." Associated Press. 12 January. http://www.tomjoyner.com/site.aspx/bawnews/neworleans0113. Accessed 3 December 2007.

Bureau of Governmental Research. 2006. "BGR Reports: City Council Planning Contract Is Out Of Bounds." 8 May. http://www.bgr.org/MainPages/2003%20pub_list.htm. Accessed 20 July 2008.

Bush, George W. 2005. Speech in Jackson Square, New Orleans. 15 September. http://www.whitehouse.gov/news/releases/2005/09/print/20050915-8.html. Accessed 7 March 2008.

Cashin, Sheryll. 2007. "Dilemma of Place and Suburbanization of the Black Middle Class." In *The Black Metropolis in the Twenty-First Century*, ed. Robert D. Bullard, 87–110. Lanham, Md.: Rowman and Littlefield.

Davis, Mike. 2006. "Who Is Killing New Orleans?" *The Nation*, 10 April. http://www.thenation.com/doc/20060410/davis. Accessed 12 December 2007.

DuBos, Clancy. 2007. "Eminently Doable." 10 April. http://bestofneworleans.com/gyrobase/Content?oid=oid%3A37928. Accessed 2 November 2009.

Farley, Tom. 2007. "There Go the Neighborhoods: Bike Paths, Parks and Sidewalks Aren't Frills, but It Turns Out They're a Bit Too 'Visionary' for Us." *New Orleans Times-Picayune*, 8 January, 5.

Filosa, Gwen. 2007a. "Ejected Public Housing Residents Return to C. J. Peete; Homecoming Lacks Utilities, Permission." *New Orleans Times-Picayune*, 11 February.

———. 2007b. "Live Updates on Demolition; Vote from City Chambers." *New Orleans Times-Picayune*, 19 December. www.nola.com/news/index.ssf/2007/12/city_hall_girds_for_public_hou.html Accessed 23 December 2007.

———. 2007c. "Nagin Wants to Run Road Home in N.O.; Congressional Panel Gets Earful on Public Housing." *New Orleans Times-Picayune*, 23 February.

Fleming, Sibley. 2006. "Rebuilding Czar." *National Real Estate Investor*. 1 March. http://www.uli.org/. Accessed 24 November 2007.

Grahamad [pseud.]. 2007. "NOLA City Council Unanimously Approves Demolition of Public Housing." *Redstar Perspective*. 20 December. http://grahamad.wordpress.com/2007/12/20/nola-city-council-unanimously-approves-demolition-of-public-housing/. Accessed 30 January 2010.

Hamilton, Bruce. 2007. "Protesters Take Over Closed Complex; Activists, Residents Begin Cleanup." *New Orleans Times-Picayune*. 16 January.

Hastert, Dennis. 2005. AP news article. 2 September. http://www.wwltv.com/cgi-bin/bi/gold_print.cgi. Accessed 21 November 2007.

Homeless Camp outside New Orleans City Hall. 2007. Associated Press story. 16 November. http://www.msnbc.msn.com/id/21840886/. Accessed 25 January 2008.

Horne, Jedidiah, and Brendan Nee. 2006a. *Detailed Description of the Lambert Process*. http://www.nolaplans.com/lambert_detail/. Accessed 8 November 2007.

———. 2006b. *An Overview of Post-Katrina Planning in New Orleans*. http://www.nolaplans.com/research. Accessed 8 November 2007.

Inniss, Lolita Buckner. 2007. "A Domestic Right of Return? Race, Rights, and Residency in New Orleans in the Aftermath of Hurricane Katrina." *Boston Third World Law Journal* 27 (Spring): 325–71.

Institute for Southern Studies. 2007. *Blueprint for Gulf Renewal: The Katrina Crisis and a Community Agenda for Action: A Special Report by Gulf Coast Reconstruction Watch*. http://southernstudies.org/2007/08/two-years-after-katrina.asp. Accessed 7 March 2008.

Jackson, Tim. 2007. "The Unified New Orleans Plan Nears Completion." 22 March. http://planetizen.com/node/23365. Accessed 22 January 2008.

Justice for New Orleans. 2007. http://justiceforneworleans.org/index.php?module=article&view=101&page_num=2. Accessed 25 January 2008.

Klein, Naomi. 2007. *The Shock Doctrine*. New York: Metropolitan.

Krupa, Michelle. 2007. "N.O.'s Plan for Rebuilding Passes Muster with LRA; Action Will Free Up Federal Money; St. Bernard Proposal Also OK'd." *New Orleans Times-Picayune*, 26 June.

Kruse, Kevin M. 2005. *White Flight: Atlanta and the Making of Modern Conservatism*. Princeton: Princeton University Press.

Lambert Plan. 2006. http://www.nolaplans.com/lambert/. 23 September. Accessed 8 November 2007.

Levy, Clifford J. 2005. "Storm Forces a Hard Look at Troubled Public Housing." *New York Times*. 22 November.

Logsdon, Dawn, and Lolis Eric Elie. 2007. *Faubourg Tremé: The Untold Story of Black New Orleans* (documentary). http://www.tremedoc.com/. Accessed 2 November 2009.

Long, Alecia P. 2007. "Poverty Is the New Prostitution: Race, Poverty, and Public Housing in Post-Katrina New Orleans." *Journal of American History* 94.3 (December): 795–803.

Lopez, Edwin. 2007. "Public Housing Supporters Speak Out against Demolition." 7 December. http://news.infoshop.org/article.php?story=2007nola-lopez-housing&mode=print. Accessed 8 August 2008.

Maggi, Laura, and Gwen Filosa. 2006. "Public Housing Dilemma: Build It Right or Build It Fast?" Newhouse News Service. 20 October. http://www.newhousenews.com/archive/maggi102006.html. Accessed 20 October 2006.

Mann, Charles C. 2006. "The Long, Strange Resurrection of New Orleans." *Fortune Magazine*, 21 August. http://www.charlesmann.org/Articles.htm. Accessed 1 August 2008.

Meitrodt, Jeffrey, and Frank Donze. 2005. "Plan Shrinks City Footprint: Nagin Panel May Call for 3-Year Test." *New Orleans Times-Picayune*. 14 December.

Nagin, C. Ray. 2007. Letter to Alphonso Jackson. December 21. http://www.nhtf.org/doc/PublicHousingIssueClarification-MayortoSecyJackson2012-21-07.pdf. Accessed 8 May 2008.

Neighborhood Rebuilding Plans. 2006–7. http://www.nolanrp.com/. Accessed 8 November 2007.

New Orleans, Louisiana: A Strategy for Rebuilding. 2005. Washington, D.C.: Urban Land Institute.

Nine Times Social Club. 2007. *Coming out the Door for the Ninth Ward.* New Orleans: Neighborhood Story Project.

Nossiter, Adam. 2007. "Steering New Orleans's Recovery with a Clinical Eye." *New York Times*, 10 April.

"Not Coming Together" (editorial). 2006. *New Orleans Times-Picayune*, 18 June, 6.

Office of Recovery Management, City of New Orleans. 2007. Target Areas. http://www.nolarecovery.com. Accessed 3 December 2007.

Ouroussoff, Nicolai. 2006. "All Fall Down." *New York Times*, 19 November.

———. 2007. "High Noon in New Orleans: The Bulldozers Are Ready." *New York Times*, 19 December.

PBS Online News Hour. 2006. "Blueprint for Rebuilding New Orleans." 11 January. http://vsx.onstreammedia.com/vsx/newshour/search/NHPlayer?assetId=71512&ccstart=2154291&pt=1. Accessed 10 February 2010.

Quigley, Bill. 2007. "How to Destroy an African-American City in Thirty-three Steps." 29 June. http://www.truthout.org/docs_2006/062907N.shtml. Accessed 3 December 2007.

Rivlin, Gary. 2005. "A Mogul Who Would Rebuild New Orleans." *New York Times*, 29 September.

Rockefeller Foundation. 2006. *New Orleans: Planning for a Better Future.* www.rockfound.org/library/no_better_future.pdf. Accessed 22 November 2007.

Russell, Gordon. 2006. "On Their Own: In the Absence of Clear Direction, New Orleanians Are Rebuilding a Patchwork City." *New Orleans Times-Picayune*, 27 August.

Saulny, Susan. 2006. "5,000 Public Housing Units in New Orleans Are to Be Razed." *New York Times*, 15 June.

Shulte, Bret. 2006. "Turf Wars in the Delta." *U.S. News & World Report*, 19 February. http://www.usnews.com/usnews/news/articles/060227/27future_print.htm. Accessed 3 December 2007.

Survivors' Village. 2007. http://www.survivorsvillage.com/about.html (now defunct). Some information, including the quotation in the text, is available at http://cwsworkshop.org/katrinareader/node/159 (accessed 26 July 2008).

Tremé/Lafitte Neighborhood. 2006. *City of New Orleans: 6th Ward/Tremé/LaFitte Neighborhood: Neighborhoods Rebuilding Plan.* http://nolanrp.com/Data/Neighborhood//District_4_Final_TremeLafitte6thWard.pdf. Accessed 2 November 2009.

Unified New Orleans Plan. 2007a. *UNOP Final Plan.* http://www.unifiedneworleansplan.com/home3/section/136/city-wide-plan. Accessed 10 February 2010.

———. 2007b. *For the (District 8) Ninth Ward Plan*, chap. 2, *Planning Process.* http://www.unifiedneworleansplan.com/home3/districts/8/plans/. Also at http://willdoo-storage.com/Plans/D8/District_08_Lower9th_Chapter_02_Planning_Process.pdf. Accessed 3 December 2007.

Warner, Coleman. 2006a. "Councilwoman Hails Planning Cash; Rockefeller Group Set to Give $3.5 Million." *New Orleans Times-Picayune*, 20 April, 1.

———. 2006b. "N.O. Blazes Trail for Grant Money: City and State Agree on Planning Process." *New Orleans Times-Picayune*, 6 July, 1.

———. 2006c. "N.O. Planning Process Puts Residents on Edge; There's No Way to Tell What Happens Next." *New Orleans Times-Picayune*, 31 August.

———. 2006d. "Schools, Streets, Trees Top Most Planning Lists." *New Orleans Times-Picayune*, 23 September, 1.

———. 2006e. "State and City to Talk Recovery: Neighborhoods Begin Crafting Their Plans." *New Orleans Times-Picayune*, 27 May.

———. 2006f. "Unanimous." *New Orleans Times-Picayune*, 21 December. http://blog.nola.com/times-picayune/2007/12/unanimous.html. Accessed 23 December 2006.

———. 2007. "N.O. Planners' Vision Will Cost $14 Billion; City Approval, Money Source Hurdles Ahead." *New Orleans Times-Picayune*, 31 January.

Warner, Coleman, and Bruce Eggler. 2006. "New Orleans to Take Request to LRA." *New Orleans Times-Picayune*, 3 November, 1.

Wolfe, Alan. 2006. "Why Conservatives Can't Govern." *Washington Monthly*, July–August. www.washingtonmlonthly.com/features/2006/0607.wolfe/. Accessed 25 June 2006.

YouTube. 2007. Videos of police and demonstrators at the City Council vote to demolish. http://www.youtube.com/watch?v=W_OUake6tao&feature=related; http://www.youtube.com/watch?v=cXJLzS4__BM&feature=related;http://www.youtube.com/watch?v=5jvhp4iZFdo; http://www.youtube.com/watch?v=oCYYPV8Nlek&feature=related, http://www.youtube.com/watch?v=1b6zGunXBas&feature=related. Accessed 15 June 2008.

NEW ORLEANS SHOTGUN
A Historic Cultural Geography

JAY D. EDWARDS

How are priorities established for saving different kinds of houses and neighborhoods in New Orleans? This issue has risen to the forefront following Hurricane Katrina because in a triage-type environment in which there is limited funding, planning commissions and governmental bodies must make Solomonic decisions about what is to be saved and what is to be bulldozed. Something on the order of 130,000 of the city's former black residents have failed to return (Browne-Dianis 2006; Livingston and Livingston 2007).[1] Approximately 75 percent of those living in low-lying, flood-prone areas of New Orleans were African Americans. These renters and owners of flood-ravaged houses have been most severely impacted, first by the flooding itself and second by the mechanisms through which recovery funding has been doled out by insurance companies and by local, state, and federal governments (see Logan 2007; Tarhakah 2005; Gyan 2007, 1A; Dreier 2006; Bohrer 2007: 17A).[2]

In New Orleans, square miles of residential neighborhoods lie significantly abandoned three years after Katrina (fig. 2.1). Numerous commentators have remarked on the fact that New Orleans is a seriously bifurcated city—large portions appear to be entirely back to normal, while others have hardly begun the recovery process. This situation impels us to consider whether we have been paying sufficient attention to the causes of the geographical differences in the recovery process. A number of factors, including topography, ethnicity, and history, have combined to render substantial portions of the city less able to recover, leading to their effective near abandonment. While other factors unquestionably play a role in creating the patterns that influence recovery, the interactions among these three have not been explored as

New Orleans Shotgun

Fig. 2.1. Rows of abandoned houses, Upper Ninth Ward, August 2008. Photo by author.

profitably as is necessary. Another insufficiently explored causal factor arises from the effects of the widely shared scale of value that decision makers have applied to different neighborhoods and different building types.

In New Orleans, interest groups are factionalized along geographical and racial lines. The removal of Jim Crow laws in the early 1960s eliminated barriers to African American advancement on many fronts but substantially intensified the process of residential segregation. Jim Crow laws did not originally limit racial mixing in neighborhood contexts. In the city's American Sector in antebellum times, blacks and whites lived in close proximity in a system geographer Peirce Lewis (1976) has called "superblocks."[3] Following the unrest and racial riots of the late nineteenth and early twentieth centuries, however, blacks were increasingly economically and geographically marginalized. Their neighborhoods were progressively pushed to the edges of the swamplands, resulting in sharper division lines by the late 1930s. Dryades Street and North Rampart–St. Claude Streets became boundaries between black and white residential zones. Today, according to Richard Campanella (2002), neighborhood segregation is largely economically driven. The principal indicator associated with African American residence in New Orleans has been topography (Campanella 2006: 303). Less expensive land was located in the city's lower-lying areas, leading to the close association between patterns of largely working-class African American residence and elevation. Before Katrina, a high percentage of African Americans lived at or below sea level.

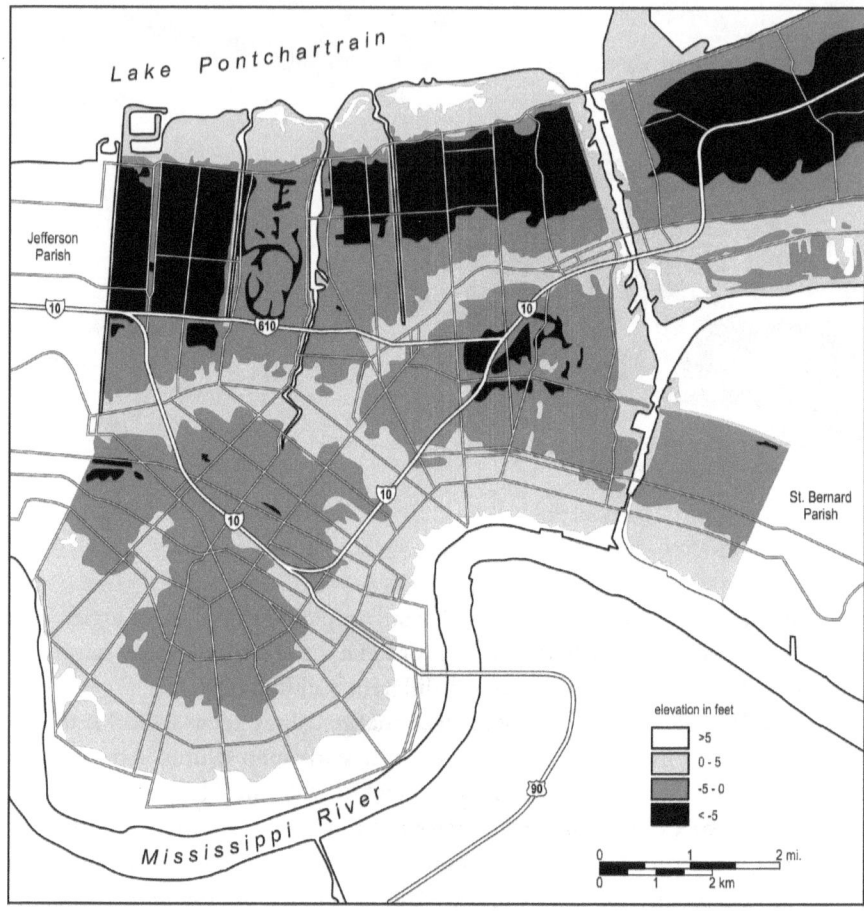

Fig. 2.2. Elevations of Orleans Parish, based on Lidar data supplied by FEMA. Sketch by Mary Lee Eggart.

This pattern is revealed through cartographic comparison. Fig. 2.2 shows a newly revised elevation survey based on Lidar data provided by the Federal Emergency Management Agency. The familiar pattern of high ground along the old natural levees is obvious. The highest ground in the city flanks the banks of the Mississippi, an area sometimes referred to as the Island. Secondary high ground is found along the Esplanade Ridge, along Bayou St. John, and along the Metairie-Gentilly Ridge complex. In between are bowls of land lying below sea level, the remnants of old cypress swamplands that were drained in the late nineteenth and early twentieth centuries. As the city pushed outward from the Creole Faubourgs, people with low incomes moved into these low-lying areas because land was cheap.[4] Much

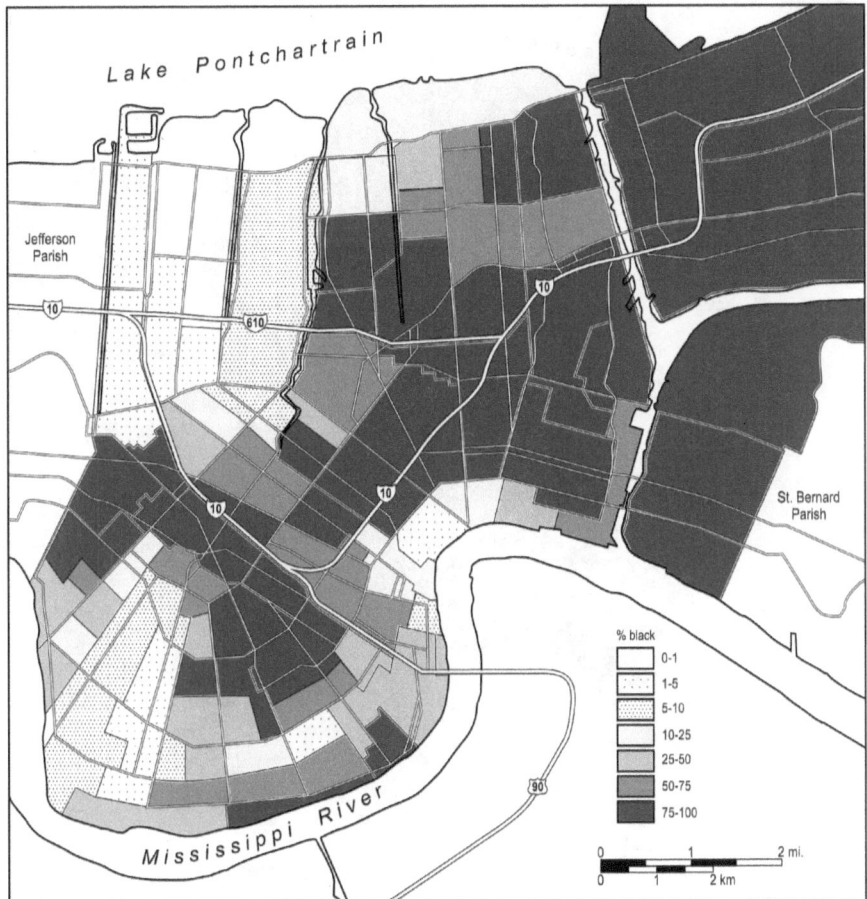

Fig. 2.3. Racial composition of Orleans Parish prior to Katrina, based on 2000 Census data. Sketch by Mary Lee Eggart.

of the old swampland experienced substantial subsidence as a consequence of the drying, rotting, and shrinking of what were previously peat-laden anaerobic soils with high organic contents.

If a map of African American residence patterns just prior to Katrina (fig. 2.3) is superimposed on the elevation map, a rather remarkable coherence appears. Although the two patterns are not completely coincident, the degree of overlap lies far beyond any possibility of random distribution. Thus, race and topography are highly correlated in New Orleans. A map depicting the failure of people to return to the city following Katrina, as measured by voter turnout in the 2006 mayoral election and by post office mail

JAY D. EDWARDS

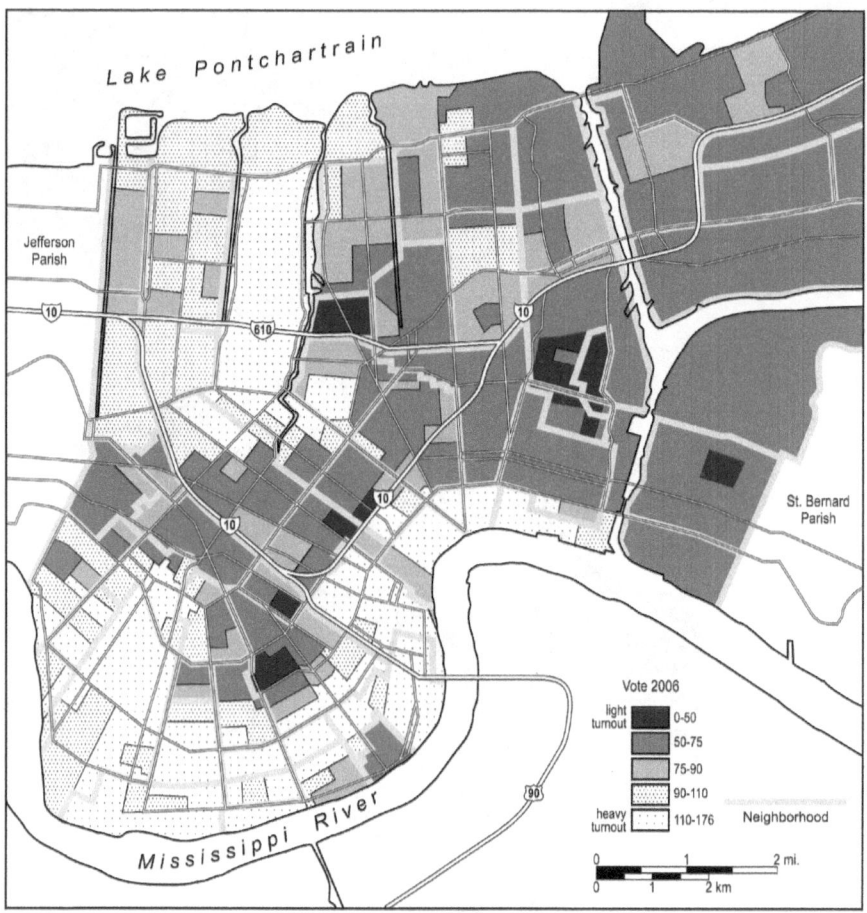

Fig. 2.4. Proportions of recovery in Orleans Parish as measured by voter turnout in the 2006 mayoral election. Sketch by Mary Lee Eggart.

delivery (fig. 2.4), shows much the same pattern and consequently provides geographical confirmation that African Americans have been differentially affected by Katrina through their inability to return to New Orleans.

Although most longtime residents can indicate fairly accurately where Creole cottages, Greek Revival mansions, porte cochere townhouses, and slab-type ranch houses may be found, to my knowledge, no geographical study of New Orleans by house type has been conducted, and no map of house type exists. Both Roulhac Toledano's *National Trust Guide to New Orleans* (1996) and the New Orleans Architecture Series of volumes written by the Friends of the Cabildo discuss house types and their locations in considerable detail, but they provide no maps of the distribution of specific

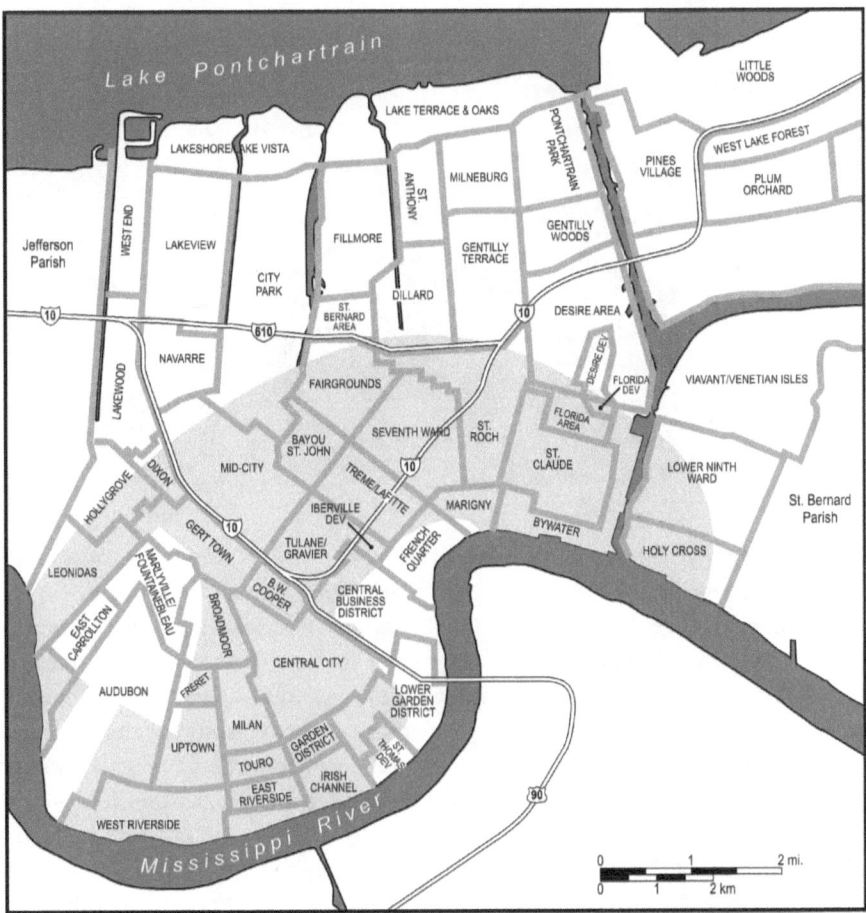

Fig. 2.5. "Shotgun Crescent" of Orleans Parish, based on 1933 aerial photography. Sketch by Mary Lee Eggart.

building forms. Loyd Vogt's two books on New Orleans architecture (1985, 2002) provide only general settlement maps. Even Campanella's detailed historic interpretations of ethnic concentrations in New Orleans provide almost no broad-based maps of building types outside of the French Quarter (2006: 113–40).

A survey of the standard architectural history literature on the city indicates that certain house types receive considerable priority in discussions of architectural value and historic significance. A marked geographical bias exists in the ranking of architectural types, with the house types of the Island and the Garden District receiving by far the bulk of the interest and publication space, while less glamorous historic houses of equal age

Fig. 2.6a. Ca. 1820s Creole cottage, 1600 block of St. Philip Street, in the Tremé neighborhood. Courtesy New Orleans Notarial Archives (084.046, elevation).

situated in the lower-lying areas of the back of town (Carrolton, Hollygrove, Gert Town, Mid-City, Tremé, New Marigny) and downtown (St. Roch, St. Claude, Desire, Bywater, and Holy Cross) receive cursory mention at best.

But where do shotgun houses cluster in New Orleans? Their zones of heaviest concentration, the "shotgun crescent," follow a pattern that closely matches the nineteenth-century expansion of the old colonial city (fig. 2.5). In other words, shotgun family houses are most common in neighborhoods developed between about 1800 and about 1930, largely before the city had expanded past the Metairie–Gentilly Ridge barrier. The crescent includes almost all of the previously swampy low-lying bowl of Mid-City and Gert Town, but shotguns also were built throughout the entire city in both middle-class and working-class neighborhoods. A comparison of all four maps shows that much of the shotgun crescent is both low and inhabited largely by African Americans. However, other areas of the shotgun crescent, including Carrollton, Audubon, and the Garden District, have large numbers of shotguns inhabited by predominately white and by mixed-race and mixed-class populations. Even in the areas that did not flood, however, most New Orleans residents do not see the shotgun as one of the city's vital cultural resources. Wooden cottages such as the shotgun generally receive lower priority in recovery efforts than do colonial houses or mansions and highly decorated cottages. The news media have taken particular note of the obvious disparity in recovery between white and black neighborhoods, as have detailed surveys and studies by national organizations (see, e.g., Kalima, Clark, and Duval-Dlop 2008; Kaiser Foundation 2007; see also Breunlin and Regis 2006; Jackson 2006).[5]

New Orleans Shotgun

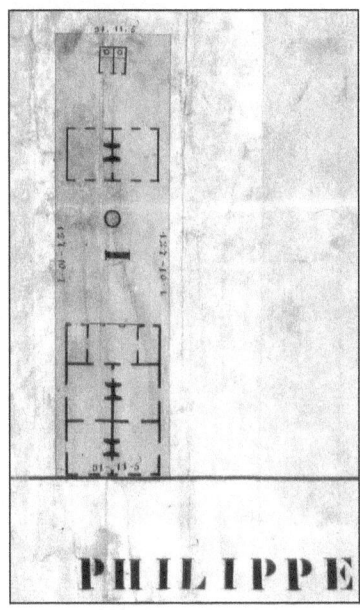

Fig. 2.6b. Plan of the 1820s Creole cottage, 1600 block of St. Philip Street. Courtesy New Orleans Notarial Archives (084.046).

THE STANDARD HISTORY OF THE SHOTGUN HOUSE

An accepted history of the shotgun house has been popularized by almost every New Orleans architectural historian. The theory began with Sam Wilson Jr., the dean of the city's architectural historians, who has been followed by most of the prominent scholars of the Crescent City, including Mary Lou Christovich, Sally K. Reeves, Roulhac Toledano, Malcolm Heard, Ellen Weiss, and Karen Kingsley. All basically agree on several crucial points.

The shotgun house is defined as a frame dwelling, narrow on the street but deep on the lot. This house type originated in the late 1830s and 1840s as a result of the progressive segmentation of city lots. While the standard French colonial lot had been 60 French feet wide (about 64 English feet), these lots had been subdivided by the early nineteenth century because of French laws that entitled every child to an equal portion of the family inheritance. By the 1830s, lots had been divided into strips 32 feet wide, 21 feet wide, or even 16 feet wide, many still 120 or 150 French feet deep.

Throughout the Spanish colonial period, New Orleans's standard small house had been the Creole cottage, of which two basic types existed. One was a gable-sided cottage with two near-square rooms opening onto the street (fig. 2.6a). Behind these rooms were two more rooms, also usually

Fig. 2.7. Single 1830s half Creole cottage, 830 N. Rampart Street. Lithograph by Childe Hassam, 1927. Courtesy Library of Congress, Prints and Photographs Division.

square, and then a cabinet-loggia range of rooms. A kitchen and service buildings were placed as detached structures behind the main building (fig. 2.6b). These houses were generally about thirty-two to thirty-six feet wide on the street. There were also half versions of the Creole cottage, one room deep or one room wide (fig. 2.7). The roof ridge of all gabled Creole cottages was parallel to the front of the house and the street. The second form of Creole cottage was a hip-roofed maisonette form with the same floor plan as the first (figs. 2.8a–b). The maisonette could have either its long or short side facing the street.

According to the standard history, during the 1830s and 1840s, residents began to experiment with new forms of houses. Archival records do not show shotgun houses much before about 1840, so they probably did not exist in significant numbers. As New Orleans's population grew wealthier and residents began to search for ways to expand their modest Creole cottages, some turned their half-width maisonettes sideways on their lots. These single Creole cottages became the prototypes for a new kind of linear cottage (figs. 2.9a–b). Longer and longer cottages, with their narrow ends facing the front, were the result. Most of these were one story high with the roof ridges now perpendicular to the street.

New Orleans Shotgun

Fig. 2.8a. Late-eighteenth-century French colonial-style maisonette, 1028/1030 Ursulines Street, in the Vieux Carré, razed in 1944. Courtesy New Orleans Vieux Carré Commission.

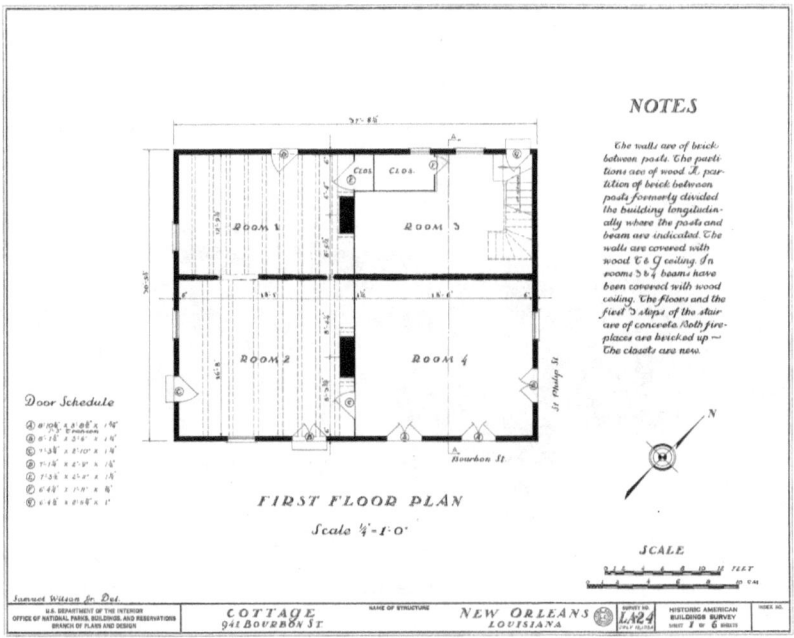

Fig. 2.8b. Plan of late-eighteenth-century French colonial maisonette, 941 Bourbon Street, from a HABS survey by Samuel Wilson Jr., 1934. Louisiana HABS LA-24, Sheet 1.

53

Fig. 2.9a. Helen Lepage linear cottage, 1024 Governor Nichols Street, in the Vieux Carré, constructed by Pierre Roup in 1823. Courtesy New Orleans Vieux Carré Commission.

Fig. 2.10a. Rebuilt pre-1840s-style *briquette-entre-poteaux* double shotgun, 1517 Governor Nichols Street, October 2005. Photo by author.

New Orleans Shotgun

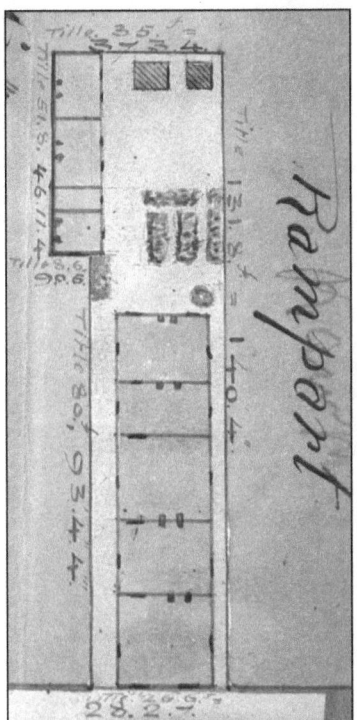

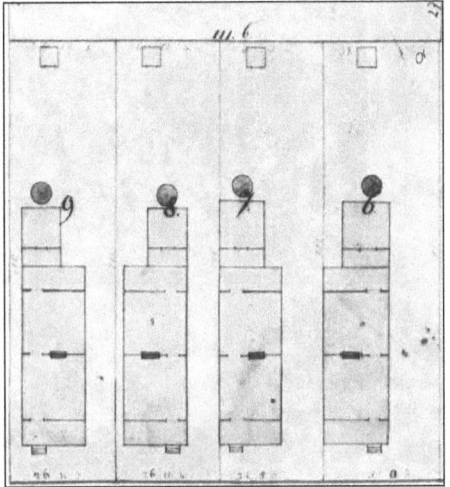

Fig. 2.9b. Plan of Helen Lepage linear cottage. Guy Seghers Office Records. Courtesy Southeastern Architectural Archive, Tulane University, Col. 41, box. 19.

Fig. 2.10b. Plans of four shotgun singles built for laborers in the Central City neighborhood, from an 1853 survey. Courtesy New Orleans Notarial Archives (064.005).

After the Civil War, the growth of the savings and loan industry stimulated demand for relatively inexpensive single-family houses. At first, many of these new cottages were relatively small—two or three rooms deep (figs. 2.10a–b). Soon, however, artisan and working-class families could afford to purchase linear wooden houses seventy to ninety feet long with four to six rooms (fig. 2.11a–b). "The Creole Cottage type proliferated throughout the city for a half century until it began to evolve into the shotgun about 1845" (Reeves 2003: 7).[6] Land developers began to build rows and entire blocks of nearly identical shotgun houses.

The standard history sounds fine as far as it goes, but several problems arise when it is considered closely. It fails to explain why the shotgun leaped across social and ethnic lines and became adopted by people of all walks of life in New Orleans in the 1840s and 1850s. It also fails to explore the origins of the shotgun house, as if the shotgun simply suddenly appeared full-blown from the mind of architects James Gallier and James Dakin (see Edwards

Fig. 2.11a. A four-room side-galleried shotgun, 2709 Camp Street, in the Garden District. Courtesy New Orleans Notarial Archives (028.022, elevation).

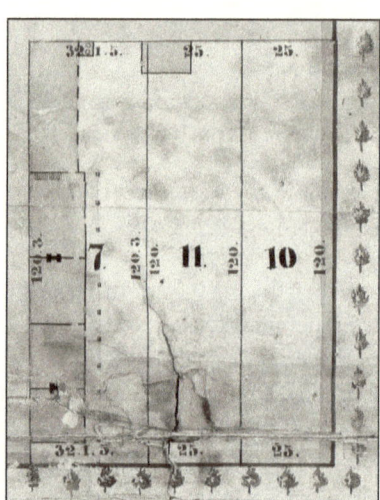

Fig. 2.11b. Plan of the Camp Street shotgun showing rear stable. Courtesy New Orleans Notarial Archives (028.022).

2008–9; Toledano 1996: 16, 26; Kingsley 2003: 27; Scully 1973). It fails to explain how a lowly form of temporary architecture, once spread around the peripheries of New Orleans, rose to become the city's dominant house type (fig. 2.12). More damaging, the standard history ignores and therefore devalues the role played by African Americans and free people of color in the development of the shotgun and New Orleans's nineteenth-century cultural landscapes.

New Orleans Shotgun

Fig. 2.12. 1803 Boqueto de Woiserie lithograph of New Orleans, as seen from the front gallery of the Marigny plantation house; a small Haitian-style linear cottage appears in the foreground. Courtesy Historic New Orleans Collection, accession number 1958.42.

The African Origins Theory

In 1975, John Michael Vlach proposed an alternate theory of the origins of the shotgun house, tracing the form back to Haiti and even to the underlying architectural principles of the vernacular architectures of Africans and African Americans. His research has often been mischaracterized and distorted. He makes two important points. First, the shotgun house originated in seventeenth-century maroon communities on the island of Hispaniola, shared today by the Dominican Republic and Haiti.[7] Vlach discovered that vernacular versions of the shotgun, usually referred to as the *ti-kay* or small house, are found throughout both rural and urban central and southern Haiti (fig. 2.13). The Haitian version is remarkably similar to the smaller early shotgun houses of Louisiana (fig. 2.12). Vlach described the *ti-kay* as a cultural amalgam of an indigenous Taino (Arawak) house form combined with West African dimensional and proportional preferences and eventually French building technologies and European-type materials. However, Vlach did not uncover very compelling evidence for the early colonial origins of the *ti-kay* in Haiti. Better evidence has appeared, some of it in New Orleans (fig. 2.14). Vlach argued that one by-product of the diasporas of the Haitian Revolution (1791–1804) was that this house form was carried to New Orleans by refugees, where it was reconstituted by experienced Haitian builders between about 1805 and 1830.

JAY D. EDWARDS

Fig. 2.13. *Ti-kay* cottages in southern Haiti, 1995. Photo by author.

Fig. 2.14. View of Les Cayes in southern Saint-Domingue, painted by a French sailor, Pierre Caillot, 1729–30, illustrating many linear cottages. Courtesy Historic New Orleans Collection, accession number 2005.11.

Vlach's second point was that although the shotgun house represents certain important aspects of West African culture, it is by no means an African house type. More interestingly, he argued almost the opposite—that house-related values and social dispositions diffuse under conditions of migration such as the African diaspora. Certain preferences and tendencies in the use of houses and in their organization survived the translation into the new environment. The small wattled and thatched houses of Saint-Domingue functioned much the same way as did the individual freestanding West African *kombet* (hut). Both groups of vernacular houses shared small interior rooms with abundant open-air living and reception spaces. Interior rooms were tiny by European standards, averaging roughly one hundred square feet. The almost ubiquitous porch on the front of the *ti-kay* functioned much like the "daytime house" (gallery) of the West African compound, and the *lacou* (yard) functioned socially much like the African *tapanca* (enclosed family compound). Groups of *ti-kay* were often built together, recalling the close association between the multiple *kombets* of close relatives within a West African compound. Although the *ti-kay* of Saint-Domingue was not an African house type, significant associations between the domestic lifestyles of West Africans and African American maroons in Saint-Domingue remained. Maroons were, of course, free to design and build their own houses and yards, but even on sixteenth- and seventeenth-century plantations, Africans were directed to construct their own houses, and they often used African styles (see, e.g., Ligon 1673).[8]

Vlach's theory has been rather universally rejected by the New Orleans architectural community. According to Reeves, former archivist of the New Orleans Notarial Archives, although that institution has some of the nation's best architectural records for the nineteenth century, they contain little evidence of shotgun houses prior to 1840. Even Vlach discovered only limited evidence for shotgun houses predating the 1840s. French Quarter architectural historian Malcolm Heard has argued that although a couple of shotgun-like Creole maisonettes existed in the 1820s, they comprised an insufficient foundation for the many thousands of shotguns built beginning in the 1840s and 1850s. Other architectural historians have made similar arguments (*French Quarter Manual* 1997: 48; see also Kingsley 2003: 25–26; Weiss 1997: esp. 276, 279–85).

POLITICAL IMPLICATIONS

The architectural historians' argument has a larger significance. If they are correct, the contributions of African Americans and free persons of color to the cultural landscapes of nineteenth-century New Orleans are minimized; instead, land developers and speculators bear most of the responsibility for the shotgun crescent. If the nineteenth-century landscapes are the product of such prosaic processes of urban development, the history of the shotgun crescent remains rather unremarkable—not something that would set the history of New Orleans apart from other American cities of the period. African Americans and Afro-Creoles then played only the less significant roles of laborers and perhaps designer-builders of their own versions of the shotgun house. But if a unique and dynamic tradition of shotgun-like houses existed among Afro-Creoles and Haitian refugees in New Orleans in the first four decades of the nineteenth century, the story is entirely different. Not only must the city's architectural history be rewritten, but the significance of the erasure of this earlier building tradition on popular perceptions—perceptions that have resulted in the current scale of value assigned to irreplaceable cultural assets—must be examined. In the latter case, the role of Afro-Creoles in the making of nineteenth-century New Orleans becomes a more central focus for investigation—something architectural history can no longer ignore. Those back-of-town landscapes suddenly deserve first-rate scholarly attention. If new ethnic histories reveal unique stories of cultural determination and innovation, then ethnic communities rise on the scale of preservation priorities. They assume a prominent place in the protective pantheon of a long overdo master plan for the preservation of New Orleans (Borah 1998).

In the post-Katrina period, spokespersons for the African American community have pointed out the injustices in the return and recovery process. In their opinion, not only has public housing been unfairly and unnecessarily affected, but large sections of the city where African Americans were both property owners and renters have failed to recover. Is there a strong possibility of a direct correlation between the lack of social and culturally based architectural histories of the shotgun crescent and the lack of social and political will to rebuild those neighborhoods? New Orleans's most widely recognized cultural institutions have flourished in these neighborhoods—jazz and the blues; social and pleasure clubs that sponsored street performances by brass bands, second lines, jazz funerals, and Mardi Gras Indians; neighborhood restaurants and bars where Creole cuisine flourished for neighborhood friendship groups (Jackson 2006). "If city planners, government officials, and developers would consider the routes that social and pleasure clubs weave throughout the city, they would discover a subaltern map—rich with physical and cultural data—that could be used to inform their own reports and recommendations" (Breunlin and Regis 2006: 760).

A close reading of the New Orleans Architecture Series gives the idea that Creole cottages, townhouses, and Victorian cottages were by far the most common house type in New Orleans. These publications discuss or illustrate relatively few shotguns.[9] Yet shotgun houses are by any measure the city's dominant house type. A rough estimate based on aerial photographs of Orleans Parish from 1933 shows about sixty thousand shotgun family houses at the height of the shotgun building boom—almost 50 percent of Orleans Parish's housing stock.[10] New Orleans is clearly the shotgun capital of the world.

Another measure of the relative disinterest in the back-of-town sections of the city by its planners and by the architectural history community is that

New Orleans Shotgun

Fig. 2.15. Duplex *ti-kay* house, Vieux Aquin, southern Haiti, 1995. Photo by author.

out of 147 specific Historic American Buildings Survey (HABS) projects that have been completed and posted online for Orleans Parish by the Library of Congress, only 8 deal with the shotgun family of house types.[11] Architectural historians have clearly expended comparatively little effort on documenting New Orleans's historic shotgun houses. They have conducted no census of shotgun houses, created no typology, written no history; geographers, folklorists, anthropologists, and architectural historians have not even agreed on a definition of the form.

In 2007, to examine the validity of the claims that the pre-1840 architectural record shows no evidence of the existence of shotgun houses, I began to construct a database of historic shotguns. I sought to document as many shotgun-like houses in existence in the first four decades of the nineteenth century as possible. This search revealed a complex and robust history of early shotgun house development.[12]

The database contains 146 properties with shotgun-like structures dated between 1790 and 1910; 47 of the structures date to before 1830, and 97 date to before 1840. The actual number of houses is higher, since several of the properties contained multiple buildings. Questionable buildings were excluded. The database provides a reasonably accurate portrait of the origins and evolution of the shotgun house. Because early shotgun-like houses varied considerably in form and in construction material, New Orleans architectural historians do not generally define these structures as shotguns, preferring to reserve that designation for the gable-fronted wooden cottages of the post-1840 period. I refer to all houses that were or that evolved directly from a shotgun prototype as linear cottages. This prototype was one room wide, was two or more rooms deep, had its narrow end and front door(s) opening directly onto the street, and had its roof ridge perpendicular to the street, path, or waterway. Linear cottages include a number of logical expansions of the single shotgun cottage, including doubles, side halls, and two-story duplexes. A similar relationship between simple single shotgun-like houses and complex forms may be seen in several Haitian cities, where linear cottages are also highly popular (fig. 2.15).

A BRIEF HISTORY OF THE LINEAR COTTAGE IN NEW ORLEANS

Sketching out an alternate history of the development of the shotgun house leads to the inescapable conclusion that the transformations of architectural form are closely linked to socioeconomic processes and symbolic meanings. Architectural transformations are closely associated with temporal fads and other trends that may survive for as little as a single decade. The development of the shotgun (or any popular vernacular form) cannot be understood without reference to the large-scale social and economic transformations that were occurring when those forms were popular. Vernacular house types are inherently social statements carrying important messages about their builders and residents, including where they stood in the fabric of urban society. Such statements include but go far beyond mere distinctions of economic power. They speak to ethnic and political tensions and a myriad of other elements in the construction of personal identity and social aspiration.

1800–1809

The Notarial Archives contain relatively few poster drawings from the first years of American sovereignty over New Orleans, but other sources help us fill in the picture of traditions of vernacular architecture. As the decade opened, the Haitian Revolution had been under way for nine years. French-speaking refugees were already filtering into the city, and many more would arrive. Under the Spanish administration, Louisiana had become a society composed primarily of three ranked castes: free citizens (white Creoles and Europeans), mostly mulatto *gens de couleur libre* (free people of color), and the enslaved, consisting largely of black Creole *negres* and *bozales* ("saltwater slaves," born in Africa). In New Orleans, the enslaved were mostly of African descent, with a significant minority of mulatto or triracial makeup. Many skilled slaves were afforded considerable freedom, a phenomenon on which the growing numbers of Anglo-Americans now pouring into the city from the North often remarked with amazement.

Fig. 2.16. Spanish colonial Creole cottages, 900 block of Conti Street. Courtesy New Orleans Notarial Archives (035.057).

Linear Cottage 1: The Appentis *Cottage*

Following New Orleans's second great fire of 1794, Spanish authorities passed a number of building codes that transformed the old city's appearance and architecture. French architects and engineers continued to design and build French-style buildings, but they now more resembled the townhouses of the suburbs of mid-eighteenth-century Paris (Edwards 1993). Houses stood at the fronts of the properties, and the earlier parterre gardens were now transformed into rear patios that functioned as service spaces. Townhouses had porte cocheres, and many townhouses were two or three stories tall with shops or commercial enterprises on the ground floor and residences in the *piano-noble* (elevated living floor). Single-story Creole cottages lined the banquettes (sidewalks), with little space between the structures (fig. 2.16). Lots were increasingly divided into narrow strips 15, 20, or 30 French feet wide but still 120 or even 150 feet deep.

In the elongated rear courtyards, shed-roofed service buildings were commonly built down one side of the lot. They were placed against a tall party wall, with the highest portion of the roof attached near the top of the wall and the lower edge of the roof on the side of the courtyard. Around 1800, New Orleans residents began to bring their linear service buildings up to the front of the street and to treat them like shotgun houses. Paired doors opened onto the banquette. These are called *appentis* (shed-roofed) cottages. They originally were supposed to be built in pairs, back-to-back, but in New Orleans it was common to have single freestanding *appentis* cottages without matching buildings on the other side of the party wall or even a party wall at all. *Appentis* cottages continued to be built through the 1840s (figs. 2.17–19).

Fig. 2.17. Freestanding *appentis* cottage single, Tremé Street. Courtesy New Orleans Notarial Archives (090.014, elevation).

Fig. 2.18. Early-nineteenth-century three-bay *appentis* cottage, 915 St. Philip Street, February 2007. Photo by author.

New Orleans Shotgun

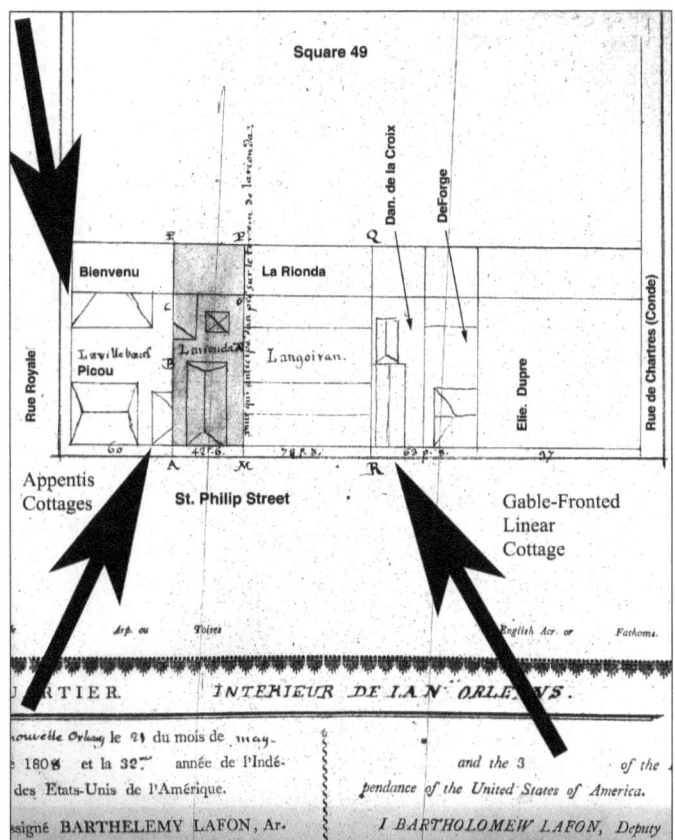

Fig. 2.19. Barthélémy Lafon survey of properties in Vieux Carré Square 49, 21 May 1808. Courtesy Historic New Orleans Collection, Mss. 408, Bk. 2.

Linear Cottage 2: Shanties and Cabanes

Another form of linear cottage was being built around the fringes of the growing city in the first decade of the nineteenth century. Though not recorded in Notarial Archive documents, tiny houses with the footprint of linear cottages began to show up in sketches and drawings before the turn of the century and continued between 1800 and 1808 (fig. 2.12). Personal field survey records of the Spanish surveyor general, Carlos Trudeau (1800–1803) and of the deputy surveyor for the Territory of Orleans, Barthélémy Lafon (ca. 1805–9), show linear cottages that appear to be in the shotgun tradition (fig. 2.19).[13] The exact purpose of some of these buildings is not known, but they are long and narrow and have hip roofs, identical in form to other shotgun-type houses for which more complete documentation exists in ensuing decades. Lafon's surveys in particular depict dozens of linear cottages in and around the French Quarter, although New Orleans historians

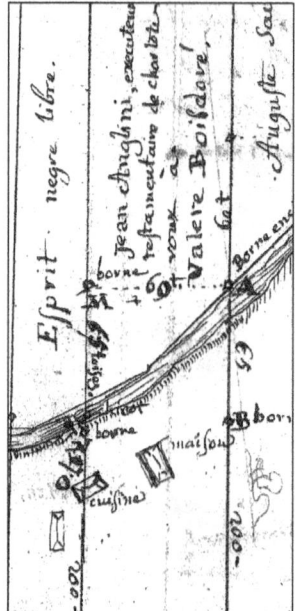

Fig. 2.20. Barthélémy Lafon Survey of the property of Valerie Boisdoré on Bayou Metairie, 16 April 1808. The survey shows two small fringe linear cottages. Courtesy Historic New Orleans Collection, Mss. 408, Bk. 2, pp. 200–202.

charting the evolution of architecture in the early American period have never used these sources.

An 1808 land dispute case, *Valerie Boisdoré v. Le Negre Esprit*, illustrates the kind of fringe architecture being erected along Bayou Metairie in the vicinity of the New Orleans Museum of Art, in what is today City Park. The case resulted in two separate surveys, eight days apart, by Lafon (fig. 2.20). Both document a pair of hip-roofed linear cottages that certainly fall within the shotgun tradition. Esprit's house is referred to as a *cabane*, while Boisdoré's is labeled a *maison*. With the exception of their relative size, they are identical.

The first extant perspective illustration of a shotgun house in New Orleans derives from Bouqueto de Woiseri's commemorative painting documenting the city at the time of the Louisiana Purchase in 1803 (fig. 2.12). The painting depicts a small Haitian-style shotgun, apparently being used as a guard house, on the Marigny Plantation at the foot of what is now Elysian Fields Avenue at the Mississippi River.

More documentary evidence indicates the presence of fringe linear cottages quickly constructed for the thousands of Haitian refugees pouring into the city at the end of the decade. Although built as a temporary solution to the problem of drastic urban overcrowding, some of these linear cottages survived until the first Sanborn surveys were conducted in 1875.

New Orleans Shotgun

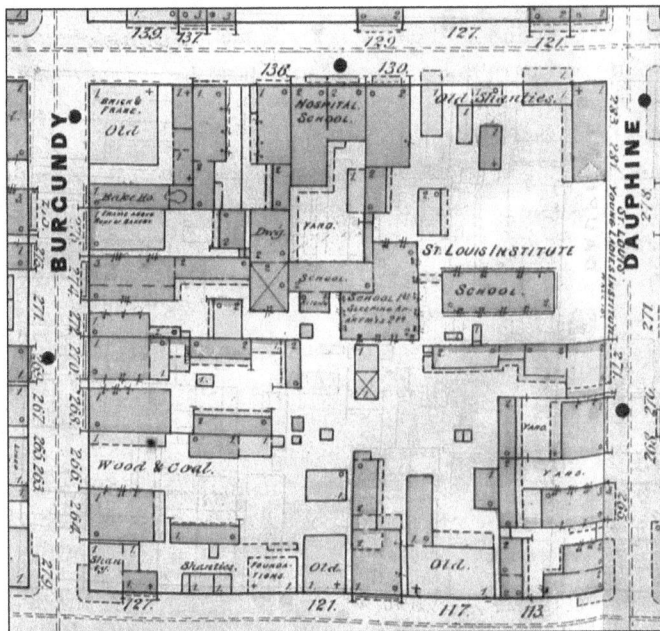

Fig. 2.21. Vieux Carré Square 83, surveyed for 1876 Sanborn Insurance Company map. The map shows "old shanties" in the 900 block of Governor Nichols Street. Courtesy Southeastern Architectural Archive, Tulane University.

Tiny shotgun-like cottages, always wooden, are generally referred to as "old shanties." By the time of the next general Sanborn survey in the 1880s, these structures were gone (fig. 2.21). They appeared both in Marigny and in the northern corner of the Vieux Carré.[14]

1810–1835

Subsequent events drastically altered the tradition of linear cottages. The Spanish government ejected French citizens from its territories when Napoleon attacked Spain in 1809. Cuba had previously received some thirty-five thousand French-speaking refugees from the Haitian Revolution, but those who would not declare allegiance to Spain were now required to leave. In 1809, therefore, more than nine thousand Haitian refugees arrived in American New Orleans, doubling the city's population. This population was divided roughly into thirds: colonial French, *affranchis* (free people of color), and the enslaved (Duplantier 2007; Dessens 2007; Bell 1997; Brasseaux and Conrad 1992).

The *affranchis* had the greatest impact on New Orleans's vernacular architecture. Their numbers more than doubled the size of the *gens de couleur libres* caste. In Saint-Domingue, the men had worked as planters, small businessmen, and artisans and for the most part resumed those occupations in Louisiana. Many had been builders and carpenters, and New Orleans suddenly had a great need for new houses, since people were crowded into attics and outbuildings. Saint-Domingue builders joined the forces working to construct more permanent houses in the Vieux Carré and in the rapidly expanding Creole Faubourgs (satellite neighborhoods): Marigny, Tremé, and the Bayou road.

By the second decade of the nineteenth century, New Orleans was growing exponentially, a process that would continue for decades. With the success of the sugar and cotton industries, Anglo businessmen from the eastern seaboard were flocking to New Orleans in search of riches. The city had few hotels or rooming houses, and good accommodations were difficult to acquire. Into this opportunity stepped free women of color, often referred to as quadroons (quarter-blooded). Most were the second- or third-generation offspring of colonial liaisons between French or Spanish planters and their slaves. Fathers often manumitted the children of these unions and provided them with considerable financial support. Girls were educated in the feminine arts and domestic skills of the day, and many were provided with residences in the city of New Orleans. They and their children preferred to settle in the city's Quadroon Quarter, the northernmost sector of the French Quarter bounded by Rampart Street and Esplanade Avenue, and the adjacent fringes of Faubourgs Tremé and Marigny.

As educated and financially independent free people of color, women of this class often hesitated to marry men of their own class. Instead, the institution of *plaçage* (formalized but extralegal hypergamy) grew up, as it had in other French colonial areas, among them Saint-Domingue, and in Saint-Louis and Gorée Island, Senegal (Hinchman 2000; Mark 2002). Teenaged mixed-race girls were introduced to and eventually contracted to wealthy white gentlemen through such institutions as Quadroon Balls (Kmen 1966). Some of these pairings were as permanent as any legal marriage, but others were not. Whatever the outcome, the white *maris* partners were obligated to provide their *placées* with small houses, most of which were located in the Ramparts or the Quadroon Quarter. Indeed, in the Spanish jargon of the time, the *placée* was called the *casa chica* (little house).

With the eventual dissolution of many of the *plaçage* relationships, quadroon "divorcees" occupied a relatively advantageous financial position. Many were homeowners and had benefitted from stipends provided by their *maris*. These women quickly turned to business, specializing in rental property and rooming houses in the rapidly expanding city. "The female quadroons may be said to have monopolized the renting, at high prices, of

New Orleans Shotgun

Fig. 2.22. Michel Fortier cottage, ca. 1820, 819 Burgundy Street, in the Vieux Carré. Courtesy New Orleans Vieux Carré Commission.

furnished rooms to the whites of the male sex. This they easily did, for it was difficult to equal them in attention to their tenants, and those tenants would indeed have been very hard to please if they had not been satisfied" (Gayarré 1866–95: 8–9).

But who built the little houses for the quadroon landladies? From the 1820s through the 1840s, numerous descriptions exist of "those pretty and peculiar houses, whole rows of which may be seen in the Ramparts" and "those peculiar little dwellings near the Ramparts" (Martineau 1981: 181–82; Saxon 1930: 57). "There are, in some streets, long blocks of one-story houses, with one or two rooms built purposely to be let out to bachelors. Indeed, there are neither hotels nor boarding-houses enough to accommodate one-tenth part of this class of male" (Register 1971: 27). Since the only other popular kind of narrow house in this part of the city in these decades was the single-wide two- or three-bay Creole cottage, which were one and a half stories tall (fig. 2.7), the houses referred to are almost certainly linear cottages.

Linear Cottage 3: The Single Maisonette

Several forms of linear cottages appear in the historical record in this period. Narrow cottages built in brick or *briquette-entre-poteaux* were commonplace,

Fig. 2.23. *Ti-kay* houses in Mirabalais, central Haiti, December 1995. Photo by author.

though not dominant in the French Quarter. The architectural histories call this form maisonettes (fig. 2.22) or occasionally *maisons longues*. In general, they have been described simply as versions of the standard French colonial urban Creole cottage turned sideways and fitted onto narrow lots. Their hip roofs were supported with heavy Norman roof trusses. The single maisonette invariably had double French-style doors that opened directly onto the sidewalk. The standard history of the shotgun claims that Creole cottages and maisonettes were socially and ethnically equivalent in this period but fails to recognize that these narrow dwellings were organized like shotgun houses rather than like Creole cottages. The standard history also fails to acknowledge that at least some of these cottages were built by immigrants from Haiti and that almost identical forms remain commonplace in Haiti today; they almost certainly were common there in the early nineteenth century as well (fig. 2.23).

Linear Cottage 4: The Double

The double shotgun house—a two-room-wide cottage with four doors facing the street, a hip roof, and ridges perpendicular to the street—appears to derive from a combination of two kinds of expansion. One form of reduced Creole cottage was only a single room deep. As free people of color increasingly found it necessary to supplement their incomes by renting rooms, the old single Creole cottage was expanded with a single set of rooms running toward the rear of the lot, with the last one or two sets separated from the rest and entered only from the outside. A gallery or hallway was constructed

New Orleans Shotgun

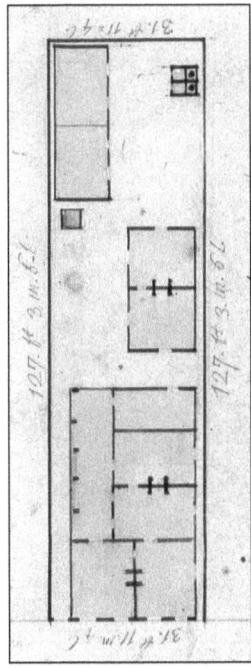

Fig. 2.24a. Plan of Phillippon cottage. Courtesy New Orleans Notarial Archives (044.035).

Fig. 2.24b. Ca. 1810 Phillippon side-gallery Creole cottage, 1016 Dauphine Street. Courtesy New Orleans Notarial Archives (044.035, elevation).

71

JAY D. EDWARDS

Fig. 2.25a. Ca. 1830 double maisonette on Frenchmen Street in Faubourg Marigny. Courtesy New Orleans Notarial Archives (048.002, elevation).

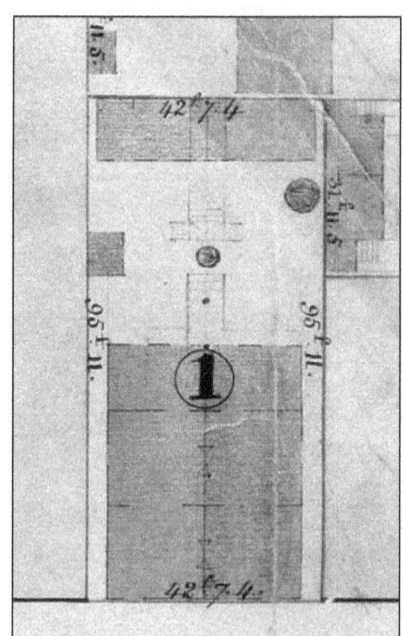

Fig. 2.25b. Plan of double maisonette. Courtesy New Orleans Notarial Archives (048.002).

New Orleans Shotgun

Fig. 2.26. Ca. 1820 linear cottage and Creole cottage, 1000 block, Union Street. Courtesy New Orleans Notarial Archives (066.009).

down the length of rear rooms to permit renters to gain access without passing through the owner's living rooms (fig. 2.24a). The resulting double maisonette closely resembled a double shotgun (fig. 2.24b). The enormous number of side-hall and side-gallery shotguns still extant throughout the city are descended from this tradition. Before long, however, true doubles began sprouting up and became an even more popular form of rental housing (fig. 2.25a–b).

1836–1860s

Linear Cottage 5: The Gable-Fronted Single

New Orleans architectural historians generally consider the shotgun to be a linear cottage with a gabled or pedimented front rather than with a hip roof. However, hip roofs were almost universal in the linear cottages of the 1805–30 period, although some gable-fronted single shotguns also existed: several appear on the Lafon surveys of the French Quarter (fig. 2.19). By the 1820s, gable-fronted frame shotguns began to appear in several of the Creole Faubourgs (fig. 2.26, right side).

Not until the late 1830s, however, did the transition between hip-roofed and gable-roofed shotguns get into full swing. In that decade, Greek Revival styling, promoted by the pattern books of Asher Benjamin (1974) and Minard Lafever (1855; 1969), swept through all ranks of New Orleans society. In 1834 and 1835, architects James Gallier Sr. (1798–1866) and James Dakin (1806–52) begin designing Greek Revival houses and mansions for wealthy clients of many ethnicities (Scully 1973). Vernacular imitations of their designs almost immediately spread throughout the city. Gable-fronted shotgun forms were among the most logical selections for the new style. The

Fig. 2.27. Ca. 1840 three-bay side-gallery shotgun with tall entablature, Brainard Street. Courtesy New Orleans Notarial Archives (088.016).

Fig. 2.28. Charles Dakin's design for the Duane Street Church, ca. 1840. Courtesy Louisiana Division/City Archives, New Orleans Public Library.

New Orleans Shotgun

Fig. 2.29. Ca. 1900 shotgun with Greek Revival trim on Chartres Street, in the Holy Cross neighborhood, May 2006. Photo by author.

massing of the more popular Creole cottage differs substantially from classical Greek temple forms. To hide the structures' rooflines from the street, builders would have had to add very tall entablatures. Even hip-roofed maisonettes are something of a problem (fig. 2.27), but the gable-fronted linear cottage was well suited to this new architectural fad since it already had the massing of the newly popular Greek temple form (compare figs. 2.28 and 2.29). Pediments, entablatures, and colonnades supporting front galleries were added to a wide variety of linear cottages, both large and small. The result was a veritable revolution in New Orleans's cultural landscapes (fig. 2.30). The greatest exuberance and devotion to the new forms appeared in the American Sector. Two-story shotgun forms, Creole townhouse forms, and doubles were all adorned with elaborate Greek Revival decor (fig. 2.31).

Linear Cottage 6: The North Shore House

Prior to the antebellum period, new Anglo residents of the Garden District begin to construct shotguns with double side galleries and with ells or tees at the rear (fig. 2.32). None remains in its original appearance. The 1840s and 1850s witnessed severe yellow fever epidemics, and New Orleans residents who could afford to do so deserted the city in summer and early fall for more rural places. Communities on the north shore of Lake Pontchartrain became popular. Mandeville, in St. Tammany Parish, developed by Bernard

Fig. 2.30. Ca. 1840 pedimented shotgun, North Robertson Street. Courtesy New Orleans Notarial Archives (019.001, elevation).

Fig. 2.31. Ca. 1840 duplex shotgun, Ursulines Street. Courtesy New Orleans Notarial Archives (002.014, elevation).

New Orleans Shotgun

Fig. 2.32. Ca. 1836 double side-gallery cottage on Euterpe Street, in the Lower Garden District. Courtesy New Orleans Notarial Archives (042.015).

Fig. 2.33. Double side-gallery duplex on Moss Street, on Bayou St. John, 2005. Subsequently razed. Photo by author.

de Marigny in 1834, eventually became the site of a new variant of the shotgun, the North Shore house. Builders seem to have duplicated a style of galleried *ti-kay* found in Haiti, though it was probably modeled most directly on New Orleans's side-galleried shotguns (fig. 2.32). Like the Haitian houses, it often had a series of doors along its flanks. It is not known whether this

Fig. 2.34a. 1820s-style *appentis* cottage single with two-story rear kitchen, 800 block of Toulouse Street, as drawn in 1858. Courtesy New Orleans Notarial Archives (045.051).

development represented stimulus diffusion, independent invention, or convergent evolution. Single- and double-gallery shotguns continued to be constructed in several parts of New Orleans until the twentieth century, though in limited numbers (fig. 2.33).

1860s–1870s

Linear Cottage 7: The Camelback

The shotgun house did not stop evolving after the Civil War. Indeed, with the spectacular parallel expansions of the urban population and the cypress lumber industry in Louisiana in the 1870s and 1880s, the number of wooden houses mushroomed. Growing working-class prosperity resulted in a variety of transformations of the antebellum shotgun house. Although the form was by now at least seventy years old, the linear cottage still had a few tricks up its sleeve.

From the 1830s through the 1870s, single-story shotguns and doubles commonly had detached two-story *cuisine/garçonnier* service buildings at the rear (figs. 2.34a–b). The kitchen was on the first floor, and the second story functioned as servants' quarters, bachelors' rooms, and rental spaces. Soon after the Civil War, retooled foundries transitioned from war production to the production of cast iron stoves, a technology that was far

New Orleans Shotgun

Fig. 2.34b. 1830s-style side-hall shotgun with a two-story detached kitchen, 1300 block of Bienville Street, in Storyville. Courtesy New Orleans Notarial Archives (090.041).

Fig. 2.35. 1848-style cast-iron box stove. Sketch by Mary Lee Eggart.

Fig. 2.36. Post–Civil War–style cast-iron stove. Sketch by Mary Lee Eggart.

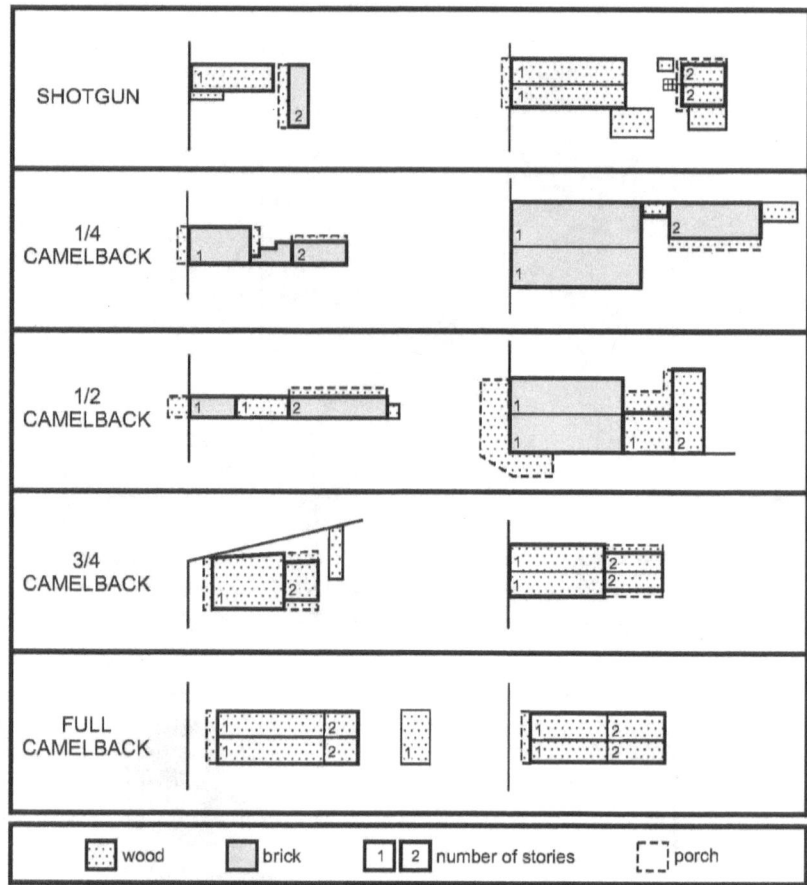

Fig. 2.37. Evolution of the shotgun into the camelback house. Data from 1876 Sanborn maps of New Orleans. Sketch by Mary Lee Eggart.

more convenient than its antebellum predecessors (figs. 2.35–36). For the first time, kitchens could safely be connected directly to rear house walls, or the two might be joined by an extension (figs. 2.37–38). When a two-story kitchen unit is attached directly to the rear of the single-story shotgun or shotgun double, the result is the curious and unique camelback house. Proto-camelbacks appear in small numbers in all stages of attachment in the 1876 Sanborns, and by the 1896 edition, camelbacks, fully formed, are commonplace (fig. 2.39). During Reconstruction, the second-floor bedroom over the kitchen, once a slave quarter or rental unit, received a new role as the secluded master bedroom. Through adaptive reuse, homeowners had

Fig. 2.38. Bargeboard camelback house, damaged by Katrina flooding, near St. Claude Avenue, in the Lower Ninth Ward, October 2005. Photo by author.

Fig. 2.39. Double camelback house in Eastlake decor at the corner of Cleveland and Gayoso, July 2007. Photo by author.

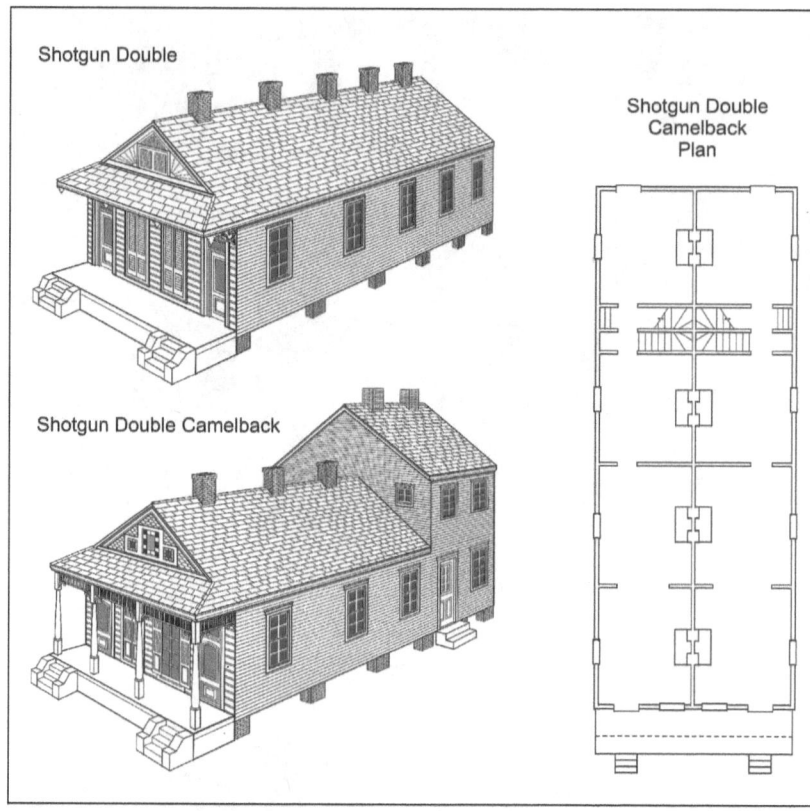

Fig. 2.40. Perspective views of a double shotgun and a double camelback with a plan of the camelback. Sketch by Mary Lee Eggart.

created a new zone of undisturbed privacy in the otherwise very public shotgun house. The rear kitchen section soon became fully integrated with the shotgun front, creating the familiar New Orleans camelback (fig. 2.39). Both single and double shotguns flourished in this period, with the second side of the double either used for rental or shared with relatives (fig. 2.40).

The history of the New Orleans linear cottage is both long and complex, the result of a richly textured weaving of influences of immigrant and local groups. The evolution of so many different forms and styles of linear cottage has not yet completely been told. The wooden, gable-fronted shotguns of the 1840s and 1850s clearly had their roots in the shanties, *cabanes*, and maisonettes built between 1805 and 1830, and many of these earlier forms clearly were the products of the hands of Afro-French Creoles, both Saint-Domingue refugees and native-born Louisiana Creoles of color.

CONCLUSIONS

In his keynote address to the Cultures of Rebuilding Conference on 6 November 2008, Andrei Codrescu suggested, only partly in jest, that the poor are uniquely the creators of culture. Although in a technical sense, cultural anthropologists might have problems with such a sweeping proposition, Codrescu makes an excellent point. Many of the numerous genres for which New Orleans is world famous arise directly from back-of-town neighborhoods populated by working-class and relatively impoverished African Americans. Indeed, several of their folk genres—Mardi Gras Indian krewes and the blues, for example—developed as direct patterns of cultural resistance to political and economic hegemonies that African Americans experienced (Jackson 2006). The shotgun house may be another of these genres.[15]

Colonial and postcolonial societies have a long tradition in which public authorities attempt to suppress or restrict folk cultural expressions and vernacular performances of all kinds, particularly those in which those authorities do not participate or those they do not appreciate. If popular cultural patterns interpreted as troublesome or simply in the way cannot be regulated so that profit may be made from them, authorities are tempted to suppress them or to replace them with something more tractable and lucrative. What is required at all costs is a top-down system of control.

When city planners run an elevated expressway through the tree-lined main boulevard of the nation's oldest African American community, almost completely destroying it, that is an expression of cultural suppression. When Catholic authorities remove the valued and beloved priest of an African American parish despite his overwhelming support from the community, that is also a form of cultural suppression. When police authorities raise the fee for a parade permit from sixteen hundred dollars to thirty-eight hundred dollars to suppress second-line parades, it is yet another example. When the Federal Emergency Management Agency withholds its support for rebuilding or when the city authorizes the razing of "blighted" houses belonging to evacuees too poor to return and rebuild, without the permission or even the knowledge of those people, such actions are also examples of cultural violence promoted under the guise of "new urbanism" or "smart growth." When the cost of living in the post-Katrina city rises 11 percent while the average income of local workers in the service and tourist-support industries drops by 22 percent, it is another form of cultural suppression. So is the early history of the shotgun house. What is remarkable about the environment of recovery is the degree to which some groups and neighborhoods have recovered and even profited while others have found themselves utterly unable to fashion a strategy for return. Part of the problem lies in the differential values placed on neighborhoods and their houses in a city that remains sharply divided along ethnic and socioeconomic lines.

History is important in no small measure because we often find ourselves living it in the present. Perhaps in no major American city has this phenomenon been more common than in New Orleans. The Crescent City increasingly survives on its cultural traditions, many of which derive directly from the nineteenth century. Yet those who have controlled the city's post-Katrina recovery policies have resisted the establishment of a design for the recovery of precisely these traditions. Planning commissions and committees apparently have seen no advantage in establishing a support system that would directly and efficiently restore those neighborhoods where the central cultural traditions of this unique city flourished before 31 August 2005. They apparently have not seen past the tourist venues to the dynamic cultural traditions that the tourist industry commodifies and from which the more recovered sectors of the city profit. By focusing on the gingerbread, they have forgotten the foundations.

In New Orleans, preservationists view post-Katrina recovery through antithetical worldviews. The majority of professionally trained architectural historians still live in Sam Wilson's view of the city's history. In part because of biases in the archival record and because of disinterest, their writings have effectively omitted a significant part of the early history of the shotgun house—its period of fluorescence. How can human-oriented historic preservation take place with little or no history to buttress it? Erasure by omission or benign neglect is still erasure—it is a form of cultural suppression. In the absence of a broad-based social and cultural architectural history, the stories of many of the creators of the city's dominant vernacular building tradition have been set aside. The imbalance that remains in the wake of an overly narrow reading of this history favors those who previously owned a history—the Anglos, the French Creoles, and the Greek Revival architects, among others. Their contributions to domestic architecture—the eastern style townhouse, Greek Revival and Italianate mansions, the raised plantation house, and above all, the Creole cottage—have become imbued with value. The dominating proportion of shotgun houses in New Orleans demands an explanation and a detailed socially sensitive history. Yet the story of the shotgun's remarkable evolution has languished, unexamined and unexplained. This erasure, I believe, has translated both directly and indirectly into New Orleans recovery politics, historic preservation policy, and neighborhood support. It is not that members of the evaluation committees for the Road Home and other grant programs to New Orleans homeowners disparaged shotgun houses and low-lying neighborhoods. In my experience, most were, in fact, genuinely sympathetic. It is, rather, that the committees were not provided with the tools that would have permitted recovery to proceed in a balanced and democratic way. It was the poorest, the least educated, the least advantaged, and the least well connected who ended up with the least support and with no practical means of returning to their devastated homes. At a minimum, there is the appearance of substantial bias being mobilized against the owners and renters of wooden cottages of the shotgun crescent. The results are reflected in part in the square miles of ghostly semiabandoned neighborhoods that now struggle to survive in an increasingly difficult and foreboding economic climate.

NOTES

1. As of 1 July 2007, New Orleans's population had rebounded to 239,124, 49 percent of the 2000 population (Clifford 2008). "In New Orleans, the Census report confirms what local officials have been saying for months: Katrina did more damage in lower-income, black neighborhoods, which has made it more difficult for those residents to return," reports William Frey, a demographer with the Brookings Institution. Post-Katrina, New Orleans's white population had rebounded to 123 percent of its prehurricane level, while the black population had risen to only 59 percent of its pre-Katrina level (Konigsmark 2006).
  The author has participated in the decision-making process for determining which homeowners living in historic districts should be granted funding.
2. Churches and NGOs have, for the most part, functioned as a counterweight, supporting the most seriously affected neighborhoods. According to Campanella, 67 percent of all blacks living in Orleans Parish were flooded, as were 51 percent of whites; among those whose houses were under water for eight days or longer, however, the figures were 60 percent of all blacks versus 24 percent of all whites (2006: 401).
3. The American Sector is that area of New Orleans settled in the nineteenth century above Canal Street. It included the Garden District, Carrolton, the Irish Channel, and the Central Business District.
4. The Creole Faubourgs are those expansions contiguous to the original French Quarter that were laid out beginning in the first decades of the nineteenth century. They include Faubourg Marigny, Faubourg Tremé, and the Esplanade Ridge–New Marigny sectors of the city. The Creole Faubourgs were originally inhabited largely by French speakers and by free people of color and blacks.
5. "Lakeview, a 7,000 home mostly white enclave in a city that is predominantly black, has emerged as a success story in the reconstruction of New Orleans. . . . In contrast, hard-hit black middle-class neighborhoods in eastern New Orleans do not have the same financial means and civic organization, and are not drawing nearly as much private investment. As a result, their recovery is crawling" (Moreno Gonzales 2007: 1D). "The Lower 9th Ward has

seen only 9.9 percent of its population return. A traditionally mixed-race neighborhood within the Lower 9th, Holy Cross, has fared better with a 37 percent return, benefitting from the work of preservationists who seek to restore the federally declared historic district. . . . The Garden District has seen 107 percent of its population return, the French Quarter 103 percent, and the neighborhood called Faubourg Marigny has a 100.3 percent return rate" (Bullard and Wright 2009: 30). "Recovery must mean the end of displacement for the people of New Orleans and the Gulf Coast. . . . What we have instead is recovery that demolishes affordable housing," testified Monique Harden of the law firm Advocates for Environmental Human Rights, before the United Nations (Moreno Gonzales 2008: 15A).

6. According to a typical statement from Toledano, a member of the Friends of the Cabildo, "One of the earliest shotgun-type houses in the city, dating from before 1846, is at 920 Spain Street, the J. B. Bordenave house." It is a frame shotgun decorated in Greek Revival style of the 1840s (1996: 52). See also Friends of the Cabildo 1984: 173, 71; Kingsley 2003: 24–25. Historical and comparative perspective calls into question the argument that the shotgun form originated as the result of expansion of the Creole cottage into long, narrow lots. Many hundreds of shotguns employed as quarters on Louisiana plantations are sufficiently widely spaced to permit the use of alternate forms. The earliest shotguns on the fringes of the Creole Faubourgs were not confined to narrow lots. In both Haiti and Cuba, the rural freestanding shotgun-style cottage antedates town cottages.

7. Maroons (Sp. *cimarrones*) were escaped slaves. Enslaved persons began escaping into the mountains of Hispaniola in the first years of the sixteenth century. Maroon slaves initially were aided by Taino natives and almost certainly intermarried with them. Maroons borrowed extensively from Taino architecture. One result, according to Vlach, was a syncretized house with a simple rectangular form and a front porch. This structure developed into the *ti-kay* (local folk shotgun house), later borrowed by African American communities in the cities of the colony of Saint-Domingue (Vlach 1990: 122–31). The French colony of Saint-Domingue began with de facto settlement in the middle of the seventeenth century in the western third of Hispaniola and survived until the Haitian Revolution.

8. In the French colonies, soon after settlement in the mid–seventeenth century, African slaves apparently developed a preference for linear shotgun-like cottages (Edwards 2005: 57–59, 71, 75–77).

9. In the highly popular volumes 4, 5, and 6 of the New Orleans Architecture Series, excluding the architectural inventories at the back of the books, those houses illustrated for discussion include multistory townhouses (44), Greek Revival townhouses (38), Creole cottages (127), Creole and American townhouses (11), Victorian cottages (10), and stores (7). These volumes have a strong bias—almost an obsession—toward Creole cottages. Only 14 shotgun houses are illustrated, and some are mislabeled Creole cottages (Friends of the Cabildo 1984: 52, 85). In other words, shotguns account for just 6 percent of the houses described in these books.

10. Complete aerial coverage for Orleans Parish in 1933 is available through the Cartographic Information Center, Louisiana State University Libraries, Baton Rouge. More recent high-resolution coverage is available through the CADGIS Lab of Louisiana State's Department of Geography and Anthropology and through Google Earth.

11. Most of the shotgun HABS projects that have been completed consist of little more than a few photographs developed for salvage documentation. There are only two sets of plans, one from a set of photocopied blueprints. The report on the 1923 Alton Lear house at 2016 Louisiana Avenue states that 48 percent of the Uptown Historic District's 10,716 buildings

"adopt a shotgun form" ("Alton Lear House" 1996). The proportion in much of the shotgun crescent is higher.

12. The most productive source was the New Orleans Notarial Archives, which hold a collection of nineteenth-century advertising posters and a database of building contracts begun by Sam Wilson and completed by Robert Cangelosi. Throughout the nineteenth century, houses offered at public auction in New Orleans were advertised on large colored posters based on accurate on-site surveys. The posters depict houses at the time of their sale, rather than at the time of their construction, but the archives' professional architectural historians have provided rough dates for most of the buildings based on criteria such as style dating (decorative features), settlement history, and construction features. The Notarial Archives holds on the order of sixteen hundred of these posters. Other valuable sources included the records of the Vieux Carré Survey, Williams Research Center, Historic New Orleans Collection; and the private records of early-nineteenth-century New Orleans surveyors (Barthélémy Lafon, Carlos Trudeau, and the Seghers Company), Historic New Orleans Collection. I also accessed the records of the Vieux Carré Commission at the commission offices in the French Quarter; legal and business records at the New Orleans Collection, University of New Orleans Library, and at the New Orleans Public Library; records of Tulane University's Southeastern Architectural Survey; and Sanborn maps of New Orleans, Geographic Collection, Library of Congress. I also conducted field surveys in the Vieux Carré and the Creole Faubourgs to identify relevant houses that appeared to date from the period of interest. I ran a chain of title searches in the records of the city of New Orleans on several of these structures, a laborious process requiring the interpretation of handwritten French- and Spanish-language documents. Fortunately, reasonably complete chains of title had been previously run by specialists for those properties located within the Vieux Carré.

13. See Trudeau Survey Book, 19 April 1800, for a survey of property on Bayou St. John, vendor Santiago Laurence, buyer Bazisio Crupy, Historic New Orleans Collection (excluded from database). For figures 2.19 and 2.20, see Barthélémy Lafon, Personal Survey Books 1, 2 (mostly property surveys and maps for the Comté d'Orleans, Territorie d'Orleans, 1803–12), Historic New Orleans Collection, MSS 408 (1806–12), acquisition no. 92-51-L.

    Dating of the vernacular buildings was supplied mostly by the architectural historians of the New Orleans Notarial Archives as recorded in their databases. In a few cases, I disagreed with their estimates and adjusted dates based on, for example, evidence of architectural features common in a specific decade. For each vernacular house proven to have existed during 1800–1830, it is likely that no less than ten similar houses existed but were not recorded. Thus, it is not unreasonable to expand the number of buildings of each type in the shotgun database by an order of magnitude to achieve a reasonable estimate of the linear cottage population.

14. The word *shanty* comes from the French *chantier* (temporary cabin). Sanborn Insurance Company maps were initiated in New Orleans in 1876. They were updated roughly every decade thereafter into the twentieth century. The Library of Congress has a nearly complete set of these maps for New Orleans. Others are held in the Tulane Library's Southeastern Architectural Archive.

15. Elsewhere, I have interpreted it as a pattern of circumventional cultural resistance (Edwards 2009).

REFERENCES

"Alton Lear House, 2016–2018 Louisiana Avenue, New Orleans, Orleans Parish, LA." 1996. http://memory.loc.gov/pp/hhhtml/hhTitles29.html. Accessed 10 February 2010.

Bell, Caryn Cossé. 1997. *Revolution, Romanticism, and the Afro-Creole Protest Tradition in Louisiana, 1718–1868.* Baton Rouge: Louisiana State University Press.

Benjamin, Asher. 1974. *The Builder's Guide.* Ca. 1838; New York: Da Capo.

Bohrer, Becky. 2007. "N.O.'s Racial Political Balance May Be Shifting." *Baton Rouge Advocate*, 15 November, 17a.

Borah, William. 1998. *A Master Plan for New Orleans: What Is It? Why Do We Need It?* New Orleans: Louisiana Landmarks Society.

Brasseaux, Carl, and Glenn Conrad. 1992. *The Road to Louisiana: The Saint-Domingue Refugees, 1792–1809.* Lafayette: Center for Louisiana Studies.

Breunlin, Rachel, and Helen Regis. 2006. "Putting the Ninth Ward on the Map: Race, Place, and Transformation in Desire, New Orleans." *American Anthropologist* 108.4 (December): 744–64.

Browne-Dianis, Judith. 2006. *This Is My Home* (documentary). Part 1. http://www.advancementproject.org/katrina/video1.html. Accessed 19 February 2007.

Campanella, Richard. 2002. *Time and Place in New Orleans.* Gretna, La.: Pelican.

———. 2006. *Geographies of New Orleans: Urban Fabrics before the Storm.* Lafayette: Center for Louisiana Studies.

Clifford, Catherine. 2008. "The Big Easy Picks Up the Pace: Census Bureau Says New Orleans Is the Fastest-Growing Large City in the Nation, Recovering from Being Wiped Out by Hurricane Katrina." *CNNMoney.com*, 10 July. http://money.cnn.com/2008/07/10/real_estate/fastest_growing/. Accessed 14 August 2008.

Davis, Mike. 2005. "Gentrifying Disaster in New Orleans: Ethnic Cleansing, GOP-Style." Associated Press. 25 October. http://www.motherjones.com/commentary/columns/2005/10/gentrifying_disaster.htm. Accessed 24 January 2010.

Dessens, Nathalie. 2007. *From Saint-Domingue to New Orleans: Migration and Influences.* Gainesville: University Press of Florida.

Dreier, Peter. 2006. "Katrina and Power in America." *Urban Affairs Review* 41.4 (March): 1022.

Duplantier, Jean-Marc Allard. 2007. "Creole Louisiana's Haitian Exile(s)." *Southern Quarterly* 44.3 (Spring): 68–84.

Edwards, Jay D. 1993. "Cultural Identifications in Architecture: The Case of the New Orleans Townhouse." *Traditional Dwellings and Settlements Review* 5.1 (Fall): 17–32.

———. 2005. "Open Issues in the Study of the Historic Influences of Caribbean Architecture on that of North America." *Material Culture* 37.1 (Spring): 44–84.

———. 2008–9. "Unlocking the History of Greek Key Architecture." *Louisiana Cultural Vistas* 19.4 (Winter): 84–90.

———. 2009. "Shotgun: The Most Contested House in America." *Buildings and Landscapes* 16 (Spring): 62–96.

Friends of the Cabildo. 1977. *New Orleans Architecture.* Vol. 5, *The Esplanade Ridge.* Gretna, La.: Pelican.

———. 1984. *New Orleans Architecture.* Vol. 4, *The Creole Faubourgs.* Gretna, La.: Pelican.

———. 2003. *New Orleans Architecture.* Vol. 6, *Faubourg Tremé and the Bayou Road.* Gretna, La.: Pelican.

Gayarré, Charles E. A. 1866–95. "The Quadroons of Louisiana." MSS. 1558. Special Collections of the Louisiana State University Library, Baton Rouge. 17 pp. Typescript.

Gyan, Joe, Jr. 2007. "Study: N.O. Population Older, Less Poor." *Baton Rouge Advocate*. 13 September. 1A, 4A.

Heard, Malcolm. 1997. *French Quarter Manual: An Architectural Guide to New Orleans' Vieux Carré*. New Orleans: Tulane School of Architecture.

Hinchman, Mark. 2000. "African Rococo: House and Portrait in Eighteenth Century Senegal." 2 vols. Ph.D. diss., University of Chicago.

Jackson, Maria-Rosario. 2006. "Rebuilding the Cultural Vitality of New Orleans." In *After Katrina: Rebuilding Opportunity and Equity into the New New Orleans*, ed. Margery Austin Turner and Sheila R. Zedlewski, 55–61. New Orleans: Urban Institute.

Kaiser Foundation. 2007. *Giving Voice to the People of New Orleans: The Kaiser Post-Katrina Baseline Survey*, May. http://www.kff.org/kaiserpolls/upload/7631.pdf. Accessed 24 January 2010.

Kalima, Rose, Annie Clark, and Dominique Duval-Dlop. 2008. *Equity Atlas: A Long Way Home: The State of Housing Recovery in Louisiana*. http://www.policylink.org/threeyears later. Accessed 2 November 2009.

Kingsley, Karen. 2003. *Buildings of Louisiana*. New York: Oxford University Press.

Kmen, Henry A. 1966. "The Quadroon Balls." In *Music in New Orleans: The Formative Years, 1791–1841*, ed. Henry A. Kmen, 42–55. Baton Rouge: Louisiana State University Press. Reprinted in *The African American Experience in Louisiana*, part A, ed. Charles Vincent, 417–27. Lafayette: Center for Louisiana Studies, 1999.

Konigsmark, Anne Rochell. 2006. "Census Outlines Face of Today's New Orleans." *USA Today*, 7 June. http://www.usatoday.com/news/nation/2006-06-07-neworleans_x.htm. Accessed 14 August 2008.

Lafever, Minard. 1855. *The Beauties of Modern Architecture*. New York: Appleton.

———. 1969. *The Modern Builder's Guide*. New York: Dover.

Lewis, Peirce F. 1976. *New Orleans: The Making of an Urban Landscape*. Cambridge, Mass.: Ballinger.

Livingston, Min, and J. Kojo Livingston. 2007. "Housing: A Crisis of Courage, Compassion & Leadership." *New Orleans Agenda*, 20 December. http://www.theneworleansagenda.com/. Accessed 11 August 2008.

Logan, John R. 2007. "The Impact of Katrina: Race and Class in Storm-Damaged Neighborhoods." http://www.s4.brown.edu/Katrina/report.pdf. Accessed 10 October 2007.

Mark, Peter. 2002. *"Portuguese" Style and Luso-African Identity: Precolonial Senegambia, Sixteenth–Nineteenth Centuries*. Bloomington: Indiana University Press.

Martineau, Harriet. 1981. *Society in America*. 1837; New Brunswick, N.J.: Transaction.

Ligon, Richard. 1673. *A True and Exact History of the Island of Barbados (1647–1650)*. London: Parker and Guy.

Moreno Gonzales, John. 2007. "Black Neighborhoods Hard-Hit by Katrina Not Getting Same Kind of Support in N.O." *Baton Rouge Advocate*, 16 March, D.

———. 2008. "U.N. Finds Racism in Katrina Recovery." *Baton Rouge Advocate*, 29 February, 15A.

Reeves, Sally K. 2003. "Contribution of Free Persons of Color to Vernacular Architecture in New Orleans before the Civil War." Paper presented at "Raised to the Trade . . . Creole Building Arts of New Orleans," New Orleans Museum of Art, 13 February.

Register, James. 1971. *New Orleans Is My Name*. 1834–35. Shreveport, La.: Mid-South.

Saxon, Lyle. 1930. *Lafitte the Pirate*. New York: Century.
Scully, Arthur, Jr. 1973. *James Dakin, Architect: His Career in New York and the South*. Baton Rouge: Louisiana State University Press.
Tarhakah, Jakuna. 2005. Interview in *Acorn: Community Forum on Rebuilding New Orleans* (DVD). New Orleans: Acorn.
Toledano, Roulhac. 1996. *National Trust Guide to New Orleans*. New York: Wiley.
Vlach, John M. 1975. *Sources of the Shotgun House: African and Caribbean Antecedents for Afro-American Architecture*. Ph.D. diss. 2 vols. Indiana University.
———. 1990. *The Afro-American Tradition in Decorative Arts*. Athens: University of Georgia Press.
Vogt, Loyd. 1985. *New Orleans Houses: A House-Watcher's Guide*. Gretna, La.: Pelican.
———. 2002. *Historic Buildings of the French Quarter*. Gretna, La.: Pelican.
Weiss, Ellen. 1997. "City and Country, 1880–1915: Shotguns, a Louisiana Building Type." In *Louisiana Buildings, 1720–1940*, ed. Jessie Poesch and Barbara SoRelle Bacot, 267–85. Baton Rouge: Louisiana State University Press.

SOUL FOOD
Katrina and the Culinary Arts

BENJAMIN MORRIS

If I'm not responsible for making a good gumbo, who is?
—CHEF JOHN BESH

May 2007, Cambridge, England. There's a restaurant, Old Orleans, not far from my house. It's a chain theme restaurant owned by the Regent Inns conglomerate in the United Kingdom. Normally I walk right past it on the way home from work, but today my friend and I are thirsty, so, stepping inside and bellying up to the bar, we mournfully survey our options—Carling, Stella, Foster's, all typical, mass-market lagers found in nearly any pub in the country. Suddenly, however, we light upon a beer whose name I have not seen in nearly two years: Dixie Beer, brewed by the Dixie Brewing Company of Tulane Avenue, New Orleans, Louisiana. How can this be? The last time I saw Dixie Brewery was in a photograph showing nine feet of floodwater in its central brewing chamber, damage that would take years at least to repair. How is it that eighteen months later I suddenly have a cold one in my hand?

The answer lies in a small note on the label: Due to the devastation of Hurricane Katrina on New Orleans, this beer has been faithfully craft-brewed in the European Union (figs. 3.1 and 3.2).[1] But this modest answer is only part of the story, a story that, to open this chapter on Katrina's effects on New Orleans's culinary industry, throws light on the many issues arising in the ongoing recovery process. The full story is beginning to take shape: Ian McNulty, a writer and restaurant critic for *Gambit Weekly*, has traced the revival of Dixie Beer on domestic shores, charting its post-Katrina history from near collapse to partial recovery by the Heiner Brau

Fig. 3.1. Bottles of New Orleans's Dixie Beer available in the United Kingdom shortly after Hurricane Katrina. Photo by author.

Brewery across Lake Pontchartrain in Covington, Louisiana, to the current arrangement by which it is contract-brewed primarily at Wisconsin's Huber Brewery (McNulty 2007b). A side of the story less well known, however, is the resurrection of Dixie internationally—how Dixie came to be found in Old Orleans restaurants, among others, so quickly after Katrina ravaged its home. And this side of the story points to the love of New Orleans's unique culture far outside the parish line and the recognition of the role the city plays not just in the American imagination but in the European imagination and perhaps even in the global imagination.

After Katrina ravaged the brewery in August 2005, Pierhead Wines (Dixie's distributor in the United Kingdom) initially allowed its local supplies to dwindle, expecting a swift recovery. In 2006, after it became clear that the recovery would be much more protracted—Pierhead eventually ran out of Dixie altogether—sales director Michael Cook reported that one option was to cross the brand off the distributor's list, amputating its European market (Cook 2007). (Brewing beer is more costly in the United Kingdom than in the United States, largely because of the higher cost of bottles and labels.) But Pierhead chose not to do so, not simply because it holds fixed

Soul Food

Fig. 3.2. Dixie Beer label inscription. Photo by author.

contracts for the supply of Dixie that it needed to honor but also because company officials hoped that the Dixie brand would stay alive—suggesting that there was something special about what the beer represented and that it would be difficult, if not impossible, to replace. Collaborating with Joe Bruno, the owner of Dixie Brewing Company, who shared the recipe for the beer, Pierhead contracted with a brewery in Sussex, England, to brew the beer, keeping the European customer base intact until the Tulane Avenue brewery reopened. "We had a contract for a supply of goods," Cook explained. But Dixie Brewing's cypress wood vats give the beer its unique taste, meaning that any attempt to re-create Dixie under contract would require a similar mechanism. Since an exact replica of such a vat was impossible either to construct or to procure in Britain, the consultant brewer found cypress chippings for the construction of the vats, and "was able to engineer a beer which, if it is not 100 percent Dixie, is at least 99.9 percent" (Cook 2007).

Cook's comments and the Dixie saga in general highlight a number of interesting questions about Katrina's effects on New Orleans's culture—not just about the economic dimensions regarding production and export of a local commodity, however historic or cherished, but about the implications of that commodity serving as a symbolic marker of culture within and between global markets. Dixie beer is but one such marker. To sit in a restaurant in the middle of one drained swamp (Cambridge) and enjoy a beer that hails from another drained swamp (New Orleans) more than four thousand miles away—a beer that by most accounts probably would not have been brewed again until years of physical rebuilding and reconstruction (as well as local, national, and international market recapitalization) had been completed—is a remarkable testament both to the presence of globalized culture and to the importance of a brand in sustaining that culture. In other words, this brief story shows that Dixie means something more than just lager: it means New Orleans, and globally New Orleans means (at least in part) an exploitable brand identity with the potential for economic development.

Still, the resurrected Dixie cannot avoid charges against its authenticity, given the changes in the brewing process. At the most banal level, brewed in a different city on a different continent using different water inside a different mechanical assembly, this "faithfully craft-brewed" beer cannot withstand the claim that it is not literally the same beer brewed until recently on Tulane Avenue. But this story also leads to the question of at what point it matters. To whom is this faithfulness important or accountable? For insofar as it throws into relief the mechanisms of global capitalism, this story also raises a host of other questions about the local lives and roles of food in a city whose relationship with the culinary arts has been passionate and intricate, celebrated and complex, inspired and embodied: as Christine Boyer has noted, culinary tourism in New Orleans has existed for at least a hundred years, probably many more (1994: 326). But this story equally illustrates the way that culture can be disrupted, reordered, and reassembled—sometimes permanently—and the way in which culture has, in late modernity, become as globalized a commodity as any other.

This chapter explores the various roles that the culinary arts have played in the rebuilding process in post-Katrina New Orleans, arguing that they have not just been "rebuilt" as part of the city's infrastructure (of hospitality, of tourism, and of heritage) but have themselves catalyzed and changed the course of the rebuilding process. In looking at the specific roles of restaurants (the physical spaces in which food is prepared, shared, and consumed) and of recipes (the documents, traditions, and performances that become iconic and celebrated as markers of personal and collective identity), I examine how both institutions have played important roles in the city's recovery. Finally, I briefly consider the future of foodways in an increasingly volatile, rapidly changing world, reflecting on the nature and meaning of "authenticity" in a society seeking to reconstitute itself after disaster and challenging Linda Civitello's claim that "the future of food is . . . unclear in America's party town, the home of Mardi Gras and the Museum of the Cocktail" (2007: 367). On the contrary, the culinary arts have returned to New Orleans with a new spirit and a new mission.

Two caveats before digging in: first, this chapter does not offer a history of New Orleans cuisine; many more and better accounts can be found elsewhere. In the same vein, this account is not intended to be comprehensive as much as representative of the issues raised by the post-Katrina rebuilding process. Because so many aspects of the story are still unfolding (perhaps most importantly, as the Brookings Institution [2008] notes, the gradually decreasing return of residents to the city), all narratives of the storm and the recovery are influenced by and must be contextualized within simultaneous and potentially conflicting narratives. Some of my claims or the trends to which I refer may be upended in time; with this awareness in mind I have tried to write cautiously rather than flagrantly about the evolving landscape(s) of post-Katrina New Orleans.

RESTAURANTS

"If I don't get back on that corner," said restaurateur Leah Chase, owner of the destroyed restaurant Dooky Chase, "there is no neighborhood" (Johnson 2006). Speaking nine months after the storm, she was not exaggerating. Dooky Chase has long been held as one of the city's most eminent Creole restaurants, sitting on Orleans Avenue in the heart of the Tremé neighborhood and patronized for years by locals, visitors, and even unpopular American presidents (Hammer 2007). But Chase's brief statement points to a salient feature of New Orleans's culinary landscape—the way that a restaurant can operate on multiple levels at once. In other words, a restaurant is less a building or a kitchen than a catalyst for what happens inside and around it: the production of culture itself and the building of community that shares that culture. "Restaurants can define urban landscapes," argue David Beriss and David Sutton, "reflecting and shaping the character of neighborhoods or even the reputation of whole cities and regions. In many cases, restaurateurs and their clients collaborate self-consciously at a variety of levels in creating this thoroughly postmodern performance" (2007: 3). In this instance, then, Dooky Chase operated on at least three levels: as a restaurant synonymous with the city itself (the level of iconicity), as an anchor of activity for a particular neighborhood of that city (the level of local community), and as a locus for the sharing of traditions, forms of knowledge, and memories within and across generations (the level of cultural heritage, of inheritance). Put into the post-Katrina context, the loss of such a widely cherished establishment (and establishments like it) would clearly have grave implications for the urban landscape as a whole, implications that every restaurant in the city would face after the storm. As Adam Nossiter (2006) noted on the reopening of Angelo Brocato's Italian Ice Cream Parlor in Mid-City, "Tastes, collectively remembered, underpin the social fabric here, as much as any precious monument or institution."

But if restaurants served these and other purposes before Katrina, they took on new roles in the storm's immediate aftermath. In the weeks during and after the flood, restaurants and bars served as meeting points, relief agency headquarters, locations for information exchange, and resupply depots for citizens, law enforcement, media personnel, and emergency workers. Andrei Codrescu memorably described the conversion of Molly's at the Market, a bar on Decatur Street in the French Quarter, from a bar into a haven for everyone in town in those first few days after the storm, including security personnel, journalists, and transvestites from the Southern Decadence Festival: "Molly's stayed open throughout [the aftermath] and it became much more than a bar; it was a community center, a clearinghouse, a gathering place for the world press, and a space for solace, comfort, and a drink" (2006: 10). McNulty echoes this phenomenon, describing how "in the months that followed [Katrina], through all the darkness and fear, the best moments of encouragement and happiness came more often from bars and restaurants than anywhere else. The city's eating and drinking places were the fires around which we circled for reminders of the city's life and culture before the storm, for company and sometimes literally for warmth" (2008: 74). In this sense, the physical sites of restaurants or bars were transformed in unexpected and remarkable ways; across the city, but especially in the areas where relief operations were staged, they became far more than just places to eat and interact with others. In a sense, they became a place to interact first and then eat, echoing Beriss and Sutton's claim that "many of the most interesting aspects of social and cultural life in our contemporary world are featured in restaurants. [They] constitute ideal total social phenomena for our postmodern world" (2007: 1).[2]

As the recovery process began to take shape, chef Emeril Lagasse (2006) argued that restaurants provided the main inspiration for rebuilding the city, offering anecdotal testimony from restaurant owners and patrons. But his claim, self-fulfilling as it may be (Lagasse owns ten restaurants, including three in New Orleans and another in nearby Gulfport, Mississippi), is not without warrant: from haute cuisine establishments such as Antoine's, Arnaud's, and Commander's Palace to the celebrated corner bars and diners of every neighborhood in the city (such as Elizabeth's in the Bywater, Liuzza's in Mid-City, or Domilese's Uptown), a great deal of fanfare has surrounded the reconstruction of New Orleans's restaurant industry. In part, Katrina renewed national and international interest in the brand of New Orleans's cuisine, interest that the city's Bring New Orleans Back Commission Cultural Committee (2006) and the state Department of Culture, Recreation, and Tourism (2006) quickly seized on and marshaled in their reports on how best to direct the cultural rebuilding process. Both of these institutions called for culture to serve as the economic engine of the city's rebirth, listing Cajun and Creole cuisine as major draws for tourism and subsequent poststorm development; in its report, the Cultural Committee even called for the worldwide export of cultural products, suggesting that "Taste of New Orleans' cultural tours could be sent across the U.S. and abroad, exporting the best of our music, cuisine, visual arts and crafts through performance tours, touring exhibitions and craft shows that would encourage others to better appreciate our creative resources and replicate some of our distinctive cultural traditions" (Bring New Orleans Back Cultural Committee 2006: 25). Such initiatives have, in time, begun to take shape; in October 2008, the Department of Culture, Recreation, and Tourism cosponsored a free Festival New Orleans at the O2 Centre in London, showcasing New Orleans's culinary traditions such as shrimp etouffeé and Bananas Foster (sponsored by McIlhenny Company, makers of Tabasco) alongside musicians such as Rebirth Brass Brand, Beausoleil, Kermit Ruffins, and Dr. John. But back home, reported Poppy Tooker (2007), this interest galvanized the city's many chefs (such as Lagasse), promoters, culinary activists, and educators, who saw an opportunity to revitalize and cultivate an industry that some observers saw as having been taken for granted. This opportunism showed its force in the scores of different benefits, fund-raisers, auctions, and charity dinners held to provide a lifeline for a culture seen as under threat as well as in the recognition of the industry's efforts to reconstitute itself in the wake of adversity. In May 2006, the James Beard Foundation awarded the entire New Orleans restaurant community its Humanitarian of the Year award.

But even with millions of dollars flowing into the city from public, private, foundation, and nonprofit sources, the road back for local restaurants has not been easy. Indeed, the damage to some restaurants, as Tom Fitzmorris (2007) has described, was so severe that their owners sold, relocated, or retired altogether. For those proprietors who have struggled to reopen and then stay open after the storm, numerous challenges have arisen. As McNulty (2007a) and others detail, trained personnel (chefs, waitstaff, managers) have been scattered across the region and the country; properties, structures, and equipment have suffered acute and sometimes irreparable physical damage; and the disruption in production industries such as agriculture and seafood, many of which are sourced from local communities (such as the Vietnamese shrimpers in New Orleans East), has rerouted or canceled the lines of supply on which restaurants depend so heavily. At the same time, however, the storm created opportunities for some restaurants to undertake works that they might not otherwise have been willing to undertake. Brett Anderson, restaurant critic for the *New Orleans Times-Picayune*, has detailed the reopening of Mandina's in Mid-City, which not only rebuilt but expanded its facilities. In doing so, the physical space changed dramatically, as two houses at the rear of the restaurant were demolished to enlarge the building, increasing both the seating inside and the parking outside. But as Anderson (2007) notes, the changes to the building could not necessarily be tied to changes in the restaurant, and a restaurant is more than just the sum of its walls: customers "were greeted to a paradoxical experience peculiar to post-Katrina New Orleans. The building has been subjected to architectural logic and modernity, and the change is shocking. But like so many of post-Katrina New Orleans' rebuilt buildings, it adheres closely enough to its former self to play tricks on the mind. Once Mandina's fills with New Orleanians, it becomes difficult to remember how exactly it is different than it was."[3]

Examining the post-Katrina culinary landscape of New Orleans, then, reveals that—perhaps contrary to the attitude of the James Beard Foundation or at least the spirit of its collective award—these individual accounts rarely are metonymic for history writ large. As each owner and establishment faced specific challenges in the recovery process, to generalize about the rebirth of the entire industry from those particular experiences is to miss out on the personal, complex intimacy of each venue and its significance for the local community (as Leah Chase pointed out). That said, paradoxically, in the midst of the recovery process, a sentiment emerged that all of the city's restaurants, taken collectively as bearers of a shared identity, were dealt a personal blow by the storm and that to reopen any one venue in particular became a means of fighting back against the devastation in general. This sentiment was perhaps expressed most clearly in an exhibition produced by the Southern Food and Beverage Museum, which had planned to open its doors in New Orleans in August 2005. (Postponed by Katrina, it has since moved into the Riverwalk Marketplace in the Central Business District, along with the Museum of the American Cocktail.) "In destroying

New Orleans' restaurants," the museum (2006) claimed, "Hurricane Katrina threatened to destroy the very identity of the city. Her restaurants are repositories of the city's cultural memory. But as people made their way back to the ruined city, it was apparent that the first and best way to rebuild New Orleans rested with the restaurants. . . . [I]n feeding New Orleanians, they are healing the spirits of the city one meal at a time." To explore how this healing process has worked—taking its boosterism with a due pinch of salt—requires adjusting the scales from the level of a restaurant to the level of an individual meal. Restaurants' long lists of post-Katrina decisions have included what to put on the menu as much as how to keep the doors open.

RECIPES

Fitzmorris, chief restaurant critic for the *Times-Picayune* and proprietor of the online culinary resource www.nomenu.com, has argued that two years after Katrina, the recovery of the city's restaurants was, in fact, completed: all establishments that were going to reopen had done so, and all those that had closed had closed for good (2007). In other words, no uncertainty about the physical landscape of the city's culinary industry remained, as the number of establishments whose fate was unknown had dwindled to a handful at most. Fitzmorris's claim provides an ideal way to account for the recovery—if the narrative is capped on both ends, as he suggests, with patent delimitations on its opening and its closing, then the methods and opportunities for analysis may become clearer. But it does not take into account the many other landscapes that overlap in the production and consumption of food: the symbolic, the mnemonic, and the social, to name but a few. Nor does Fitzmorris's claim, writ large, take into account what is occurring inside these kitchens: that is, how Katrina changed the recipes themselves, both physically and symbolically. One of the clearest and most ubiquitous examples of this process comes in looking at one of the murkiest examples of New Orleans's cuisine: gumbo. It is also to ask, as both tourists and residents alike have enjoyed asking for years: What *is* a gumbo?[4] But to ask this question post-Katrina invokes a range of new and different narratives about gumbo making and gumbo eating and by extension the preparation and enjoyment of any "traditional" New Orleans recipe.

One of the more celebrated instances of post-Katrina gumbo eating came in the introduction of the Fox network television series *K-Ville*, a fictional police drama set in New Orleans in the months after the storm. Chris Rose (2007) has amusingly described how the tradition of a neighborhood gumbo party depicted in the show never actually existed either pre- or post-Katrina—unlike, for instance, a crawfish boil—but that this naive yet earnest onscreen depiction led many New Orleanians who enjoyed the series to take up the "tradition." Residents would gather each Monday night during the run of the series for bowls of gumbo (displacing, Rose points out, the tradition of red beans and rice on Mondays) for a collective viewing and satirizing of the beloved drama. Acknowledging that part of the show's appeal was the local willingness to celebrate for any reason, Rose still suggests that it is "amazing, really, that nobody thought of it before." What exactly is being consumed in this instance—a network television series, a bowl of gumbo, and/or a fictionalized narrative about the city—is not easy to unpack. But the phenomenon shows that the dialogue about the future of the city's culinary arts after the storm relied in part on the stereotypes of what constituted "typical" or "unique" New Orleans dishes, in which case the question became not merely what *is* gumbo but what is its importance—in other words, *Why* gumbo? These questions were met by an overwhelming response from local activists, chefs, and restaurateurs. Chef Paul Prudhomme said it perhaps most poignantly, in the first Carnival season after the storm. After noting his experience during Katrina and then rebuilding his French Quarter restaurant, K-Paul's, he asked, "What brings them back, the longtime residents and worshipful tourists? Maybe it's those herbs and spices that are so essential to our cooking. They clear away the sad memories of the weeks after floodwaters ravaged our city and get us ready for a new chapter in the life of New Orleans" (2006: 72).

That new chapter has taken a number of different forms. Immediately after the storm, the much-reviled Meal, Ready-to-Eat (MRE), distributed widely by relief personnel, became fuel for improvisation and experimentation in classic New Orleans style. Locals frequently developed new ways to cook and eat MREs, McNulty writes: "For instance, the pouches and heating elements included in each MRE could easily be put to use to make a poached egg—not an easy trick to otherwise pull off in a house with a destroyed kitchen and no gas or electricity" (2008: 79). Since these dark days, however, the culinary landscape has continued to evolve. New restaurants have opened, among them Hicham Khodr's Table One (one of the first new post-Katrina restaurants, since closed) and Donald Link's critically acclaimed Cochon, with its emphasis on locally sourced meat and produce and innovative nouveau southern dishes. In older restaurants, changes in supply lines and availability have led many chefs and bartenders to come up with new creations, new menu items, and new experiences for their patrons. One particularly interesting phenomenon is the emergence of Katrina-themed menu items (or in some cases, the renaming of old items with new reference to Katrina), a practice McNulty (2007c) has called "unappetizing." One restaurant changed the name of one of its traditional sushi dishes to the FEMA Roll, and Slim Goodies, a diner that reopened weeks after the storm, served a large Contractor's Breakfast and a Katrina Combo, among other similarly titled items (Andrews 2005). Regardless of whether it is also an effective marketing tool, as in the case of Absolut New Orleans (a limited-edition mango-flavored vodka whose bottle was engraved with a harmonica and whose profits went to recovery efforts), is consuming one of these dishes in some way "consuming" the storm, overcoming or showing control over the loss and adversity created by the storm by ingesting its namesake? If so, it echoes the widespread practice described by Marlene Otte (2007) of people seeking hurricane-themed tattoos as a means of "owning" their experience of grief, displacement, and loss.

But far more important than any of these emergent (and probably temporary) creations are those recipes that do not just come from New Orleans but mean New Orleans. As Pat Caplan (1997) has argued, the links between food and identity are many and complex, but in this context, celebrated dishes clearly have helped individuals, families, and wider communities maintain a sense of identity despite the disruption and loss inflicted by Katrina. A year after the storm, Rick Brooks outlined a number of initiatives that had reconnected people to recipes that they had prized but that had been lost, abandoned, or destroyed in the storm: one former Lakeview resident reported that she spent hours searching online for lost recipes because she "wanted to provide something of normality for my kids and my husband and to feel like we're not on the road anymore" (2006: A7). This expression of specific dishes (in this case, a sweet-potato casserole) becomes a marker not just of place but of home, of normalcy and of continued identity, especially to the population of New Orleanians still in diaspora, as Justin Lundgren's Katrina Dinner 2006 project aimed to show.[5] Inspired by the Passover seder and intended to reach displaced New Orleanians all over the country, Lundgren proposed holding a complete dinner on 29 August 2006, featuring recipes, rituals, and even appropriate local musical selections. "How powerful would it be," Lundgren wrote, "If every New Orleanian currently living in Houston, Dallas, Atlanta and every other town across the country sat down at the same time to recognize the losses of the last year and to reaffirm their connection to the city? . . . The entire New Orleans diaspora could sit down simultaneously, fork in hand, to tell the world that this was a special place, a special community, one worth fighting to restore" (Walker 2006: C1). This impulse to revisit known traditions comes through even in fiction: in Tom Piazza's recent novel, *City of Refuge*, Wesley Williams, an evacuee from the Lower Ninth Ward, ends up in Albany, New York, under the care of two strangers who have opened their home to him. Wesley's desire for New Orleans's cuisine manifests itself twice while he is cooking at their house, first when he requests Crystal sauce (a local hot sauce) to add to his bland pot roast and later as he prepares pork chops and cabbage for his host: adding lemon juice is "a trick of his Uncle J's" (2008: 212, 223). When Codrescu wrote a "Letter to America" informing all the families hosting displaced Katrina evacuees, "Your food will get better," could he have known that he was also speaking to people who exist only within the pages of a novel? (2006: 271).

Fictive gestures notwithstanding, many of these initiatives reflect the abiding sensibility that although Katrina has forever changed the landscape of New Orleans's culinary arts, change is itself always a part of the city's culinary landscape. If, as Nossiter noted, tastes underpin the social fabric "as much as any precious monument or institution"—though what are Dooky Chase or Willie Mae's Scotch House if not precious monuments or institutions?—then this social fabric must be seen as undergoing constant revision and self-assessment, and not always smoothly. Such processes became apparent in the summer of 2007, when, addressing the presence of mobile taquerias (taco trucks) catering to the growing immigrant population from Mexico and Central America, health inspectors in Jefferson Parish changed the laws regarding food distribution permits in an attempt to force these trucks to relocate to Orleans Parish. Widely panned in the press for the decision, the Jefferson Parish Council stuck by its decision, sparking a controversy in which the battleground was not economics or sanitation as much as culture. At one point, city councilman Oliver Thomas wondered publicly, "How do the tacos help gumbo?" (Elie 2007: B1).

Betraying a remarkable resistance to the infusion of yet one more influence into the city's mosaic of culinary influences as well as a disregard for day laborers undertaking much of the strenuous manual effort of rebuilding the city, the council's decision (and Thomas's words) were met with an overwhelming show of support for the taco trucks, including by the editors of the *New Orleans Times-Picayune*, whose argument, "Tacos and Po-Boys Can Coexist," closed by claiming, "New Orleans is no stranger to food on-the-go—from Lucky dogs to po-boys to sno-balls. And a city that has melded French, Spanish, African, Italian, Irish, Vietnamese and a host of other cultures to beautiful effect ought to be willing to add one more" (2007). This claim acknowledges the city's rich culinary heritage at the same time as it anticipates a revitalized and continually evolving future.[6] But this instance clearly illustrates how the culinary arts contribute to New Orleans's rebuilding process, not just by nourishing the individuals doing the physical work but also by reinforcing its history, its heritage, and its image as a unique place where diverse traditions productively collide and commingle to produce new outcomes, new ideas, and new opportunities.

CONCLUSION

May 2008, Cambridge, England. As I put the finishing touches on this chapter, it feels somehow appropriate to head down to Old Orleans and enjoy another Dixie. But on arrival I find, with surprise and even a little regret, that this particular branch—ironically, the first to open in the United Kingdom—has inexplicably closed. Not that I had any special fondness for the place—in fact, the only time I ever visited Old Orleans was the time I was surprised to find Dixie Beer there. But this closure stirs the recognition that foodways are just as subject to forces outside their control (whether hurricanes or global market dynamics) as any other part of our culture, despite food's special relationship to emotion, to community, and to memory and even despite place's singular importance to social and collective identity. In other places, we eat to live, but in New Orleans, so the saying goes, we live to eat. And the restaurants and the dishes we love will be there to sustain and inspire us, even if the recipes might have changed a little. What is, after all, a recipe but a suggestion? The last .1 percent of authenticity that Michael Cook says the new Dixie Beer lacks is, I now think, not an ingredient that one tastes but a belief that one adopts. A surprising lesson to be drawn from a kitsch-filled wannabe–juke joint: change does not defy but rather defines culture, and culture both responds to and creates change in a messy, beautiful, ecological relationship that will always require further thought and care. This is not to say that all changes must be viewed through such a sanguine lens, however, or escape a raised eyebrow: after its reopening in September 2007, Dooky Chase began serving Starbucks-brand coffee.

NOTES

I could not have written this chapter without the assistance of many different individuals. In New Orleans, I thank M. B. Hackler, Lauren Lastrapes, John Lawrence, Karen Leathem, Ian McNulty, Gerald Patout, and Poppy Tooker; and in the United Kingdom, I thank Robin Boast, Michael Cook, Marie-Louise Stig Sørensen, and Dacia Viejo-Rose, all of whom have shown hospitality both beyond their means and beyond my ability to repay it.

1. Lind (2007) notes that the American bottle has two inscriptions. The first reads, "The nearly century-old Dixie was almost destroyed by Katrina but restoration is under way. With the help of our friends, we're working hard to re-beer New Orleans and the rest of the country." The second is, "Dixie Beer captures the essence and is characteristic of the gracious charm and joy of living so inherent in the proud New Orleans and Southern way of life."
2. In many cases, restaurants were literally transformed to outside their walls: many chefs set up operations in parking lots, neutral grounds, and tent cities to feed emergency personnel and first responders (see Prudhomme 2006). The same was true after Hurricane Gustav in September 2008 (see Anderson 2008).
3. The expansion also involved considerable loss in the form of the two historic homes that were demolished.
4. Roahen (2008) is the latest to take a stab at answering this question, developing her own classification of five different gumbo families.
5. A similar idea was put forth in "diaspora gumbo," promoted by the Crescent City Farmers' Market, in which you would "pick your diaspora by choosing from the following foods, depending on personal preference and availability to obtain ingredients in your evacuation site" (2007). This chapter does not address the New Orleans–themed restaurants opened by evacuees, such as Blue Orleans in Chattanooga, Tennessee; or the Augusta in Oxford, Iowa.
6. As Schwartz (2008) has detailed, one recent and promising development has been the revival (and in some cases creation) of neighborhood markets to support locally grown goods, such as the Sankofa Market in the Lower Ninth Ward. Though the long-term sustainability of these projects remains unknown, they are unquestionably a step in the direction of rebuilding the city's neighborhoods and livelihoods.

REFERENCES

Anderson, Brett. 2007. "Mandina's Rising: A Five-Part Series Chronicling the Ruin and Restoration of a Classic New Orleans Restaurant." *New Orleans Times-Picayune*, 10 September. http://blog.nola.com/brettanderson/mandinas_rising/. Accessed 1 October 2007.

———. 2008. "'People Are Hungry, and I'm Going to Feed Them.'" *New Orleans Times-Picayune*. 4 September, C1–C2.

Andrews, Betsy. 2005. "On the Line in New Orleans: Rebirth and a Rustic Guy." *Food and Wine*. http://foodandwine.blogs.com/neworleans/2005/12/a_rustic_guy.html. Accessed 1 March 2007.

Beriss, David, and David Sutton, eds. 2007. *The Restaurants Book: Ethnographies of Where We Eat*. Oxford, Eng.: Berg.

Boyer, Christine. 1994. *The City of Collective Memory: Its Historical Imagery and Architectural Entertainments*. Cambridge: MIT Press.

Bring New Orleans Back Commission. 2006. *Report of the Cultural Committee*. 2006. 10 January. http://www.bringneworleansback.org/. Accessed 10 January 2006.

Brookings Institution. 2008. *The New Orleans Index Anniversary Edition: Three Years after Katrina*. August. http://www.brookings.edu/reports/2007/08neworleansindex.aspx. Accessed 1 September 2008.

Brooks, Rick. 2006. "Comforting Food: Recapturing Recipes Katrina Took Away." *Wall Street Journal*, 26–27 August, A1–A7.

Caplan, Pat. 1997. "Approaches to the Study of Food, Health, and Identity." In *Food, Health, and Identity*, ed. Pat Caplan, 1–31. London: Routledge.

Civitello, Linda. 2007. *Cuisine and Culture: A History of Food and People*. Hoboken, N.J.: Wiley.

Codrescu, Andrei. 2006. *New Orleans Mon Amour: Twenty Years of Writings from the City*. Chapel Hill, N.C.: Algonquin.

Cook, Michael. 2007. Interview. 30 May.

Crescent City Farmers' Market. 2007. *Diaspora Gumbo*. http://www.crescentcityfarmersmarket.org/index.php?mact=News,cntnt01,detail,0&cntnt01articleid=18&cntnt01origid=55&cntnt01returnid=55. Accessed 12 June 2008.

Elie, Lolis Eric. 2007. "The Gumbo Just Gets Better." *New Orleans Times-Picayune*, 9 July, B1.

Fitzmorris, Tom. 2007. *The New Orleans Menu*. http://www.nomenu.com/FAQ/default.html#restaurants. Accessed 13 September 2007.

Hammer, David. 2007. "Bush Shares Gumbo with Nagin, Brees." *New Orleans Times-Picayune*, 28 August. http://www.nola.com/news/t-p/frontpage/index.ssf?/base/news-9/1188367335232970.xml&coll=1. Accessed 15 October 2007.

Johnson, Suzanne. 2006. "Culture Shock." *Tulanian*, 18 December. http://tulane.edu/news/tulanian/culture_shock.cfm. Accessed 15 March 2007.

Lagasse, Emeril. 2006. *Bringing Back the Bayou* (documentary). The Food Network. Aired 26 August.

Lind, Angus. 2007. "Refreshing Sight." *New Orleans Times-Picayune*, 13 July, C1–C3.

Louisiana Department of Culture, Recreation, and Tourism. 2006. *Louisiana Rebirth Plan Executive Summary*. 24 March. http://www.crt.state.la.us/. Accessed 24 March 2006.

McCaffrey, Kevin. 2007. *We Live to Eat: New Orleans' Love Affair with Food* (documentary). ePrime Productions for the Historic New Orleans Collection.

McNulty, Ian. 2007a. "Chewing over 2007." *Gambit Weekly*, 26 December, 55.

———. 2007b. "Confederacy of Suds." *Gambit Weekly*, 20 February. http://www2.gambitweekly.com/dispatch/2007-02-20/feat.php. Accessed 1 March 2007.

———. 2007c. "Rolling in Mid-City." *Gambit Weekly*, 26 June, 70.

———. 2008. *A Season of Night: New Orleans Life after Katrina*. Jackson: University Press of Mississippi.

Nossiter, Adam. 2006. "Spumoni Fills a City's Void, and Its Belly." *New York Times*, 1 October. http://www.nytimes.com/2006/10/01/us/nationalspecial/01icecream.html. Accessed 1 October 2006.

Otte, Marlene. 2007. "The Mourning After: Languages of Loss and Grief in Post-Katrina New Orleans." *Journal of American History* 94.3 (December): 828–36.

Piazza, Tom. 2008. *City of Refuge*. New York: HarperCollins.

Prudhomme, Paul. 2006. "At Home on the Range." *U.S. News & World Report*, 27 February, 72.

Roahen, Sara. 2008. *Gumbo Tales: Finding My Place at the New Orleans Table*. New York: Norton.

Rose, Chris. 2007. "Gumbo Party Time! 'K-Ville' Spawns a New Monday-Night Tradition." *New Orleans Times-Picayune*, 7 October. http://blog.nola.com/chrisrose/2007/10/gumbo_party_time_kville_spawns.html. Accessed 1 November 2007.

Schwartz, Jeffrey. 2008. "Making Groceries: Food, Neighborhood Markets, and Neighborhood Recovery in Post-Katrina New Orleans." Master's thesis, MIT.

Southern Food and Beverage Museum. 2006. *Restaurant Restorative*. http://www.southernfood.org/content/index.php?id=366. Accessed 31 October 2006.

"Tacos and Po-Boys Can Coexist." 2007. *New Orleans Times-Picayune*, 30 June, B6.

Tooker, Poppy. 2007. Interview. 24 July.

Walker, Judy. 2006. "A Meal to Remember." *New Orleans Times-Picayune*, 24 August, C1.

MAKING GROCERIES

Food, Neighborhood Markets, and Neighborhood Recovery in Post-Katrina New Orleans

JEFFREY SCHWARTZ

On 30 August 2005, yahoo.com published two photographs showing people wading through Katrina's floodwaters, groceries in tow. Superficially, the only difference between the two images is that one depicts a young black man, while the other portrays two young white adults. Yet in what became one of the better-known story lines of the immediate aftermath of Hurricane Katrina, the captions' characterizations of the storm victims' activities differed markedly. With no context provided in either the photograph or the caption, the African American man is said to have "looted" from a grocery, while the white male and female merely "found" their bread and soda in the same store.

The captioning caused a furor among many observers who found these images to be an example of institutionalized bias and racism. While many commentators dismissed the divergent captions as the differences between two press agencies' policies (one image and caption came from the Associated Press, while the other came from the Agence France Presse), I find the disparities between the photographs and the public response to them provocative for what they say about who is entitled to even basic necessities of life in a postdisaster context. The race of the pictured victims and the potential institutionalized biases of large media organizations stoked the controversy, but it obscured what struck me as an even more basic and obvious affront. In the wake of Katrina, these individuals were forced to scavenge for what is otherwise such a mundane consideration as to be almost invisible in daily life in cities: food.

As a New Orleanian looking at the images, knowing the precise location of the photographs and the history of that place, the differences in the captioning assume a much more nuanced significance. When I look at these images now, the many interrelated histories of the images suggestively connect to one another, as if in montage. The grocery store referred to in the caption is the Circle Food Store, a venerable grocery in the heart of Tremé, the country's first free neighborhood of color. The store is situated at the intersection of North Claiborne and St. Bernard Avenues, the epicenter of what used to be one of the nation's wealthiest African American commercial corridors. The Circle Food Store was once the St. Bernard Market, a significant public market owned by the City of New Orleans as a part of the most extensive public market system in America. The interstate overpass from which the photographs were safely taken is an urban renewal project of the 1960s that devastated most of the black-owned businesses on Claiborne Avenue. Almost three years after the storm, Circle Foods has yet to reopen. Looking back at Katrina through these two images evokes deep-seated questions about the ways in which actors' political, social, and economic decisions contribute to how disaster is not only experienced but also produced.

The episode evokes a number of questions that are specific to New Orleans but that have much wider implications about the relationship of food access to urban development, the vulnerability and resiliency of individuals and neighborhoods, and the cultures of particular communities. What does it mean that the Circle Food store was once a public market and that New Orleans therefore once possessed a public interest in the food access of the people of Tremé? What does it mean that over the course of the twentieth century, that store was privatized and then placed in the shadow of the Interstate 10 overpass, which was bulldozed through a formerly vibrant African American commercial corridor? That from this platform floating above Claiborne Avenue journalists could photograph three American citizens struggling to provide for their sustenance in 2005? What is the effect on a community when a grocery store does not reopen after a disaster, or when a neighborhood had no grocery for three decades prior to a catastrophe? What is the significance of a community's food access before, during, and after a disaster?

This chapter examines why a surprising number of neighborhood markets were created in New Orleans as a response to Hurricane Katrina, the extent to which this market creation seeks to compensate for a lack of fresh food access, and the political, social, and economic significance of these markets in narratives operating on various levels, from the individual to the neighborhood to the city.

Food, Markets, and Neighborhood Recovery

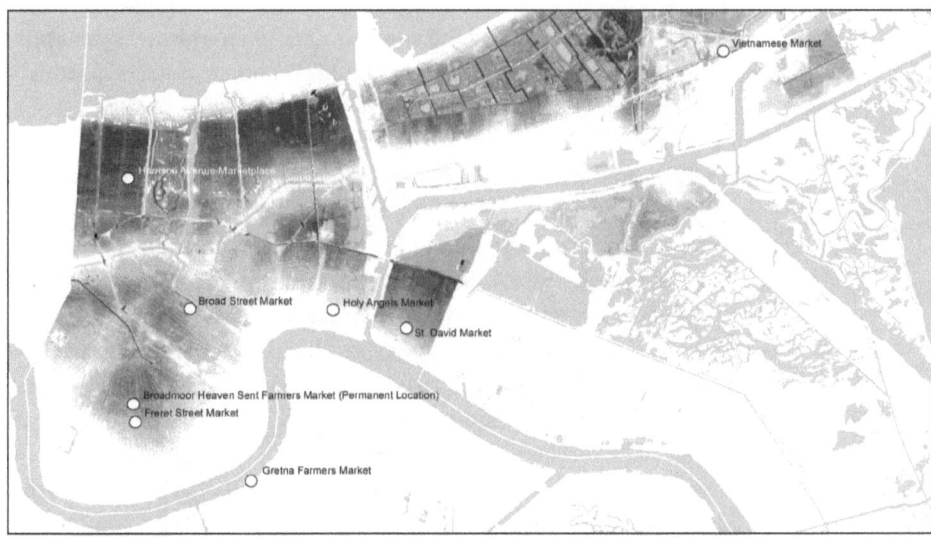

Fig. 4.1. The neighborhood markets studied in this paper, overlaid on Katrina flood depths. All of the markets established after the storm were created in neighborhoods that experienced some flooding. Created by author using data from City of New Orleans, ArcGIS.

New Orleans had five farmers' markets before the storm, only one of them run by a neighborhood organization. Yet after Katrina, despite the fact that only three of the prestorm markets have reopened, neighborhood organizations have created at least eight neighborhood markets. In a city as notoriously apathetic at the grassroots level as New Orleans and one largely without a recent history of neighborhood markets, the creation of these markets is notable.

MARKETS DEFINED

While markets defy easy categorization, the neighborhood markets studied here were created or reinitiated after Hurricane Katrina, are operated by neighborhood-level organizations, and are confined exclusively to the geographic borders of the neighborhood. This definition excludes the two Crescent City Farmers' Markets, which are managed by the nonprofit but non-neighborhood-based MarketUmbrella organization. Because this chapter is in part an inquiry into the importance of food access looking through the lens of neighborhood markets, it also excludes the myriad other festivals—neighborhood and otherwise—that are a celebrated part of the culture of southern Louisiana.

Not all of New Orleans's neighborhood markets are farmers' markets. Markets can be classified according to the kind and amount of products available, the ownership structure, and the sellers and can thus be categorized into terminal markets, public markets, or farmers' markets (Brown 2001: 670). Prior to the twentieth century, public markets were almost always run by municipalities; therefore, while the neighborhood markets studied here are not run by cities, they should be understood as falling in a direct lineage with the public municipal markets that generally persisted in this country until the turn of the twentieth century. Because they are managed by neighborhood organizations and offer varying levels of fresh food access as well as a variety of fresh and prepared foods, arts and crafts activities, and social interaction, these neighborhood markets fall on a spectrum between public and farmers' markets.

The organizations that manage the neighborhood markets are by no means identical. Some markets are operated by neighborhood community development corporations, others by nonprofit neighborhood organizations, and still others by collaborations between neighborhood improvement associations and other neighborhood institutions (such as churches or other nonprofits). The variation among neighborhood market operators presents an opportunity to explore the reasons why ostensibly disparate neighborhoods and neighborhood organizations have found cause to pursue similar neighborhood market undertakings.

THE MEANING OF NEIGHBORHOOD MARKETS

Neighborhoods have created farmers' markets not only to meet some of residents' food accessibility needs but also to provide tools for neighborhood validation, self-determination, and political identification and to contribute to both a neighborhood's vulnerability and resiliency prior to and in the wake of disaster. In this context, *resilience* is typically defined as the ability of a system—such as a neighborhood or a city—to recover after a catastrophe or to cope with threats and hazards, and *vulnerability* is the related exposure to risk and inability to avoid potential harm (Pelling 2003: 5). In the context of food geography, the concept of neighborhood resiliency also includes food accessibility. What is the relationship between neighborhood markets and uneven patterns of food access in the city? The food system—especially food access—plays a critical role in neighborhood vulnerability and resiliency before, during, and after disasters. Differences and similarities between neighborhood markets reflect not only the disparities of the post-Katrina period but also the uneven development of New Orleans's food geography over the twentieth century.

The neighborhood markets created after the storm are windows into neighborhood disparity and difference, revealing cleavages and commonalities among diverse New Orleans communities. The varying experiences of neighborhood food access play a significant role in determining neighborhoods' fate after disaster. In that sense, the differences between markets reflect the larger distinctions that existed among New Orleans's neighborhoods on the eve of the storm, the extent to which those differences resulted from uneven development of the food system, and the ways that these disparities can be ameliorated.

It is important to go beyond markets' purely economic functions to understand the social, political, and symbolic roles that neighborhood residents ascribe to their markets. Even before the mandatory evacuation preceding Katrina, food access affected individuals' capacity not only to respond to catastrophic disaster but also to provide for their physical well-being, psychological health, and ability to reach out to neighbors. For individuals, markets are a potential source of reconnection and newfound rootedness after disaster. As one of the many responses to the storm, neighborhood markets address the practical food needs of a particular community as well as the larger need for visual, significant interventions during recovery. For a city reeling from the storm, markets are low-cost, high-visibility projects that are practical as well as symbolic. Neighborhood markets are a common undertaking that nonetheless has different significances and meanings in different neighborhoods.

It is eminently telling that food, which is so central to many New Orleanians' conceptions of their city, remains utterly neglected as a topic of public policy. Markets, which are also a part of the city's culture, are held only weekly or once a month. While many of the visions for neighborhood markets are grand, the on-the-ground reality shows communities' continuing vulnerability more than four years after the storm. The experience of neighborhood markets shows how elusive recovery remains, especially in the most deeply affected neighborhoods.

Though urban planners and policymakers have historically neglected the food system, it is critical for understanding the different trajectories of American communities, particularly urban ones. Disaster not only accentuates these disparities but also is in part produced by them. The changing geography and politics of food must be understood as a part of the larger panorama of decentralization, suburbanization, Euclidean zoning,[1] and privatization that has unfolded over the past century. Communities have

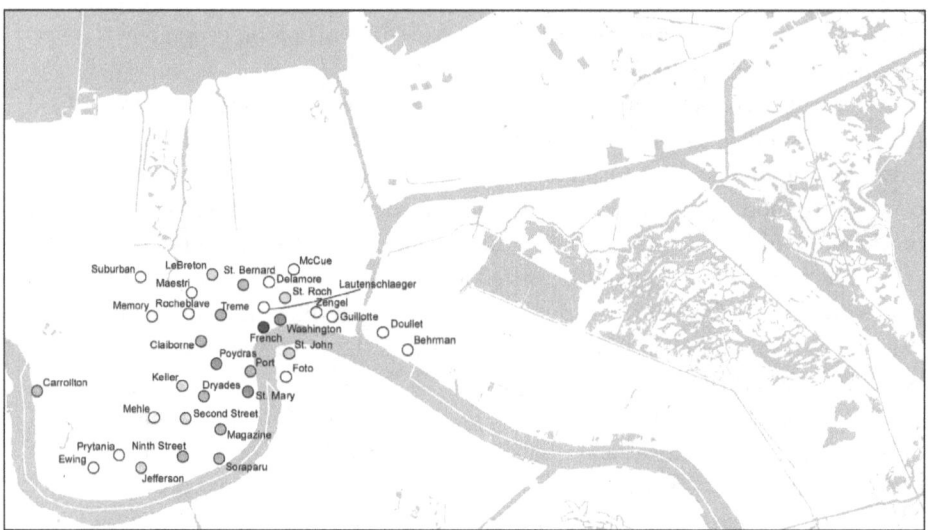

Fig. 4.2. New Orleans's public market system was the most extensive in the country in 1911. Created by author, using City of New Orleans data; after Sauder 1981.

been differentially affected by the changing landscape of food; for this reason, the food system and the cultural pathways it supports should be placed in the emerging literatures of urban resilience and sustaining urban places (Eckstein 2006: 4).

As a relatively new literature in the domain of planning, resiliency is most often applied to the disaster context on a macrolevel scale; very little has been done—especially in the global North—to understand how resiliency and its counterpart, vulnerability, are produced in neighborhoods and local communities to answer the question of how resiliency and vulnerability play out on the ground. Food access in general and post-Katrina neighborhood markets in particular problematize these facile definitions to understand how they interrelate and how resilience is a characteristic of individuals and communities that is manifest not just after a disaster but also before. Changes in food access and the sociopolitical and economic relationships tied to food access thus can affect a community's resiliency.

NEW ORLEANS'S FOOD GEOGRAPHY

It is perhaps unsurprising that New Orleans, with all of its other idiosyncrasies, also has a unique public market system and a food access history different from those experienced by other American cities. For longer than any other American city, food access in New Orleans was provided by public, municipally owned markets and was complemented by a network of independent grocers. As a result, New Orleans's food system was characterized by pervasive equal access to food in every neighborhood in the city well into the twentieth century, a latticework that supported the development of the city's unique cultural and food-related pathways. However, as the city suburbanized, the geography of food access became increasingly uneven.

NEW ORLEANS'S PUBLIC MARKET SYSTEM

New Orleans's system of public markets was notable for the markets' ownership and operation, their relationship to neighborhoods, and the persistence and extensiveness of the system long after most other municipal public market systems had failed. Before becoming part of the United States, New Orleans established what later came to be called the French Market in 1781. By law, food access in the city was centralized there to protect consumers from high prices and poor-quality food by eliminating middlemen and regulating the handling and selling of perishables (Sauder 1981: 283). The Cabildo (the Spanish colonial administration) expressed in the legislation that founded the French Market the hope that the new market "would result in untold goods to the public" (Tangires 2003: 25). The Cabildo might also have mentioned that while the open-air market was amenable to market vendors, it provided a financial windfall for the colonial and later city governments. Under the pretense of protecting public health and sanitation, New Orleans's Spanish and municipal governments had found a lucrative source of revenue for the general fund. While their low-cost, public health benefits and food quality and access were important factors in establishing markets, city market revenues were a dominant consideration in every subsequent decision to open a public market in New Orleans (Reeves 2007: 26–27).

Rather than directly run markets, New Orleans operated what would today be considered a public-private system of ownership and management that was unique in this country. The municipality built and owned markets, but they were managed following the European system of "farmer of the market," in which "bidders competed at auction in order to become 'farmer' or prime contractor" (Reeves 2007: 29). These farmers were then responsible for subleasing the entire facility to butchers, fishmongers, and fruit and vegetable dealers, "furnishing a surety, and paying the city on a monthly basis" (30). The markets were heavily regulated: the city controlled everything from the times that the markets could be open (the meat market closed at ten o'clock in the morning in the summer), the location of sales, the use of open flame (permissible only in a few instances, including making coffee), as well as prohibitions against liquor and oysters (the latter were the strict purview of the oystermen on the Mississippi levee). Revenues from the markets grew from more than twenty thousand dollars a year in 1815 to more than two hundred thousand dollars annually in the 1880s (30). When New York City was facing pressures for laissez-faire reform of its butcher shops and meat markets in 1854, that city's comptroller advocated unsuccessfully for a New Orleans–style system of market management, which he estimated would have brought in five hundred thousand dollars a year (Tangires 2003: 88).

Until refrigeration and other late-nineteenth-century developments made it untenable for New Orleans to maintain a monopoly on the sale of perishables in the name of public health, meat, fish fruit, and vegetables could be sold only in public markets. Private grocers were limited to selling dried, barreled, or canned goods—so-called groceries not available at the public markets (Reeves 2007: 29). The relationship remained uneasy, but grocers eventually thrived, at first in close proximity to markets and then after markets went into decline. As with most other American cities in the middle of the nineteenth century, private grocers began growing slowly in New Orleans after a municipal ordinance enabled private grocers to sell—subject to general sanitary requirements—fruits, vegetables, meats, and fish in 1866. The city also experimented with turning over some public markets entirely to private control in the last quarter of the nineteenth century, sweetening the deal by granting a food access monopoly within six blocks of these markets. The experiment was short-lived; the markets were back under municipal control by 1900, and no private grocer could sell any perishable (except potatoes and onions) within nine blocks of a public market (Sauder 1981: 286–87). Despite the legislation that enabled private markets to compete to an extent with public markets, George Washington Cable observed in 1880 that "much of the larger proportion of the retail supply of meats, poultry, fish, and vegetables is from the public markets, sales from the private stores and stands being comparatively unimportant" (quoted in Sauder 1981: 286). Thus, public markets played a vital role in the daily livelihoods of New Orleanians even as such markets began to wane in importance elsewhere.

Public markets prospered in New Orleans until the second decade of the twentieth century. In the 1918 Census of Markets, New Orleans had twenty-eight (nineteen public, nine quasi-public); Baltimore, which had the second-highest tally, had only eleven (Sauder 1981: 288; Tangires 2003: 201). However, New Orleans's market system was in almost total disrepair by the end of the 1920s, reflecting both internal disorganization within the city and increasing competition from private and chain grocers (Department of Public Markets report 1932; Sauder 1981: 289). As in most American cities, New Orleans's food geography was changing in favor of cheaper canned goods found in independent and especially chain grocers (Mayo 1991: 134). Before succumbing, the city's public market system underwent one last round of investment in the 1930s. Works Progress Administration funding was used to rebuild nine of the remaining markets and renovate eleven others beginning in 1931, but the city largely ignored the local real estate board's recommendation that "if you put buildings on all present market sites, many having become obsolete because of the movement of population, you will soon find that they are absolutely unable to produce income for their maintenance, no matter who operates them" (quoted in Sauder 1981: 290).

Even before all of the renovations were completed, New Orleans began declassifying the public markets and selling them to private businesses. The Department of Public Markets was liquidated by 1946, when the last of the public markets was auctioned off, marking the end of the city's public market system. Today, eighteen of the public market structures are still standing, but only the French Market remains in operation (Sauder 1981: 290).

THE PUBLIC LIFE OF PUBLIC MARKETS AND CORNER STORES

Public markets in New Orleans were central to the cultural, economic, and political life of the city's neighborhoods. As the city grew, "the public market system simply grew with the city" (Sauder 1981: 287). Other American cities did not experience the same process. From 1784 until 1911, when the last public market was built, New Orleans had a total of thirty-four markets; other cities typically had a few central markets—as many as ten in the largest American cities (Tangires 2003: 98; Pyle 1971: 179). (Philadelphia briefly had thirty-five to forty markets in the middle of the nineteenth century, but that number quickly dwindled.) Markets were located in newly created neighborhoods, and the periods of market expansion thus reflect the periods of the city's growth. As New Orleans burgeoned from 1830 to 1860, public markets were built almost exclusively in the American Sector downriver of Canal Street; the first market constructed outside the French Quarter was the St. Mary Market, which was built in 1836 and named after the area's original moniker, Faubourg St. Marie. Later, as development encroached on the city's back swamps at the end of the nineteenth and beginning of the twentieth century, the city still actively constructed markets. Indeed, the greatest period of expansion of public markets in New Orleans occurred from 1880 to 1911, while newly drained lands were being developed, the same era when most other cities were closing their markets (Sauder 1981: 284–85). For practical, political, cultural, and financial reasons, the city guaranteed that markets were physically located at the center of neighborhoods.

Markets were one of the most important institutions in the daily lives of New Orleans neighborhoods. Sally K. Reeves has called the public markets "well-dispersed centers of food and society," noting the many roles that they filled in their communities: "Market employment served as a professional stepping-stone for young people, immigrants, and free people of color. The market was also a bastion of preservation for languages, culinary traditions, social occasions, and the drinking of coffee. City ordinances made no distinctions in class, gender, or race among vendors or shoppers. . . . Citizens flocked to the markets on Sunday mornings to shop for the week's most important meal while enjoying the social occasion" (2007: 29).

Many of the culinary and social traditions for which New Orleans is famous are intricately intertwined with the public market system. New Orleans's passion for coffee and cafés in part evolved with the public market system, to which Café Du Monde remains a testament: brewing coffee was one of the only permissible uses for cooking flames in the public markets. The operators of many of the city's famous French-Creole restaurants—Antoine's, Tujagues, Begue's, and Maylie's—had family members or close relations who worked in butcher shops; when the meat markets closed each day, some of the best cuts of meat were taken to the restaurants (Reeves 2007: 32). Even into the 1920s, when the French Quarter had lost some of its former luster, New Orleans's Sicilian community was centered at the French Market, and the invention of the muffuletta sandwich at Central Grocery Company—at 923 Decatur Street, across from the French Market—can be traced to this period. Central Grocery is still there, serving up muffulettas daily (Campanella 2006: 315–17).

When the public market system faded in New Orleans after 1930, many corner stores continued to anchor aspects of the social and economic lives of their surrounding communities. First and most important, the corner stores and other private (usually independent) grocers had some of the highest-quality food available in the city. Chain stores typically offered canned and less fresh food (Mayo 1991: 40). But these independent grocers also served a variety of socioeconomic functions in their communities. Although A & P eliminated credit in 1910, many smaller grocers maintained credit lines for some of their customers through World War II and beyond (86). This practice had a beneficial income-leveling effect for the community; although stores no longer run credit lines, the few remaining corner groceries, such as Matassa's Market in the French Quarter and the Brown Derby on Freret Street, look out for their customers by extending them credit to buy groceries when times are hard (Mulrine 2006).

Moreover, independent markets and corner groceries were social spaces. A friend of mine whose grandmother started a corner market during the 1930s fondly remembers how the store served as a meeting place for neighbors, and he attributes its closing in the 1950s not only to competition from larger chain stores but also to the fact that the installation of air-conditioning systems in private homes obviated neighbors' need and desire to congregate outside their residences. A better-known example of the salience of corner groceries in the fabric of the city is Matassa's Market, located at 1001 Dauphine Street in the French Quarter. Cosimo Matassa, whose father, a Sicilian immigrant, bought the grocery in 1924, started what eventually became the J & M Recording Studio in the back of the store. The renovated grocery store the family bought two blocks away on North Rampart Street in 1944 witnessed the recording of the first rock-and-roll song (Fats Domino's "The Fat Man") as well as seminal sessions by Little Richard, Professor Longhair, Jerry Lee Lewis, and Ray Charles. Matassa no longer produces music, and independent corner grocers have largely faded from New Orleans's neighborhoods; a few stores, including Matassa's, retain a level of quality foods and social and economic relevance for their communities, but they are now rare exceptions.

POSTWAR CHANGES

As with most other American cities, New Orleans changed dramatically after World War II, and these changes had sweeping implications for the geography of food. Development of the food system occurred along two axes: consolidation and unevenness. Settlement in New Orleans had previously been confined to the high ground created by the Mississippi River and its distributaries. After A. Baldwin Wood turned on the screw pumps for the Sewerage and Water Board in 1911 and drained the back swamps, the city began to expand north toward Lake Pontchartrain. Thereafter, settlement of the city took a fundamentally different form. The city overtopped its historic constraints and rapidly spread north and east; in 1960, only 9 percent of the city's population lived east of the Industrial Canal, but by 2000, a quarter of New Orleanians lived in an area that had been developed entirely after 1960 (Campanella 2007: 6). As was the case with every American city, neighborhoods built after the World War II were designed around automobility, and the "distribution of grocery stores increasingly tended to be spatially decentralized as cities expanded" (Mayo 1993: 49). The contemporary communities north of Interstate 10, east of the Industrial Canal, and west of the Seventeenth Street Canal are post–World War II, car-oriented neighborhoods, embodying a pattern of urban development that entailed an entirely different food geography. Attendant to this changing geography, New Orleans rapidly transitioned from a pervasive, public market/corner grocery system that relied on walking or taking the ubiquitous streetcar system to a consolidated supermarket system that almost entirely depended on the automobile for access. According to James M. Mayo, "The grocery store was transformed from a shopkeeper's domain that was a community social institution to a factory of consumption designed by economic reasoning. . . . By the 1930s, an overwhelming majority of grocery stores in the nation belonged to either a corporate chain or an affiliated independent, and this movement brought an end to the shopkeeper's age. Grocers were no longer self-reliant or specifically organized to meet the needs of a local community or neighborhood" (1991: 115–16, 128).

By almost any measure, food access in the city dwindled over the twentieth century. The number of public markets dropped from the high of thirty-four in 1911 to twenty-eight in 1928 and none by 1946. The number of food access points peaked at twenty-two hundred in 1932 but dropped to just under four hundred on the eve of Katrina in July 2005. Even more tellingly, the number of markets selling nutritious food, making them comparable to the grocers of the interwar period, was less than fifty. In strictly numerical terms, New Orleans lost 80 percent of its food access points as smaller, neighborhood-based stores disappeared, resulting in the extraordinary consolidation of the food system that attended the suburbanization of the city.

According to Mayo (1993: 140), a typical chain store prior to suburbanization and automobility measured about 500 square feet, meaning that in 1932, New Orleans had 1.1 million square feet of food retail space for 458,762 people. In 2005, the city had thirty-six grocery stores averaging approximately 30,000 square feet, for a total of 1.08 million square feet of food retail space. New Orleans's 2005 population, 437,186, was nearly unchanged, meaning that the food retail space per capita was virtually the same. The quality of food has remained comparable; thus, a massive physical realignment of food access had taken place, with profound implications for neighborhoods and citizens. However, the pattern of food access has changed dramatically: because food access is now predicated on the automobile, large portions of the population lack any food source within half a mile of their homes, and many communities have no access at all without cars. Each store is vastly more efficient, and the costs per customer presumably have declined with the efficiencies of scale. But what was lost in this restructuring of the food system?

Consolidation did not occur evenly. As the number of stores in the city dwindled, some areas retained relatively high levels of access to fresh food, while others suffered diminishing levels of food accessibility. This development cannot be fully understood except as part and parcel of the process of American suburbanization. Areas that had never suffered from any shortage of access to fresh foods now had such problems. Many of the neighborhoods that became famous for their plight during and after Katrina were those that suffered the steepest decline in access to fresh food: prior to the storm, food access in the Upper and Lower Ninth Wards, Broadmoor, Central City, Mid-City, Gentilly, and New Orleans East had drastically diminished, while food access had remained relatively robust in areas of Uptown, and the Esplanade Ridge. Moreover, the areas with the largest decreases in food access are also those that have the highest proportions of minorities, lower wealth, and less access to an automobile. Food access locations have been decided by potential profit, not need: "The desire for profits shaped every spatial decision, not any sense of the public good" (Mayo 1991, 71).

Changes in New Orleans's food access also illustrate the changing conceptualization of the food system. This system, which touches so many facets of quality of life in New Orleans, as in all cities, moved from one characterized by public consideration and creation of food access to one driven by private motivations of profit and provided exclusively by private markets. Food access transitioned from a public utility to a retail industry. The implications of this pattern of development of food access, especially in times of disaster and particularly in the marginalized communities that are typically on the losing end of the uneven geography of development, are striking.

THE EVE OF KATRINA

In August 2005, New Orleans had thirty-six grocery stores and the four Crescent City' Farmers Markets. As a result, vast swaths of the city could be considered food deserts, with no direct access to fresh foods. Many of those areas, such as the Lower Ninth Ward, significant portions of New Orleans

East, and Central City, were predominantly African American, although the pattern also extends to Lakeview, which was almost entirely white.

AFTER KATRINA

As in so many other areas, the prestorm trends in food access have continued after Katrina. Thirty months after the storm, most neighborhoods in New Orleans remained desperate for food access, and many of these areas had been hardest hit by the previous trends of consolidation and unevenness. Two and a half years after Katrina, only eighteen of New Orleans's supermarkets had reopened. Most of the large groceries that have reopened are located in the "sliver by the River"—the historic high ground that remained relatively unscathed. And the distribution of open and closed supermarkets is highly correlated with race and poverty. A March 2007 National Public Radio story identifies how disparities in food geography affect citizens' daily lives: "About a quarter of New Orleanians do not have cars, and with public transportation still spotty, a trip to that 'sliver by the River' can take all day" (Troeh 2007).

The national average for the number of people per grocery store is eighty-eight hundred; prior to Katrina, the ratio in New Orleans was twelve thousand to one; it is now eighteen thousand to one (New Orleans Food Policy Advisory Committee 2008). Food banks such as Second Harvest are stretched thin by the consistently high volume of demand: Second Harvest still receives as many as thirty calls an hour (*Demand Skyrockets* 2008). A 2007 survey of low-income residents by Tulane's School of Public Health explored access to healthy foods among low-income New Orleanians. The results reflected the combination of poor neighborhood design and lack of fresh food access: low-income residents shopped at convenience stores almost three times a week, and only a fifth of these residents ate the recommended five fruits and vegetables a day. Only a third of neighborhood stores sold fruits or vegetables, and a mere 6 percent of residents said that they lived within walking distance of a supermarket ("City Council" 2008). Food access has almost completely disappeared from many of the hardest-hit neighborhoods.

The experience of the Mardi Gras Zone in the Bywater neighborhood is emblematic of the haphazard manner in which neighborhoods have attempted to meet their food access needs after Katrina. The store opened five years before the storm as a trinket emporium, selling Mardi Gras beads and costumes. When it reopened immediately after Katrina, the owner, Benny

Naghi, an Iranian immigrant and New Orleans resident for twenty-six years, found that the neighborhood wanted groceries. He expanded the store from six hundred to six thousand square feet to meet the neighborhood's demand for food (Troeh 2007). The Mardi Gras Zone even garnered a *New York Times* article describing its growth (Eaton 2008).

Some neighbors admire the store as a symbol of the can-do, grassroots attitude that has helped the city rebuild, but others believe that Naghi is using the lack of close oversight of development after the storm as a way to skirt zoning and land-use issues. He recently applied for a liquor license, thereby testing the neighbors' devotion to the grocery store:

> *Many neighbors were delighted by the Zone, and still are. "Benny was a lifesaver," said Howard Allen, who made a point of saying how much he liked the place, which has become a local hangout. If it were to close, Mr. Allen continued, he would have to drive miles to go to a supermarket in the suburbs....*
>
> *But the prospect of a 24-hour liquor store in their midst has infuriated some residents. "The neighborhood really does need a grocery, so we figure we would put up with it," said Marie K. Erickson, a law librarian whose two-story house fronts Royal Street. "It's the 24/7 liquor license which has got us all cranked up." (Eaton 2008)*

FOOD ACCESS INITIATIVES

The city, nonprofit groups, and other organizations have attempted to address New Orleans neighborhoods' food access needs. While some of the initiatives are relatively large in scope and in resources, there has as yet been no comprehensive attempt to address the deficiencies in New Orleans's food system.

Nonprofit efforts to address shortcomings in the food system have been a hodgepodge of smaller undertakings to fill niches, but none has appreciably affected the food access landscape. Several neighborhoods have created or restarted community gardens, including a few that grow food for sale at neighborhood markets. SeedCo, a technical assistance provider that worked with small businesses in Lower Manhattan after the 11 September terrorist attacks, began its post-Katrina work in New Orleans by offering financing and assistance to restaurants along St. Claude Avenue. The Green Charter School started an edible schoolyard, modeled after the schoolyard Alice Waters began at the Martin Luther King Jr. Middle School in Berkeley,

California. The schoolyard not only will preserve local foodways and traditions but also will be used in every facet of the school's curriculum (Price 2006). These vibrant and varied grassroots efforts highlight the deficiencies and opportunities in New Orleans's food system and embody the creativity of private citizens and nonprofit organizations working to meet food access needs. But these initiatives also raise in sharp relief the ways in which food access is not being comprehensively addressed.

To their credit, the city and its partners have undertaken a number of public initiatives to address food access needs since the storm. On 3 May 2007, the New Orleans City Council paid heed to the city's food access issues by adopting a resolution that created the Food Policy Advisory Committee (FPAC), declaring that "everyone deserves equal access to healthy and nutritious foods" (New Orleans City Council Minutes 2007). Tulane's School of Public Health and Tropical Medicine and Philadelphia's Food Trust co-led the FPAC's initial work, and the FPAC released its first report to the public in March 2008 (New Orleans Food Policy Advisory Committee 2008). The FPAC's broadest recommendations included reducing regulatory barriers and adding incentives for the sale of fresh foods; encouraging fresh food access in economic development and transportation-related considerations, especially in underserved areas; promoting locally grown and produced foodstuffs; and establishing a financing program for developing supermarkets (New Orleans Food Policy Advisory Committee 2008: 3). While the FPAC's policies take into account many of the food access issues and the financial incentives and regulatory hurdles that need to be surmounted to deliver food to neighborhoods, the committee deliberately constrained its focus to food retail and eschewed markets' larger social and political roles, dealing with them only implicitly. The FPAC report is by far the most comprehensive public effort to deal with food access issues before or after the storm, but it is also focused only on a narrow band of the spectrum of functions that markets play within a community.

The FPAC report has additional resonance because the recommendations were announced to the public at the Circle Food Store. The press conference featured the owner of the store and a resident of the Tremé neighborhood in addition to the public health officials who drafted the report. Eric Baumgartner of the Louisiana Public Health Institute, which is a nongovernmental partner in many of the city's public health initiatives, spoke on the committee's behalf of the connections among public health, food access, and the built environment: "Louisiana has rates of being overweight, and diseases and conditions related to being overweight, that are among the highest in the nation. . . . Health research shows that by changing the environment—the neighborhood—to one that has more access to fresh, nutritious foods, that in fact it will improve diets" ("Group Wants" 2008).

Community resident Ed Buckner asked the critical question: "The world keeps telling me as a black man to eat healthier and I'll live longer. Well, where am I going to get the fresh vegetables and fruit to eat healthier so that I can live longer and help my community be a healthier community?" (*Demand Skyrockets* 2008). Finally, the owner of the Circle Food Store, Dwayne Boudreaux, spoke of impediments he faced in reopening: "We have realized that the costs of operating a grocery store post-Katrina are higher than it was before. It is difficult to find affordable financing, and insurance issues are very tough. I was concerned about security before, and now security is a major objective" ("Healthy Food" 2008). Given not only Circle Food's post-Katrina experiences but also its history in a black neighborhood that was negatively affected by decades of uneven development, a more fitting site could not have been chosen.

The city has also undertaken two other programs to address food access needs since the storm. The corner store initiative has sought to put more fresh foods—and to feature them more prominently—in thirteen stores and two produce trucks dispersed over a wide portion of the city. Similar programs have succeeded in cities as disparate as Oakland and Boston, and the New Orleans initiative, which began in September 2007, also seems to be working (Strobel 2007; Louisiana Public Health Institute 2007a).

The city's second effort is the renovation of the French Market. After decades of selling Mardi Gras kitsch to tourists rather than fresh food to residents, the French Market has undergone a five-million-dollar renovation. In planning for the rehabilitation, city officials decided that "they wanted the market more to be more like it used to be, when they used to sell a lot of fresh food at the market, and prepare fresh dishes for people to eat" (Associated Press 2007).

In addressing current needs, the French Market sought out past solutions and the reintroduction of fresh food. And some of the French Market vendors are cognizant of food's importance to the market and the larger community: according to one vendor, "Everything is indigenous to here. . . . Pralines came right into market by slaves. These are old products. It's just like the red beans and rice and gumbo, it makes New Orleans what it is. We can't forget it" (Associated Press 2007).

JEFFREY SCHWARTZ

A PLACE FOR NEIGHBORHOOD MARKETS

Neighborhood markets have assumed a large role in the landscape of post-Katrina recovery, in which almost every neighborhood planning process has expressed a need for local food access. According to the FPAC, "Throughout the UNOP [Unified New Orleans Plan] planning process, residents consistently ranked access to healthy foods as critical to neighborhood recovery efforts. Nearly every neighborhood plan created as a part of UNOP's Citywide Strategic Recovery and Rebuilding Plan has included the location of a supermarket or grocery store in the immediate area" (New Orleans Food Policy Advisory Committee 2008: 6).

The Danzey-Lambert Neighborhood Rebuilding Plan, the planning process that originated with the city council and that focused exclusively on the city's forty-two flooded neighborhoods, mirrored this emphasis. According to the plan's executive summary, "As neighborhoods rebuild, providing services previously absent will become essential amenities to complement the quality of life for residents as they return. Residents will evaluate the availability of services as a barometer of neighborhoods' growth and vitality.... One of the economic development initiatives that many residents ranked higher than even the restoration of neighborhood schools or health care, was the return of the neighborhood supermarket and pharmacy" (*New Orleans Neighborhoods Recovery Plan* 2006). Indeed, 94 percent of the residents interviewed for the Danzey-Lambert planning process rated grocery stores as "required essential services," higher than any other essential service and more important than health care, assisted living care or day care, or restaurants (*Executive Summary* 2006).

Moreover, food access represents a source of potential entrepreneurialism and activism on the part of individuals and neighborhoods. Johanna Gilligan, the New Orleans Food and Farm Network's community organizer, elaborated, "There's a lot of money to be made in food in the city right now because every neighborhood we travel to people talk to us that they don't have the food access that they need, so it can really be profitable" (Troeh 2007). Dr. Edward Blakely, head of New Orleans's Office of Recovery and Development Administration (ORDA), has supported this vision of neighborhood markets, expressing his hope that they become centers for grassroots entrepreneurialism (2008).

Neighborhood markets also present an opportunity for recovery officials and city planners. One of the primary interventions suggested for the "target areas" selected by the Office of Recovery Management (later renamed ORDA) as the initial recipients of concentrated public investment is food

Food, Markets, and Neighborhood Recovery

Fig. 4.3. Former public markets and current neighborhood markets superimposed on ORDA's target areas. The correlation between neighborhood markets and the city's designated areas of investment is intentional; the alignment of target areas and neighborhood markets with the former system of public markets is not and is therefore highly suggestive. Created by author using City of New Orleans data, ArcGIS.

access. The FPAC notes that "supermarkets and green grocers are featured as part of the redevelopment efforts in most of" the target areas (New Orleans Food Policy Advisory Committee 2008: 6), and at-large city council member Arnie Fielkow has pointed out the connection between neighborhood recovery and fresh food access: "The more grocery stores that exist, the more residents will be willing to move in" (quoted in Moises 2007).

Not coincidentally, nine of the seventeen target areas contain former public market sites. Such a development is not necessarily surprising for the target areas in which the former markets are a part of the city or neighborhood plans (as is the case for the St. Roch Market); however, most of the target areas were selected for past and prospective viability. That many of these areas prioritized for public investment used to have public markets suggests that the urban design and socioeconomic structures of neighborhoods still reflect some of their past orientation toward public markets. Public markets are sites of former vibrancy, and returning to these centers of neighborhood activity as areas of public investment carries not just practical economic implications but also cultural and political resonance. Moreover, in seven of the target areas, the market structures remain standing (Sauder 1981: 283). Former public markets and more recently created neighborhood markets could have renewed relevance in a post-Katrina context.

Neighborhood socioeconomic and political functions visibly and symbolically address many of the issues that have arisen as a consequence of the uneven development of food access and the aftermath of Katrina. In understanding this role, Lawrence J. Vale's concept of neighborhood resource centers is germane: "As the citizens of New Orleans struggle to repopulate decimated neighborhoods, the neighborhoods require a rededication to small-scale institutions that can provide both identity and resources to support the viability of hundreds of sub-neighborhood districts that have services as well as residences" (2006: 159).

New Orleans's neighborhood markets seem to fulfill just these functions in the wake of Hurricane Katrina, and at least one response to Judy Walker's question—"In what ways will the new New Orleans resemble its former self?" (2007) —is a system of neighborhood markets and localized food access.

THE EXPERIENCE OF NEIGHBORHOOD MARKETS

Two interrelated questions lie at the core of this research: To what extent do neighborhood markets compensate for a lack of fresh food access? And what socioeconomic, symbolic, cultural, and political functions do the neighborhood markets have?

Food plays a larger role in cities than is typically appreciated, especially in times of emergency. Even before the Katrina-related evacuation, food access affected how New Orleanians would respond to catastrophe by coloring citizens' ability to reach out to neighbors, their physical well-being, and their psychological health. During a disaster, access to food can be a life-and-death consideration, as the images discussed at the beginning of this chapter attest. Food also plays a role after disaster: those neighborhoods that enjoy the practical and social amenities embodied in markets are more likely to provide for their residents' welfare. Neighborhood disparities in access to fresh food are accentuated during disaster, dramatically affecting how neighborhoods experience catastrophe. Thus, insofar as neighborhood markets are attempting to address their neighborhoods' food access and socioeconomic needs, they are also providing glimpses into the ways in which vulnerability and resiliency are playing out on the ground.

But markets typically come up short in their attempts to meet their communities' food access and resilience needs. This statement is not an indictment of the markets or their shoppers, vendors, or organizers. Rather, neighborhood markets are emblematic of the larger issues of recovery and resilience, and that process has been problematic and lacking on many fronts.

Fig. 4.4. Gretna Market, 2008. Though the market is housed in a former rail depot, the building is strikingly reminiscent of the earliest public market structures. Photo by author.

THE VALUE OF MARKETS

Neighborhood markets unquestionably meet some social and economic development needs and provide some social and psychological benefits. Markets can be a tremendously affirmative experience for individuals. For many New Orleanians, deciding whether to rebuild was difficult, and seeing friends and new faces at the markets is often a validation of the decision to return or stay. The act of participating in the market in some ways helps transform vulnerability into resiliency; in some senses, neighborhood markets are sites for the production of resiliency. Far from seeing markets as frivolous entertainment, many vendors and shoppers find the socializing, food, and music to be bound up with their aspirations for their neighborhood. As was the case with New Orleans's historic food system, food access at the neighborhood markets is inextricably tied to larger neighborhood social networks. Such is the power of food access. Going to markets thus promotes not just physical but also psychological well-being.

One of the defining aspects of markets is that they have become places of respite. Perhaps because markets only take place on a weekly or monthly basis, individuals enjoy the food and shopping that markets offer as a break from the incessant difficulties of rebuilding. Post-Katrina shoppers in New Orleans can often be heard to say, "The market is a nice break"; as one Lakeview market shopper put it, "The market gives me the night off from cooking." Even when the market is not providing fresh food access, the prepared foods often offer a convenience that shoppers greatly appreciate. A

JEFFREY SCHWARTZ

Fig. 4.5. Upper Ninth Ward/"Holy Angels" Market, 2008. Photo by author.

Gretna market shopper found psychological benefits to spending some time at the market: "Without community, you sit in your house all day by yourself and focus on the long list of things you have to do. That's not New Orleans style."

Many shoppers and vendors characterize their experiences as centering amid the frenetic pace of recovery. That is, neighborhood markets and food shopping more generally provide not just the sustaining aspects of food but also spaces for socializing and individual reflection (Troeh 2007). Greta Gladney of the Renaissance Project notes that its Upper Ninth Ward Market is located within one block of both an assisted living home and a senior living center. Seniors who visit the market benefit from the contact and interaction, and the multigenerational character of the Renaissance Project markets is actually a priority for Gladney (2008; Louisiana Public Health Institute 2007b). Richard McCarthy, the director of the Crescent City Farmers' Market, has observed that after the storm, friends reconnected with one another at markets: "If government failure was one of the major stories of Katrina, civic engagement was the other" (quoted in McNulty 2007). He notes, "You have to consider the amount of stress people are under right now. . . . They're going to the market for a break from our house-gutting lives and to see a glimpse of the gentleness that can exist in our city. This is about more than shopping. It's more than markets. It's a public declaration of commitment and togetherness. It's saying, 'We're here.' There's a local solidarity that develops from that and people get pretty emotional about it, too. People are engaging and connecting with each other and becoming aware of why they live here in a way that other cities would kill for. I think markets are places that help express that" (quoted in McNulty 2007).

At bottom, much of recovery is a problem of collective action. Almost all challenges faced by cities rebuilding after disaster—from housing to schools to municipal services to food access—encounter the question of whether

Food, Markets, and Neighborhood Recovery

Fig. 4.6. Freret Market, with fresh food vendor in foreground, 2008. Photo by author.

demand by residents should precede supply of services or whether services should precede demand, an often paralyzing chicken-and-egg dilemma. On the neighborhood level, this problem is often epitomized by the solitary occupied house on an otherwise vacant block—the jack-o'-lantern effect. In many ways, neighborhood markets represent a partial solution to these trenchant difficulties of rebuilding. At the Lakeview Market, for example, the Beacon of Hope invites the Lakeview Civic Improvement Association as well as a group of real estate agents to sit in two tents to provide residents with information about rebuilding. The agents in particular have been providing homeowners with information about the little advertised and even less understood options with the state's Road Home program, which offers rebuilding grants to homeowners.

Finally, markets provide some limited community economic development benefits. While most of the smaller markets have an almost negligible economic impact on the surrounding community, some of the larger markets, among them Freret and Lakeview, provide an economic stimulus to their neighborhoods that has the potential to carry over into the creation of new business. One of the vendors from the Freret Street Market used the income he generated there and at other markets to open a retail storefront. Market organizations hold up precisely this sort of example as a positive economic impact of the neighborhood market, but such instances are few and far between.

In addition to their many pragmatic purposes, neighborhood markets are also highly symbolic spaces that signify a community's ongoing recovery and vitality. In some neighborhoods, including Broadmoor and Village L'Est, several individuals and market managers specifically placed markets to defy the BNOB's plans to turn their neighborhoods into green space. Perhaps most importantly, markets are held regularly, marking out the time of recovery and symbolizing neighborhoods' increasing viability and vibrancy.

Several of the post-Katrina neighborhood markets, including both the Lakeview Market and the Broad Street Market, are held in parking lots of shuttered grocery stores, a juxtaposition that both comments on the specific food access issues still facing neighborhoods and offers a more general indictment of the pace of recovery and a symbolic affirmation of a neighborhood's renewal.

Other neighborhood markets enable connections between communities by providing the space for that process to unfold. Markets often occupy liminal spaces at the intersection between neighborhoods, partly because major streets in New Orleans often serve as dividing lines but also because neighborhoods are often segmented into disparate areas. Markets therefore help to identify community spaces. Indeed, many market managers have expressed an overt goal of bringing neighborhoods together or breaking down walls.

Food access adds another level of symbolism to some New Orleans neighborhood markets. Because of the city's unique food system, many markets use that tradition as a way to remedy previous inadequacies or challenges. According to Gladney, "Once upon a time, the municipal government took responsibility for food access. The city managed the system to ensure that there was food access across neighborhoods. [This is so] exciting because I think we are returning to that now poststorm, partially because of work from neighborhood markets" (2008). Moreover, she notes, "In the Lower Ninth Ward, "we haven't had a grocery store in over thirty years" (DocNO 2006). For many people, resiliency is not just reconstruction but is reclaiming what was lost or claiming what was never previously present.

Similarly, the Vietnamese market in New Orleans East is a bastion of cultural promotion and preservation. Almost all Village L'Est market vendors are elderly women who began their relationships in Vietnam and who continue those connections at the market. While the Vietnamese Market has important practical and food-related roles in the community, it also plays a critical role in sustaining cultural pathways. As Christopher A. Airiess and David L. Clawson observe, "The re-creation of a garden landscape reminiscent of rural Vietnam represents a familiar past environment in the tangible

Fig. 4.7. Vietnamese/Village L'Est Market, 2008. The Vietnamese Market is an ethnic neighborhood market whose vendors are almost exclusively the elders of the community who are sustaining social ties that began in Vietnam more than three decades ago. Photo by author.

present. . . . The elderly are thus afforded opportunity to create order in a new socioeconomic environment. . . . For any immigrant group, traditional foods represent a connection to the past, function to maintain ethnic identity, and assist in reducing the effects of acculturation" (1994: 19–20). The neighborhood organization that runs the market also views it as a tool for preserving and promoting cultural traditions among members of younger generations and is thus planning to build a new urban farm on twenty underutilized acres in the neighborhood. The proposal has support from several prominent New Orleans chefs, including John Besh, who has promised to spend as much as possible of his restaurants' four-million-dollar grocery budget there (Peck 2008).

In this way, neighborhood organizations are employing the political facets of neighborhood markets to guide urban reconstruction. Establishing a market in a sense constitutes a neighborhood's attempt to ensure that the story of recovery is told in that particular setting. Markets can thus be seen in part as attempts to put specific neighborhoods on the agenda for urban development. For all of these reasons, neighborhood markets are valuable institutions on the landscape of recovery in New Orleans.

THE FAILURES OF MARKETS

For all of their merits, however, the manner in which markets fall short of meeting their communities' material needs is a commentary on the fragile status of rebuilding in the city. Post-Katrina neighborhood markets are largely limited to psychological and symbolic functions rather than economic development or improving food access. A great gulf remains between markets' aspirations and the reality of neighborhood recovery.

These failures are a partial indictment of the culture of New Orleans, which for too long has settled for ephemeral events rather than fostering community economic development. It has simply been easier to have an event than to rebuild buildings and supermarkets. Despite the importance of markets, festivals, and New Orleans's spontaneous spirit, neighborhood markets cannot replace more regular avenues of food access. Food access may not require building supermarkets but does require markets that are held on at least a weekly basis—rain or shine—and that have a plethora of fresh food options.

FAILURE OF GOVERNMENT

While acknowledging the difficulties facing city government after a disaster of such magnitude and the sometimes bungling response of higher levels of government, the experiences of neighborhood markets represent in several respects local government's failure to respond effectively to the storm. In particular, the continuing struggles of neighborhood markets offer regular reminders that something as fundamental to recovery and resilience as food access remains largely neglected.

The city council as well as recovery officials recognize that many New Orleanians' food access needs are not currently satisfied, but in the first thirty months after the storm, the council's only action was to charter the FPAC study (New Orleans Food Policy Advisory Committee 2008). And whatever the merits of FPAC's recommendations, the city has done very little to remedy the deficiencies in New Orleans's food system. As one ORDA employee tautly acknowledged, "The FPAC didn't come up with anything the city council could do" (Cody 2008).

Moreover, ORDA has recognized since its inception the potential value of neighborhood markets and the importance of food access yet remains unable or unwilling to act effectively to address those community needs. Blakely eloquently describes how neighborhood markets have factored into the planning for recovery "target areas": "You have to start with the market. These markets accidentally are located along the spine of the city. When I was choosing the target areas, after I chose the second or third one, I said, 'Wait a second—these were market centers.' Just look at the spacing—it's the same distance in the old days that people would walk. These are ideal places for anyone who was going to market something to eat. . . . These are of course the locations where markets were before and where we're bringing them back" (2008).

Another ORDA official also noted neighborhood markets' potential role in arriving at what he calls "sustainable, daily retail space" for food access. One of his suggested policy interventions echoes Gladney's vision: "One of the things that the city might do instead of subsidizing individual private businesses is set up the [public] markets again. We pay the entire infrastructure cost, build the building, put the roof on, give it a water supply. We have a stall, you sign up.... It's potentially viable. We're rebuilding the target areas with an awareness of where the traditional market areas were in the city, and I would guess that the locations where those used to be are fairly good locations now" (Cody 2008).

Yet the city has been incapable of addressing the challenge of food access and the potential for neighborhood markets. It is telling that the first projects undertaken through the city's post-Katrina recovery plan were food related. These "trigger projects" were meant to galvanize interest and investment in the areas ORDA identified as salient. The first occurred two years after the storm when the city helped to sponsor a onetime market day in the parking lot of the still-shuttered Circle Food Store to assess the demand for reopening the grocery.

The second of such trigger projects was the funding of the Freret Street Market, for which the city gave $9,010 in start-up funds. Both Mayor Ray Nagin and ORDA's director, Blakely, were present at opening day, and Blakely insisted that the effort represented a "crane in the sky," a symbol of New Orleans's rebuilding (City of New Orleans 2007).

The city's relationship with the neighborhood markets is an indictment of its recovery policies and actions since the storm. On the practical side, the experience of the markets shows ORDA's problematic focus on large-scale projects despite the fact that the few projects that it has supported quickly have been associated with neighborhood-level markets. The city indeed needs to rebuild infrastructure and promote private development, but it is also missing out on an opportunity. Geoff Coates, director of the Urban Conservancy, which focuses on local economic development, characterizes the poststorm situation as continuing bad prestorm policies: "The city has been abandoning small businesses for decades.... The city spends a lot of time, money, and effort going after large projects that more than often never materialize, and they don't invest the small amounts that could really do something" (2008). Yet he remains optimistic about neighborhood markets and what they represent: "I've seen more interesting, better projects in the last couple years than at any time since I moved down here.... Before the storm, several neighborhoods asked the Crescent City Farmers' Market to set up a market for them, and now, the Crescent City Farmers' Market still won't, but neighborhoods did it anyway" (2008).

The experience of neighborhood markets is also an indictment of the city's larger laissez-faire approach to recovery. As the markets have shown, many of the issues associated with rebuilding after a disaster are chicken-and-egg problems of coordinating expectations and managing collective action. Apart from designating areas for redevelopment, the city has been woefully inept at helping to guide the city's overall redevelopment and has been deliberately silent on policy issues related to guiding private development. It is emblematic of the larger process of recovery that despite recognizing the myriad problems related to the city's urban food system and the potential of neighborhood markets to help address neighborhood food access and resilience, New Orleans's leaders have done almost nothing to support neighborhood markets.

So far, neighborhood markets have only partly fulfilled their promise to meet the needs of their communities. Markets have hardly made a dent in food access needs in most neighborhoods, and while they have certainly provided a social gathering space, that space is ephemeral and far too infrequent. Said one shopper at the Freret Market, "If this is all we can do two and a half years after Katrina, then leadership is seriously lacking. We need much more and sooner."

CONCLUSION: MAKING GROCERIES

The experience of post-Katrina neighborhood markets attests to the salience of food in the daily life of cities. That New Orleans's communities turned in part to markets among all of the possible neighborhood activities speaks to the inextricable importance of food access in the larger culture and vitality of urban places. From the vibrant social worlds surrounding New Orleans's public market system through the narratives of recovery and resilience after Katrina, analysts, observers, writers, and planners need to better account for the geography of food in our cities.

Above all else, the experience of neighborhood markets in New Orleans after Katrina demands that planners and policymakers take full account of the food system. This entails understanding how the planning and policy choices we make are intertwined with the health, vibrancy, and resiliency of our communities. Only in the last few years has planning as a discipline begun to acknowledge the importance of food. In the *Policy Guide on Community and Regional Food Planning*, adopted by the board of directors of the American Planning Association in April and May 2007, the association argues that "food is a sustaining and enduring necessity. Yet among the basic essentials for life—air, water, shelter, and food—only food has been absent over the years as a focus of serious professional planning interest. This is a puzzling omission because, as a discipline, planning marks its distinctiveness by being comprehensive in scope and attentive to the temporal dimensions and spatial interconnections among important facets of community life" (2007).

Food plays a variety of roles in the communities in which planners work, but only recently have planners and policymakers begun to consider the role of urban design and urban food access in public health. An extensive study of Chicago's food system sponsored by LaSalle Bank explored the relationships among race, health, and food access. The researchers found that vast swaths of Chicago could be characterized as food deserts, where affordable, healthy food was difficult or impossible to procure while fast food was omnipresent (Gallagher 2006: 5). The presence of food deserts correlates with poverty, race, and the lack of mobility, issues that planners typically consider. It is no coincidence that Chicago's food deserts coincide almost exclusively with that city's African American communities or that Chicago's African American citizens must travel almost twice as far to grocery stores as to fast food restaurants or corner stores (7). Residents of poorer urban neighborhoods typically pay a larger proportion of their income for food and are more likely to "have premature death and chronic health conditions" associated with chronic afflictions such as obesity, diabetes, and cardiovascular disease (Pothukuchi and Kaufman 2000: 214; Gallagher 2006, 9). The Chicago report also alludes to the sociopolitical implications of food deserts on communities, noting that *desert* is an act as much as it is a place: "The lack of access to good food in some areas is not a natural, accidental phenomenon but is instead the result of decisions made at multiple levels by multiple actors" (Gallagher 2006: 5). This finding ties directly into the resiliency literature, which seeks to understand how disasters and vulnerability are produced, not merely how they are experienced.

"Making groceries" is a distinctly New Orleans phrase for going grocery shopping. It derives from the French *faire son marché*, where *faire* means "to do" or "to make," from a time when New Orleanians literally had to assemble meals in a city system of public markets and private corner groceries. These food access outlets were the vibrant centers of their neighborhoods, and food shopping was intertwined with community life. After Katrina, the phrase speaks to the manner in which neighborhoods have tried to use procuring food at markets as a creative, social, and political act. In New

JEFFREY SCHWARTZ

Orleans, one cannot buy food without talking to someone; after Katrina, those connections with neighbors and strangers hold more weight than was previously the case. While the reality of neighborhood markets does not yet always reach their aspirations, a city or a neighborhood could do worse than to remake itself in the image of a market. Critical observers of the city would do well to learn how to make groceries too.

NOTES

1. Euclidean zoning is the zoning system used in most U.S. towns and cities and is characterized by a segregation of land uses into particular types ("residential," "commercial," "industrial," and so forth), each of which stipulates the activities permissible within each classification. This zoning was first adopted in the town of Euclid, Ohio, and was upheld in a landmark 1926 Supreme Court decision, *Village of Euclid v. Ambler Realty Co.* (272 U.S. 365, 71 L.Ed. 303, 47 S.Ct. 114).

REFERENCES

Airiess, Christopher A., and David L. Clawson. 1994. "Vietnamese Market Gardens in New Orleans." *Geographical Review* 84.1 (January): 16–31.
American Planning Association. 2007. *Policy Guide on Community and Regional Food Planning.* www.planning.org/policyguides/food.htm. Accessed 29 March 2008.
Associated Press. 2007. "In New Orleans, French Market's $5 Million Makeover Nearing Completion." *International Herald Tribune*, 4 June. www.iht.com. Accessed 3 May 2008.
Blakely, Edward. 2008. Interview. 26 March.
Brown, Allison. 2001. "Counting Farmers Markets." *Geographical Review* 91.4 (October): 655–74.
Campanella, Richard. 2006. *Geographies of New Orleans: Urban Fabrics before the Storm.* Lafayette: Center for Louisiana Studies.
———. 2007. *Above Sea-Level New Orleans: The Residential Capacity of Orleans Parish's High Ground.* New Orleans: Tulane/Xavier Center for Bioenvironmental Research.
"City Council Calls for Increasing Access to Healthy Food in New Orleans." 2008. *New Orleans CityBusiness.* www.neworleanscitybusiness.com. Accessed 11 January 2008.
City of New Orleans, Mayor's Office of Communications. 2007. "Target Recovery Area Project to Kick Off on Saturday: Freret Market Will Include Art, Food, and Thrift Shopping." 4 September. www.cityofno.com. Accessed 24 February 2008.
Coates, Geoff. 2008. Interview. 24 April.
Cody, David. 2008. Interview. 7 March.
Demand Skyrockets at Local Food Banks. 2008. www.wwltv.com. 14 March 2008. Accessed .
DocNOProductions. 2006. *Ninth Ward Farmers Market.* http://www.youtube.com/user/DocNOproductions. Accessed 25 March 2008.
Eaton, Leslie. 2008. "Raising the Ante with Liquor Sales Bid." *New York Times*, 18 April. www.nytimes.com. Accessed 18 April 2008.

Eckstein, Barbara. 2006. *Sustaining New Orleans.* New York: Routledge.
Executive Summary: New Orleans Rebuilding Plan Survey. 2006. http://www.nolanrp.com/Data/Neighborhood//Resident%20Survey%20Executive%20Summary%20Formatted.pdf. Accessed 10 February 2010.
Gallagher, Mari. 2006. *Examining the Impact of Food Deserts on Public Health in Chicago.* Chicago: LaSalle Bank and Mari Gallagher Research and Consulting Group.
Gardner, Peter. 2008. Interview. 10 April.
Gladney, Greta. 2008. Interview. 9 March.
"Group Wants to Bring Healthy Food Closer to You." 2008. www.wwltv.com. 18 March.
Ingram, Michelle. 2008. Interview. 4 April.
Louisiana Public Health Institute. 2007a. *Corner Store Initiative: Steps to a Healthier New Orleans.* http://www.stepsla.org/home2/section/3%3Cn%3E153-153/the-corner-store-initiative. Accessed 11 February 2010.
———. 2007b. *Healthier Food Options Are Just Around the Corner.* 17 September. lphi.org/home2/section/2-158/announcement-archive/view/108/. Accessed 11 February 2010.
Mayo, James M. 1991. "The American Public Market." *Journal of Architectural Education* 45.1 (November): 41–57.
———. 1993. *The American Grocery Store: The Business Evolution of an Architectural Space.* Westport, Conn.: Greenwood.
McNulty, Ian. 2007. "Market Makers." *Gambit Weekly,* 18 September. www.bestofneworleans.com. Accessed 23 February 2008.
Moises, Christian. 2007. "Food Policy Advisory Committee Hopes to Help with Food Access." *New Orleans Citybusiness,* 4 June. http://findarticles.com/p/articles/mi_qn4200/is_20070604/ai_n19202391/. Accessed 11 February 2010.
Mulrine, Anna. 2006. "The Long Road Back." *U.S. News & World Report,* 19 February. www.usnews.com. Accessed 16 April 2008.
New Orleans City Council. 2007. *Minutes of the Regular Meeting of the Council of the City of New Orleans.* 3 May. http://library3.municode.com/minutes/home.htm?infobase=30001&doc_action=whatsnew. Accessed 10 February 2010.
New Orleans Food Policy Advisory Committee. 2008. *Building Healthy Communities: Expanding Access to Fresh Food Retail.* http://www.sph.tulane.edu/PRC/Files/FPAC%20Report%20Final.pdf. Accessed 1 February 2010.
New Orleans Neighborhoods Rebuilding Plan. 2006. 31 October. http://www.nolanrp.com/final.php. Accessed 11 February 2010.
Peck, Renee. 2008. "In New Orleans' Vietnamese Community, Gardening Is a Way of Life." *New Orleans Times-Picayune,* 27 September. blog.nola.com/reneepeck/2008/09/in_new_orleans_vietnamese_comm.html. Accessed 11 February 2010.
Pelling, Mark. 2003. *The Vulnerability of Cities: Natural Disasters and Social Resilience.* Sterling, Va.: Earthscan.
Pothukuchi, Kameshwari, and Jerome L. Kaufman. 2000. "The Food System: A Stranger to the Planning Field." *Journal of the American Planning Association* 66.2 (Spring): 113–24.
Price, Todd A. 2006. "Edible Schoolyards." *New Orleans Magazine,* December, 54–57.
———. 2007. "The Go-Between." *OffBeat Magazine,* 1 November. offbeat.com/artman/publish/article_2695.shtml. Accessed 11 February 2010.
Pyle, Jane. 1971. "Farmers Markets in the United States: Functional Anachronisms." *Geographical Review* 61.2 (April 1971): 167–97.

Reeves, Sally K. 2007. "Making Groceries: A History of New Orleans' Public Markets." *Louisiana Cultural Vistas*, Fall, 24–35.

Sauder, Robert A. 1981. "The Origin and Spread of the Public Market System in New Orleans." *Journal of Louisiana History* 22.3 (Summer): 281–97.

Strobel, Hillary. 2007. *The Future of Food Security in New Orleans*. http://www.uas.coop/node/181. Accessed 11 February 2010.

Tangires, Helen. 2003. *Public Markets and Civic Culture in Nineteenth-Century America*. Baltimore: Johns Hopkins University Press.

Troeh, Eve. 2007. *Food-Shopping a Challenge in New Orleans*. 28 March. www.npr.org/templates/story/story.php?storyId=9182476. Accessed 11 February 2010.

Vale, Lawrence J. 2006. "Restoring Urban Viability." In *Rebuilding Urban Places after Disaster: Lessons from Hurricane Katrina*, ed. Eugenie L. Birch and Susan M. Wachter, 149–67. Philadelphia: University of Pennsylvania Press.

Walker, Judy. 2007. "Urban Agriculture: The Fruits (& Veggies) of Our Labor." *New Orleans Times-Picayune*, 30 August. http://blog.nola.com/judywalker/2007/08/urban_agriculture_the_fruits_v.html. Accessed 11 February 2010.

LOSING GROUND
The Cultural Politics of Cultural Landscapes in Plaquemines Parish

W. D. WILKERSON

The weeks following Katrina brought floods of discourse nearly equal to the floods of brackish water drowning Louisiana and Mississippi. National sorrow, indignation, and rage at the conditions of life in New Orleans eventually receded into deep concern over the city's continued existence, particularly the survival of the city's rich and unique cultural life (*Louisiana Rebirth* 2005: 4). One of the most significant ideas to come from this disaster is a nationwide popular and political opinion that "culture" is important and worth saving, the culture of New Orleans particularly so. This sentiment is even more remarkable given the apparent vagueness of the concept of culture. The discourse on culture in the popular media and several state-sponsored publications on the subject suggests that cuisine, jazz music, visual and performing arts, architecture, Mardi Gras Indians, brass bands, and Mardi Gras krewes are all parts of a greater cultural whole (see esp. Mt. Auburn Associates 2005; Bring New Orleans Back Commission 2006; *Louisiana Rebirth* 2005). Throughout, these elements are integrated into a unified concept of culture as a "way of life," as the introductory paragraph of the Bring New Orleans Back Report attests: "Culture expresses a people's sense of what is worthwhile, what is beautiful, and what is meaningful; it suggests solutions to the challenges of living in a specific time and place, and those solutions are distilled, over generations, into a vision of a civilized way of life" (Bring New Orleans Back Commission 2006: 1).

Unfortunately, the concept of culture as a way of life seems to have definite geographic boundaries that reach only as far as the borders of Orleans Parish. Beyond the parish line, there is little discussion of a cultural rebirth.

The attention given to New Orleans after Katrina has almost completely obscured the cultural crises unfolding daily in the less populous parishes that were also devastated. This chapter explores how pre-Katrina cultural policy, coupled with post-Katrina environmental (mis)management and disaster recovery policies, has desperately endangered the cultural life of one comparatively marginalized parish. Rather than attempt to survey the damage done and being done in all parishes, this chapter will focus on the plight of Plaquemines Parish, the ninety-mile strip of land south of New Orleans where Katrina first made landfall.

While the idea of cultural policy is often as vague as the notion of culture itself, the cultural policy referred to in this chapter specifically deals with state and federal initiatives put into place to enhance, promote, conserve, preserve, use, and/or financially support the cultural life of a given place—in this instance, Plaquemines Parish. The primary problem with the state cultural policy as formulated in the *Roadmap for Change*, the *Louisiana Rebirth* plan, the Bring New Orleans Back Report, and *Louisiana: Where Culture Means Business* is that while these policies introduce culture as a way of life, they quickly move to reframe the idea of culture as being variously a resource pool, a salable commodity, a business plan, or an economic engine. The state's current cultural policy is overt; that is, cultural policy as formulated in these documents and current governing policy efforts is directly related to cultural work and cultural resources as linked to the state's economic health. The ideas behind this overt policy seem to work well when dealing with a city such as New Orleans, which even after Katrina has the physical and financial infrastructure to cater to tourists and other consumers demanding cultural products as well as a resident population base that has a degree of economic wherewithal sufficient to supply these products.

Plaquemines Parish has very little of either, so this overt policy does not apply. In contrast, the current policy at work in Plaquemines is covert, which is to say it does not directly feed into the state's current plans but does directly affect the way that the state views culture in the parish and subsequently the work done to conserve that culture. For Plaquemines, culture may be understood as a way of life. As such, it defies the easy definition and commodification evident in the iconic aspects of New Orleans culture, such as jazz, Sazerac cocktails, and so forth. Framing culture as a way of life within the context of Plaquemines results in culture as the lived experience of daily life that is defined by its relationship to the landscape. Plaquemines's culture is directly linked to residents' relationship with the environment, because their way of life depends largely on fishing, farming, and oil and natural gas. This way of life creates not only shared cultural values but also a shared cultural historicizing and prioritizing of the local landscape and ecology. This landscape is simultaneously the land's physical and ecological features and the cultural significance that the landscape holds for the people who live on and interact with it.

The primary issue at stake for the parish is the atrocious environmental degradation washing away the Plaquemines landscape. This erosion has three main causes. First is the lack of alluvial flooding needed to replenish the lost soil, brought about by the heavily engineered levee system controlling the Mississippi River. Second are the access canals that the oil companies have dug into the marshland, which allow more water to flow through the marsh, washing away the land as it goes. Third is the increasing number and frequency of hurricanes, which batter the Gulf Coast and wash away miles of coastline. The environmental degradation problems endanger the landscape as well as the lives and livelihoods of the people who live and work on it. Without people, there can be no culture, and without a healthy landscape, the people of Plaquemines cannot thrive. State policy needs to address this cultural landscape and can do so only if it also addresses the environmental degradation eroding this landscape.

In their introduction to *Preserving Cultural Landscapes in America*, Arnold R. Alanen and Robert Z. Melnick explain that cultural landscapes "exist virtually everywhere that human activities have affected the land" (2000: 3). Cultural landscapes include not only topography, soil, vegetation, and water but also buildings, bridges, fences, roads, gardens, and parks. Landscapes are often imbued with social or spiritual values; for the people who live on them, these landscapes hold "cultural meanings directly linked to the past, present, and future, as well as to the health and well-being of their culture" (6).

All landscapes can be considered cultural landscapes in one way or another, and many of them come into being "without the direct involvement of a professional designer, planner, or engineer." Some landscapes may be considered particularly vernacular in nature. The defunct Burrwood military installation in Plaquemines Parish is one such landscape. These ordinary, vernacular landscapes generally evolve "unintentionally and represent multiple layers of time and cultural activity, [and] are fundamental to our very existence" (Alanen and Melnick 2000: 5) because humans inevitably alter their environmental surroundings to make life more amenable or at least tolerable. Other landscapes may be considered primarily ethnographic in nature, such as that in the village of Grand Bayou, another Plaquemines Parish community. Multiple cultural groups—"particularly people bound together by a common history, identity, or ethos" (6)—simultaneously use ethnographic landscapes. Neighborhoods, villages, and even entire parishes are readily subject to evaluation and interpretation by applying the theories of the cultural landscape. Cultural policy that does not include the state's efforts to enhance, promote, conserve, preserve, use, and/ or financially support a parish's cultural landscape is thus incomplete and ineffective.

State and federally commissioned cultural resources investigations have failed to take into account precisely these cultural landscapes. Since the late 1970s, the state has commissioned several cultural resource investigations in Plaquemines Parish, with the studies conducted by archaeologists and overseen by the Division of Historic Preservation, to ensure that significant cultural resources are not negatively affected by state and federal road, levee, or freshwater diversion projects. Intended to conserve the Plaquemines culture, these efforts have also created narrow definitions of cultural resources and a narrow scope of endeavor.

In recent years, researchers from Louisiana State University (LSU), the University of New Orleans (UNO), and the University of Louisiana at Lafayette have undertaken ethnographic research to document the lives, occupations, traditions, and concerns of the members of the cultural groups residing in the parish. These documentation projects have stressed the threats environmental degradation poses. With the notable exception of LSU anthropologist and folklorist Carolyn Ware, whose work was initiated by a grant from the Louisiana Folklife Program, little research has examined the family, community, and occupational traditions nurtured by people's relationship to the land.[1] The result is that the groups seem vague and insubstantial—no one knows exactly who they are, but by all accounts they should be saved.

Both historic preservation and ethnographic inquiry endeavors acknowledge the degradation and landscape attrition caused by coastal erosion, though the two types of cultural work deal very differently with the subject. For Plaquemines, appropriate cultural policy must address the preservation of cultures that lack the economic justifications provided by easily commodifiable products that characterize the bulk of contemporary cultural policy in Louisiana as well as the issues of environmental degradation and restoration. It is thus important to examine how historic preservation and ethnography have influenced and been influenced by the concept of culture that underlies the state's covert cultural policy in the parish and to determine what needs to change to bring Plaquemines's cultural needs into overt statewide cultural policy.

HISTORIC PRESERVATION

The bulk of the state's cultural policy efforts in Plaquemines seem to be intertwined with the myriad cultural resources surveys undertaken through the Division of Historic Preservation. The parish contains historically significant sites, and a wide variety of state and federal land development projects have taken place there. The *Louisiana Comprehensive Statewide Historic Preservation Plan* published in 2000 reaffirms the long-standing mandate for cultural resource investigations of all sites targeted for state or federal development projects (1). Specifically, the state wants to identify and preserve ruins, artifacts, land-use patterns, and other historically significant remnants of Native American, early settlement, and Civil War material culture. The investigations are conducted by archaeologists, and the results and recommendations are then taken into consideration during the preplanning stages of each land-development project. The plan further mandates the need to seek out, recover, and restore historically significant places in the state's underconsidered rural parishes, among them Plaquemines.

But because historic preservation comprises the largest segment of cultural policy activity in the parish, this one branch of the state's cultural administration has the largest say in shaping and articulating the concept of culture that is applied to cultural resources. The concepts used as criteria to determine what is culturally significant and meaningful often obscure other important cultural aspects, such as lived culture and the cultural landscape.[2] A number of cultural resources investigations have taken place in Plaquemines Parish, with fifteen having taken place between 1982 and 2005 (Pelletier 2001; Pearson 2001; U.S. Army Corps of Engineers, New Orleans District 2000; Hinks 1994; Inon 1993; Hunter 1992; Goodwin 1992; Hunter and Reeves 1990a, b; Goodwin and Associates 1985, 1989, 1990; Jones 1989; Poplin, Poplin, and Armstrong 1987; Gilmore 1983). Three of these investigations do a particularly good job of representing the aim, scope, goals, activities, methodologies, and conclusions that are typical of these investigations in Plaquemines Parish and that demonstrate the pattern of logic that organizes the prevailing concept of culture. The Fort Jackson Vicinity and Citrus Lands projects and the Burrwood evaluation are useful because they discuss and reexamine the findings of previously identified sites in the areas being assessed in making conclusions about the current investigation, which in turn dictate the research recommendations made regarding the project areas. The first two indicate the ideas about culture, cultural resources, and landscape that dominate the state's cultural efforts in the parish, and the third demonstrates the shortcomings of these ideas.

Undertaken in the late 1980s, the Army Corps of Engineers–backed cultural resources investigation of the vicinity of Fort Jackson (Jones 1989), located in the southern half of the parish, gives a useful overview of the ideas shaping archaeological work in Louisiana, in particular in Plaquemines (Hunter and Reeves 1990a: 28–29). The investigation sought to determine if the effort to borrow soil from the vicinity of Fort Jackson to shore up levees in lower Plaquemines would disturb a culturally (that is, historically) significant site. Two sites of historic relevance had been discovered in the area prior to the investigation: the Point Pleasant Camp and Empire Oil Field No. 1. Both sites "consisted of abandoned wooden frame buildings with associated historic debris that dated the sites to the late 19th and early 20th centuries" (29). Subsequent investigations found that "the area had been impacted by recent construction" and that it "contained cultural debris, but that it was of such a recent age, that it did not warrant designation as an archaeological site" (33). The division is responsible for "recording all 50 years+ properties on survey forms," primarily to assess eligibility for inclusion on the National Register of Historic Places (*Louisiana Comprehensive Statewide Historic Preservation Plan* 2001: 8, 12). Not all discovered properties will qualify for the register, but many of them may be identified as property types that the state wishes to recover. The plan calls for the preservation of sites related to Louisiana's historic oil and gas industry, yet Empire Oil Field No. 1 was dismissed as a culturally insignificant site because it was less than fifty years old at the time of the investigation.

In 1990, the Citrus Lands investigation assessed the impact of a hurricane protection project on an area in northern Plaquemines (Goodwin and Associates 1989). The researchers noted three previously identified sites comprised of "highly disturbed surface scatter," dating from the nineteenth to mid-twentieth centuries. According to the report, two of these sites "lacked integrity; neither site was thought to possess the quality of significance" (Goodwin and Associates 1990: 11). Reinvestigation of the third site, which contained a prehistoric mound component, a mission chapel, and a cemetery, yielded mixed recommendations. The chapel was still in good condition and "may still possess research potential," but the mound component and the cemetery were not good candidates for further research because both "lacked integrity" (11). This investigation determined that the hurricane protection project would not disturb the sites because the chapel area was well beyond the boundaries of the affected area, and the sites that could or would be affected lacked integrity, so there was nothing within them to preserve (13).

All fifteen investigations were archaeologically based and conducted in accord with standard operating procedure, consisting of intensive pedestrian survey with shovel tests carried out "at 50 meter intervals to the depths of at least 30 cm." (Goodwin and Associates 1990: 38). It is fair to question whether pedestrian surveys conducting shovel tests to a depth roughly equivalent to twelve inches taken roughly 164 feet apart could yield culturally significant material in an area fortunate enough to be regularly inundated with fresh alluvium. This inundation would and could have washed away any culturally significant material, but it is just as likely that the material is still present but buried deeper than one foot. Archaeologists might have considered digging deeper and more frequently. In these investigations, integrity creates a double bind for researchers. If standard operating procedure does not yield the results that would be present in a site with archaeological integrity, then further research on the site cannot be justified, even if common sense suggests that more detailed excavation could yield what the researchers need to find to confirm the site's historic merit.

In these reports, *culture* is nearly synonymous with *history*, which is artifactual in nature. According to researchers' recommendations, archaeological integrity must be present to quantify historical merit. The idea of integrity is central to the archaeological enterprise because scattered artifacts rely on context for interpretation. A china shard in the dirt is garbage; a china shard found with several other shards in a confined space with other types of artifacts can be from a cup, a plate, a washbasin, a necklace, or a lampshade, and origins indicate something of the original context. This original context will always be a sort of reconstruction, but context always shapes that reconstruction into something understandable, recognizable, and plausible; the product of this process is history. The act of reconstructing history through excavation and interpretation of material remains creates a concept of history as that which is artifactual when it could just as easily be recognized as that which is reconstructed. In these reports, where this logic has led to a narrow interpretation of culture as history and even more narrowly as history quantified according to archaeological standards of artifactual integrity, it becomes impossible to recognize culture as anything that is not artifactual in nature.

Using archaeological integrity as the parameter of historical merit confirms for researchers and the policymakers for whom those researchers work that history is an artifact; thus, the landscape containing historical artifacts comes to be regarded in the same way. Sites that lack physical integrity are dismissed from the enterprise of history even when myriad artifacts are present because those artifacts cannot be arranged into a coherent history. A landscape judged according to its level of artifactual integrity cannot be seen as anything other than static and timeless. One must conclude that any changes to that landscape only corrupt both history and culture.

These cultural resources investigations have no room for recent or even contemporary materials in the construction of the historic past. That there may be a different context, another history, is not considered, as in the Fort Jackson vicinity and Citrus Lands investigations and in 1988 surveys of the Woodland levee site and the Bohemia revetment site, both also within Plaquemines Parish. The Bohemia investigation revealed several sites containing an array of late-nineteenth and early-twentieth-century artifacts, but all sites were denied archaeological site status because "investigators concluded that these scatters represented the remains of eroded and redeposited trash dumps" (Goodwin and Associates 1985: 12). The sites do not attest to the presence of original ownership or original context, but they do attest to inhabitants' land-use patterns: Where did this accretion come from, and why was it put here? Why were these particular things thrown out?

These questions are not relevant when seeking a definitive, static, artifactual history product but are useful when trying to ascertain the landscape's cultural significance to the people living on it. In this case, culture refers to a dynamic way of life rather than to a historical artifact. Sites lacking integrity but indicating clear patterns of reuse present the possibility of a living landscape that reflects a dynamic and living culture. The present consequently becomes disconnected from the past, and history is permanently disassociated from lived culture. History does have an artifactual basis, but its importance lies in its impact on the lives of those who interpret it—that is, observe and recontextualize it in accord with their values and ideas about their own lived culture. A culture's relationship to history is as dynamic and vital as its relationship with the land on which it lives. The uses, values, and interpretations the people of Plaquemines ascribe to their lived landscape have not been taken into account. These sites are cultural resources because they are landscapes that reflect the relationship between the generations of residents in Plaquemines and their land. Archaeological integrity cannot begin to quantify the worth of these sites as cultural resources. The Plaquemines investigations have heretofore occluded a view of Plaquemines Parish as a vital cultural landscape that deserves to be considered on its own terms.

Throughout the reports, the importance of Plaquemines's role in Louisiana's history has been seriously marginalized, in large part because the nature of the history sought is static and artifactual. Primary source documents—munitions lists, diaries, letters, and official eighteenth-century colonial correspondence—that illustrate the lived experiences of people in Plaquemines from colonization through the present day do not figure into the evaluation of Plaquemines's historical or cultural merit.

The report on the Fort Jackson vicinity, for example, offers a brief and thorough historical overview of the parish; it mentions prehistory, Native American influence, early European contact, military and strategic importance, the Civil War era, and a few details up to the present. The first paragraph concludes, "The area of Plaquemines Parish has for most of its history been a commercial and strategic appendage of New Orleans" (Goodman 2001: 25) and dismisses entirely the parish's role in creating contemporary Louisiana. But the parish has been and is much more important to the history of Louisiana than any mere "appendage" could possibly be, as is illustrated by the fact that Plaquemines was where La Salle claimed the Louisiana territory for France (7); that the presence of Native Americans (Manning 2005: 1) and one of America's oldest Croatian settlements (Ware 1996: 24) creates a unique cultural mix that tenuously survives to this day; that seventeenth-, eighteenth-, and early-nineteenth-century struggles between different colonial and military powers played out at the mouth of the Mississippi River seriously affected and often endangered the development of New Orleans; and that the presence of one of the largest sulfur mines in America brought Nazi U-boat incursion inland as far as Point à la Hache (Goodwin and Associates 1985: 174–75, 186–87).

Collapsing Plaquemines Parish history into a historical footnote to the rise of New Orleans is unfair and depletes rather than enriches the history the state of Louisiana seeks to recover. Given the view of history and culture that has governed the state's interest in the parish and the reliance on conventional archaeological methods and guidelines to assess that interest, it is not surprising that the Fort Jackson report eventually concluded that the investigation "produced no culturally significant material" (Hunter and Reeves 1990a: 38).[3] Because these reports marginalize Plaquemines's historical importance and have led to a perception that the parish lacks culturally significant material, state agencies have difficulty recognizing the scope of the parish's cultural policy needs.

The state Division of Historic Preservation, which regulates most cultural work in the parish, relies on archeology to evaluate the importance of the sites. If the archaeologists conducting this research cannot understand the significance of post–Civil War artifacts, they will not recommend that the Division of Historic Preservation further investigate and preserve these and similar sites. These sites cannot be reclaimed; rather, their role and place in the cultural landscape is reduced to a potential obstruction of land development projects. Such a view impoverishes the parish's cultural life, and the Louisiana Division of Historic Preservation needs to rethink its approach if state and federal agencies are to better assess the cultural work that needs to be done.

One instance of how the state's cultural policy activities in the parish could have been significantly affected by viewing sites in Plaquemines as cultural landscapes rather than simply as artifactual and historical resources can be seen in the 1985 evaluation of the Burrwood facility. Burrwood was constructed in 1908 along the Southwest Pass in the mouth of the Mississippi River as an Army Corps of Engineers refueling and maintenance station for the dredge boats that kept the pass clear for boats coming upriver. All of the buildings and residences on the site were built prior to 1920, and virtually all "may be considered site-adapt structures" (Goodwin and Associates 1985: 92), meaning that site was arranged in accordance with the features of the landscape and that buildings were added and rearranged as the facility's needs grew to include schools, shopping, and social clubs. The Burrwood economy was strong enough to supply seasonal work and trade opportunities for the hunters, fishermen, and trappers residing in the nearby village of Hollywood. During World War II, the facility served a dual purpose of maintaining the dredging of the Mississippi and of keeping watch on the river for German naval activity. From 1942 to 1943, German U-Boats patrolling the Gulf of Mexico sank fifty-six merchant ships and damaged fourteen others. Eight of these destroyed ships were taken in from the mouth of the Mississippi (Wiggins 1995: 3), and oral history reports made during the evaluation offer firsthand accounts of the rescue of survivors of some of these attacks (Goodwin and Associates 1985: 174–75, 186–87).

Following the war, the Burrwood facility declined in importance. Wartime advances to naval technology, such as improved fuel and faster and sturdier boats, made the Burrwood facility obsolete. The families left when the army decommissioned the site and turned the facility over to the weather bureau (Goodwin and Associates 1985: 120), leading to the demise of Hollywood, whose residents no longer had seasonal work and trade opportunities. The facility was closed in 1965, and the buildings were auctioned off as army surplus (122). At the time of the 1985 evaluation, only substructures, slabs, the disintegrating wharf, and a few stick-frame buildings remained standing.

The archaeological survey of the area was disappointing: "Subsidence, overbank flooding, spoil dump overburden and anthropomorphic adaptations to the site for utilitarian reasons have profoundly affected the archaeological context or integrity of the site" (Goodwin and Associates 1985: 151).

A quarter of the original site was lost to shoreline erosion, and only physical features taller than three feet were visible above the spoil fill dumped onto the site. The researchers were disappointed by the "paucity of artifactual remains" encountered during subsurface testing at the site (151). The wooden structures left by the hunter-trappers and the Burrwood families had undergone changes: "Recent 'repairs' to these structures, which served as shelter for cattles [sic], have made use of driftwood and scrap lumber"; the wharf remained in use; and one of the slabs was being used for storage (156).

The report acknowledges that Burrwood "is closely associated with two significant themes in the history of South Louisiana, . . . the commercial growth of the port of New Orleans and the development and evolution of navigation on the Mississippi River," but concludes that the "ongoing destructive process of erosion, subsidence, and filling" has "eliminated [the] archaeological context of the site" so that it no longer possesses "integrity of design, setting, materials, workmanship and feeling." Although Burrwood "clearly was associated with events that have made a contribution to the broad pattern of our history," the lack of integrity and research potential mean that it "cannot be considered eligible for nomination to or inclusion on the National Register of Historic Places" (Goodwin and Associates 1985: 160). For these reasons, further work on the site was not recommended because it "is not likely to yield archaeological information important in history" (160).

Burrwood's lack of artifacts should not exclude it from relevance to Plaquemines's cultural and historical life, however. Given the same evidence and applying the concept of the cultural landscape, researchers would have reached far different conclusions about the site that integrated previously undocumented aspects of Plaquemines culture into the investigation and validated the cultural and historical merit of Burrwood as a cultural landscape. Per the Comprehensive Statewide Historic Preservation Plan, sites associated with the growth of the port of New Orleans, the development of navigation on the river, and national military engagement are prioritized for state preservation—criteria Burrwood meets. The fact that it was closely related to the traditional occupations of trapping, hunting, and fishing adds another cultural and historical dimension of interest to the state. But the most interesting historical facet of all is the role that Burrwood played in monitoring the river during World War II. This is the only site in Louisiana and one of the few sites in the continental United States that was directly affected by German incursion, giving Burrwood historic significance for the entire nation, not only for the state of Louisiana. Most Americans have no idea how close the Axis powers got to the United States, nor do they realize the damage U-boat activity caused to trade through the port of New Orleans. Visitors to Burrwood can stand in a place that experienced German naval attack and thus realize that World War II was not fought entirely on foreign shores. The site's proximity to the National World War II Museum, ninety miles north in New Orleans, only foregrounds the fact that allowing Burrwood to further deteriorate works against the best interests of Plaquemines, Louisiana, and the United States.

The lens of cultural landscape also affords a more complex view of the contemporary relationship between the Burrwood site and the people living nearby who are reusing it. Burrwood has always been and remains a thriving vernacular landscape. The fact that the original structures on the site were constructed in response to geographical limitations and social necessities demonstrates how Burrwood itself was fashioned to fit the land rather than planned out beforehand and then imposed on it. These are the key characteristics of a vernacular landscape. In present day, those living nearby have likewise adapted their reuse of the site to the landscape features. The structures have been ingeniously reappropriated and repaired by use of vernacular materials, recontextualizing Burrwood as a site of continued economic and social significance as a cattle range. The parish is recognized as being primarily maritime. Pointing out the presence of cattle operations in Plaquemines demonstrates the economic and cultural diversity of this peninsula: cowboys exist alongside oyster farmers, shrimpers, fishermen, and oil field workers. The continued use of the wharf and the concrete slabs demonstrates that people in Plaquemines use the land in an economically and culturally significant way. While the site lacks archaeological integrity, it still clearly possesses "integrity of design, setting, materials, workmanship and feeling" as long as this sort of integrity is recognized as being dynamic and cultural rather than historical and artifactual in nature (Goodwin and Associates 1985: 160). Burrwood is not an archaeological footnote in the state's artifactual history but a vernacular landscape that demonstrates the continued cultural vitality of the site as well as the continued vitality of the people of Plaquemines.

The Burrwood report marks the first time the Division of Historic Preservation broached the topic of subsidence as a factor in the disintegration of cultural sites. Though the specter of subsidence was present in the fourteen other investigations, the connection between the two was never made. What seems invisible in Citrus Lands, Fort Jackson, and myriad other cultural resources investigation reports is for the first and only time stated outright in the Burrwood evaluation: subsidence attributed to coastal erosion and accelerated alluvial redistribution are major factors in the disintegration of these important sites. The reports consistently do not recommend further excavation, but at no point is the disintegration caused by erosion addressed as a problem in its own right. The sites have not simply been disturbed by human activities such as reappropriation and reuse and construction projects; they have been mortally compromised by landscape changes wrought by coastal erosion. Recommending against further work is concomitantly a recommendation against reclamation and environmental recovery of these sites. The thinking is circular: even though restoring the natural environment will halt the erosion of these sites, they should not be recovered because they have suffered too much damage as a consequence of environmental decay; because they are so decayed, they are not worth recovering since further decay of the sites caused by erosion is inevitable.

The Burrwood report demonstrates that state cultural policy in Plaquemines has endorsed a relationship between the natural landscape and culture that frames the landscape as a series of inevitably doomed sites to be investigated and evaluated according to their archaeological merit. When recognized and read as the cultural policy documents that they are, the investigations very clearly strip landscape away from lived culture, an undertaking that has had dire consequences for the parish's cultural landscape. In dismissing the merit of the cultural sites heretofore investigated, the state sidesteps and then separates cultural issues (represented in the form of Plaquemines's cultural landscape) from the natural landscape (represented by the subsidence and coastal erosion plaguing the parish). The processes of recovery and development of sites such as Burrwood rely on efforts to restore the coastal environment of Plaquemines. A quarter of Burrwood has disintegrated as a consequence of human and environmental factors, but three-quarters remains, and if the state undertook to restore the site as well as the natural environment containing it, this cultural landscape could also be reclaimed as a historic site. The painful irony is that of all the state and federal cultural policy agencies, the Division of Historic Preservation is in the best position to connect environmental degradation to cultural issues because these resources are located on and exist in relationship with the landscape. But doing so would require the division to adjust its methodology to account for a vital and dynamic cultural landscape.

ETHNOGRAPHY

As used here, *ethnography* is the observation and dialogic inquiry into and subsequent reportage of cultures being studied. An ethnographer is one who undertakes such work. The word *ethnographic* has a double meaning, describing both fieldwork and interpretation done by ethnographers and a landscape that is read, interpreted, and valued according to the point of view of the cultural groups living in relationship with it. Understanding the nuances of these terms is vital for better understanding the cultural issues at stake and the people charged with identifying and assessing those issues.

Ethnographic fieldwork in Plaquemines has been taken on largely by trained academic professionals in the fields of folklore, anthropology, sociology, and geography under the auspices of state agencies and universities as well as Jean Lafitte National Park. These ethnographic activities comprise the state's second major genre of cultural policy. Of the subjects studied in Plaquemines Parish, the thriving Croatian community, primarily concentrated in central Plaquemines, and the village of Grand Bayou, a small ethnic settlement located on the gulfside bayou west of the Mississippi near Port Sulphur, had been the primary subjects of ethnographic documentation, with the majority of study focusing on Grand Bayou. While ethnographic work was associated with the Burrwood evaluation project, the interviews were tangential to the major investigatory concerns and both too brief and too few in number to bear closer evaluation. The major issue raised by these interviews is that although all respondents mentioned the state's involvement in World War II, the Division of Historic Preservation did not follow up on that information. Even then, the passing ethnographic interest had come too late—many potential respondents died before the Burrwood evaluation. Ida Mae Scarabin, a former resident of Burrwood answering questions on the wartime recovery of German U-boat casualties, said, "You should have come about five or ten years ago. Because the people down here when all those bodies were brought up—they were here. But all those people are gone. . . . You see, we're the old people now!" (Goodwin and Associates 1985: 187). Indeed. Though Grand Bayou has a different cultural history and relationship to the land than does Burrwood, both sites are plagued by environmental degradation, and both sites have received insubstantial and narrowly focused attention from state agencies.

My involvement with Grand Bayou came in 2004, when I was a graduate student at UNO and working as an ad hoc intern for the Greater New Orleans office of the Louisiana Regional Folklife Program, hosted by the university. I undertook the documentation of Plaquemines's cultural landscape vis-à-vis environmental degradation problems because no ethnographic work had been applied specifically to Plaquemines as a cultural landscape. I received neither pay nor reimbursement for my efforts. Most of the other fieldworkers in Grand Bayou are professors at UNO and Louisiana State University, serving on a predominantly volunteer basis and receiving neither funding nor reimbursement from their home institutions. Most university-based researchers recognize that fieldwork is central to their work and that it offers significant rewards, particularly when it leads to publication. Nevertheless, the commitment to ethnographic work on the part of these researchers comes from their own initiative rather than any direct university-mandated interest in the parish. In the case of ethnographic inquiry directly related to folklore and folklife, the Louisiana Division of Folklife has made grants of up to five thousand dollars to researchers not affiliated with or working through the Regional Folklife Program, but such amounts can hardly sustain long-term, in-depth research. I was by no means the first ethnographer to visit Grand Bayou, and my fieldwork has a different focus than most fieldwork performed there, but I reached many of the same conclusions regarding the cultural landscape of Grand Bayou as previous researchers.

According to Plaquemines Parish historian Rod Lincoln, the ethnically and culturally unique community of Grand Bayou has existed more or less since the eighteenth century (2004).[4] French trappers, hunters, and fishermen were among the first European residents of the peninsula, and in several cases they married local Native Americans. Slavery later came to the parish, adding African Americans to the ethnic mix when escaped slaves from nearby Woodland Plantation came to live in the village. The Grand Bayou community primarily claims ancestry from the Atakapa-Ishak and Houma Native American tribes, adumbrated with French, Spanish, and in some cases African American ancestors. Before Katrina, Grand Bayou boasted between fifty-five and sixty-five residents, some of whom speak French and English, and the entire community is linked through extended family ties.

Grand Bayou is geographically unique. The homes, school, and church lie on the bayou's banks, meaning that residents use boats to get back and forth to link up to the highway. Driver Paul Sylve Jr. explained that the communal yellow school boat serves all village residents' public transit needs in addition to ferrying children to and from the bus stop on Highway 23. Those who do not own boats time their comings and goings to coincide with the school boat's schedule. Grand Bayou lacked modern utilities such as running water, plumbing, electricity, and telephone service until the 1990s. Village life was rustic and at times inconvenient, but residents had always adapted well to their environment. For example, Rachel Sylve remembered that "when they first got the phone, nobody knew what to do. It was like, 'What is that noise? Oh. It's the phone'" (2004). Before phones came, village residents had learned how to gauge wind, weather, and volume so that shouted greetings and requests to borrow household goods could be heard across the bayou. The need for this skill disappeared with the introduction of the telephone, but many of the villagers can still do it.

The village has always struggled to stay afloat financially and has always relied on its occupational folklife to survive. The folk traditions of fishing, hunting, and trapping have sustained the village through most of the past three hundred years. In the twentieth century, fishing lay at the core of life in Grand Bayou. Paul Sylve recalled, "Growing up, this was just a fishing village, and that was all we ever did." When Paul and his three brothers were old enough, their father took them out of school to go trawling and crabbing, a Grand Bayou family tradition for many generations. In the last few decades, illegal shrimping, cheap imports, and a glut of commercial fishermen in the parish have all contributed to low market prices. The parish's commercial fishing environment is highly competitive. Since the 1990s, big outfits from outside the village have increasingly frequented Grand Bayou's fishing grounds. Scores of sportfishing companies have taken over areas, including Grand Bayou, that were formerly controlled by small- and medium-scale commercial fishermen, creating enormous competition between sport and commercial fishermen and depleting the fish stock in those formerly rich areas. Land developers have shown an interest in purchasing the land from the villagers to turn Grand Bayou into a sportfishing resort, as has been done in Happy Jack, a small fishing community just to the south populated primarily by retirees and weekend sportfishermen. At present, about two dozen independent recreational fishermen have built camps in the village on sites where locals' homes once stood.

Even though the traditional profession of fishing has become decreasingly profitable for the small-scale and individual fishermen, it remains the mainstay of the village economy. Despite the growing difficulties of making a living, Rachel Sylve supports her husband, Scott, in his vocation as a fisherman: "Thing is, it's in him." They have agreed that he can keep fishing as long as he can make ends meet. Scott has created a market niche by catching minnows rather than shrimp or big, food-grade fish. He supplements the family income through fishing oysters, trapping alligators, and occasional shrimping, but his main income comes from catching the minnows and selling them to bait shops and to the sportfishermen who flock to Plaquemines. Scott is also working to acquire a captain's license that will enable him to augment his living by piloting sportfishermen down the bayou, using knowledge gleaned from his family to help locate good fishing spots. Many of Grand Bayou's fishermen have similarly diversified their occupations. To survive the bayou's tough economic conditions, the people of Grand Bayou are adapting traditional fishing skills to capitalize on the economic opportunities afforded by the tourist market.

Though Grand Bayou's economic conditions have always been tough, the biggest threat by far is the severe and relentless erosion and subsidence problem. Seasonal work inland, diversified fishing strategies, and a captain's license cannot mitigate this threat. The erosion of the coastline is rapidly eating away at the village as well. According to Kim Sylve, the village's residences had makeshift bulkheads built into the shoreline in front of their houses to slow erosion, though the backs of houses continued to dip into the mud (2004). But the rest of the bayou was still disintegrating out from under them because the village was surrounded by a network of ever-widening access canals cut into the bayous by oil companies. The locals first realized the extent of the erosion when Hurricanes Isidore and Lily hit in 2002. Most Grand Bayou residents had never experienced flooding in their homes, but these hurricanes brought almost a foot of water into all houses. A year later, Tropical Storm Bill needed less than thirty-five minutes to bring nearly four feet of mud and water into almost every home in the village. Though Grand Bayou was largely spared the havoc of 2004's Hurricane Ivan, the threat of the next big hurricane loomed. Katrina came the next summer and washed away almost all of the buildings and much of the land.

Prior to Katrina, attempts to gain state and federal intervention and restoration failed in part and succeeded in part. While state and federal environmental management support eluded the community, an increasing number of UNO and LSU researchers became involved in the village's struggle. Help from UNO came on three fronts. In 2003, UNO School of Business Management professor Sandy Hartman helped the village establish a 501(c)3 nonprofit organization, Grand Bayou Families United, to coordinate writing grants for economic development and environmental restoration (2004). Shirley Laska, a member of the UNO Sociology Department and head of the UNO-affiliated Center for Hazards Assessment Research and Technology, has conducted essential ethnographic fieldwork in Grand Bayou and is applying it toward the goal of "allowing the marginalized community to negotiate with FEMA and other government agencies in order to take responsibility for its response to Katrina. This participatory approach has been proven to build community resiliency" ("Laska" 2006). As director of the LSU Disaster Science Management program, former Department of Environmental Science professor and researcher John Pine oversaw ethnographic documentation that he has used to create a community-formulated strength and risk analysis to develop long-term sustainability and disaster mitigation practices (*Bayou Community's* 2008).

Despite the involvement of UNO and LSU professors and several church and nonprofits from outside of Louisiana, Grand Bayou has been unable to rally. The villagers are eligible for the assistance provided by the Road Home program, a joint state and federal program designed to compensate Louisiana homeowners affected by Hurricanes Katrina and Rita. The program will pay out up to $150,000 to enable owners to get back into their homes, but red tape has deterred Grand Bayou families from participating. The people of Grand Bayou are and always have been poor and thus cannot afford to clean up and rebuild without Road Home funding. As a result, the Grand Bayou families remain scattered throughout Louisiana and Texas. Associated Press correspondent Cain Burdeau reports that the nearly empty village has become particularly appetizing to land developers. Grand Bayou previously had fended off developers seeking to buy the land to build weekend fishing camps for sale at high prices to out-of-towners, but now "the uncomfortable circle of outsiders and development is drawing tighter" (2008). Precisely this process has taken place across the bayou in Happy Jack. If Grand Bayou does not begin to recover, developers will turn it into another resort. In Paul Sylve's words, "If they . . . leave Grand Bayou to die, it would be just like shutting off the Mississippi River." Grand Bayou Families United president Myrtle Phillips has concurred: "You can't separate us from the land, this is who we are, we know and love the land, the water, and the birds. To live anywhere else is to die. We have a vested stake in what happens here" (Pine and Phillips 2008). Dwight Reyes Sr. laments that trawling the bayou for shrimp at night "makes you sick. You don't see a light in none of the houses. You don't see nobody outside hollering at you, asking if you're doing any good" (quoted in Burdeau 2008).

The village's contemporary circumstances strongly indicate that Grand Bayou is an ethnographic landscape. The villagers, large-scale commercial fishermen, sportfishermen, and land developers value Grand Bayou in accord with their individual—and competing—goals, aims, and values, and these different views afford vastly different interpretations and meanings. The families that have lived there for three hundred years recognize Grand Bayou as the source of their way of life; they take their livelihoods and identities from this landscape. Land developers see the bayou as a lucrative investment, and visitors from outside respect the bayou's recreational activities and lifestyle. The federal government sees Grand Bayou as yet another collection of displaced individuals waiting for their Road Home disbursements. The highly vernacular character of this landscape—ramshackle wooden houses, jerry-rigged wharves, and scraped-together bulkheads to keep the bayou at bay—results entirely from its ethnographic nature.

Grand Bayou is an ethnographic and hence cultural landscape, so state and federal culture agencies have governance over it as such. The Division of Historic Preservation has inadequate and counterproductive criteria for judging these landscapes, which undervalues and jeopardizes rather than preserves and protects them. Yet the inadequacies in the case of ethnographic landscapes—in particular, Native American landscapes such as Grand Bayou—differ because they are rooted not only in inappropriate definitions of culture but also in a narrow and inadequate recognition of Native American tribes and the role that they have played and continue to play in Louisiana's history and culture.

The *Louisiana Comprehensive Statewide Historic Preservation Plan* stresses Native Americans' cultural and historical importance, stating that "Indian groups in Louisiana are experiencing a revival, with the result that they are finally taking their rightful place among the many diverse cultures which comprise our state's rich cultural heritage" (2001: 44). One facet of this revival is state recognition of the Houma tribe, one of the tribes from which people in Grand Bayou claim descent. Despite this revival, the comprehensive plan mandates that only "prehistoric" Native American cultural sites dating from before 1540 are eligible for historic preservation activities (61). The plan does not account for more recent uses, much less contemporary uses.

As per Louisiana state historic preservation policy, the historical importance of these sites is assessed through archaeological analysis, which leaves no room for the consideration of history and culture as dynamic, living processes. Despite the fact that Grand Bayou has been continuously inhabited by the same Native American group for about three hundred years, far more than the fifty-year minimum necessary for the Division of Historic Preservation to become involved, the site does not meet the standards for historic preservation activities because it is not solely prehistoric. History and culture are a living and dynamic process in Grand Bayou, making the site ineligible for state intervention. Given this view, it almost seems that Grand Bayou must become extinct before the state can justify a cultural resource investigation. This extinction is very close to happening. Moreover, even if Grand Bayou ceased to exist, the state could easily dismiss its importance as a cultural resource because the village seems too recent a site for investigation. Moreover, any archaeologically based investigation would likely dismiss its findings because erosion would destroy the site's integrity.

The opposite is true when the case of Grand Bayou is viewed from a federal level. The National Park Service (NPS) can identify, assess, and protect contemporary, vital, occupied ethnographic landscapes such as Grand

Bayou. The NPS, which oversees the National Register of Historic Places, has much clearer and more appropriate provisions for recognizing and preserving cultural landscapes. The NPS defines a cultural landscape as "a geographic area . . . associated with a historic event, activity, or person exhibiting other cultural or aesthetic values" ("Defining Landscape Terminology" 2008). The NPS defines ethnographic landscapes as those that "contain a variety of natural and cultural resources that associated people define as heritage resources." Vernacular landscapes "have evolved through use by the people whose activities or occupancy shaped that landscape" ("Defining Landscape Terminology" 2008).

Grand Bayou clearly meets the NPS standards but faces one enormous obstacle in becoming a national historic site. Sites must be nominated by the relevant state cultural and preservation agencies. Because Louisiana's Division of Historic Preservation has policy provisions that explicitly do not account for the historic and cultural significance of Grand Bayou as a cultural resources site, the village cannot be nominated to the National Register. For the village to qualify, the Division of Historic Preservation must change its provisions to include cultural significance, vernacular character, and ethnographic meaning as well as archaeological merit. Such a move would also eliminate the obstacles to proper evaluation of other sites identified by the division as cultural resources and perhaps could be used to justify a reinvestigation of sites such as Burrwood.

Grand Bayou serves as an excellent indicator of the necessary scope and endeavor of cultural policy in Plaquemines Parish, demonstrating a clear relationship between cultural policy and environmental policy. Qualifying for the aid of state and federal cultural agencies such as the Louisiana Division of Historic Preservation and the NPS would force both agencies to acknowledge the need to act against the environmental degradation that threatens cultural landscapes. If these problems were resolved, the people of Grand Bayou could turn to both state and federal agencies for help in preserving their home. Should the village become a national historic site, the state and federal historic preservation agencies would be forced to undertake restoration and preservation attempts to return Grand Bayou to a livable and stable landscape. The village cannot be restored without the aid of environmental agencies, and the environmental restoration projects undertaken by those agencies would by extension mitigate the landscape attrition of Fort Jackson, the Citrus Lands, and Burrwood, among other sites. Bridging the gap between environmental policy and cultural policy in Plaquemines Parish would ensure the protection of cultural sites and create another avenue for pursuing environmental restoration.

Grand Bayou is also an excellent indicator of the shortcomings of current state cultural policy in Plaquemines. The case for the preservation and restoration of the village can best be made through the Division of Historic Preservation. However, the village has yet to be evaluated through any cultural resources investigation. The problems in the village have been uncovered entirely through ethnographic fieldwork, all of which addresses the need to restore the environment of Grand Bayou to preserve this unique cultural landscape. Because ethnography deals with lived culture and experiences of a cultural group, the ethnographic activities have opened the door to an understanding of the cultural landscapes of Plaquemines Parish—in particular, Grand Bayou. As a result, the work being done has produced significant innovation in developing models for community involvement in the policies that affect landscapes in general and the cultural contexts in which they are located. Yet all of this fieldwork has received little funding from the state universities or from state agencies other than the Division of Folklife, which has defrayed only some of the costs.

The case of Burrwood raises similar issues. The cultural resources investigation to determine the eligibility of the site for inclusion on the National Register of Historic Places included only two ethnographic interviews, both of which confirmed the important role Plaquemines in general and Burrwood in particular played during World War II. This information is some of the most interesting, historically significant material any fieldworker could hope to find, yet it disappeared after the investigation. Though the Louisiana Folklife Program was not founded until 1999, the Division of Historic Preservation could have referred the matter to the Louisiana Folklife Commission, the state Endowment for the Humanities, the Louisiana State Museum, or the LSU anthropology, English, or history departments, any of which could have followed up on these interviews. But the Division of Historic Preservation saw no need to do so because of its reliance primarily on artifactually based notions that defined culture as history. Had the Division of Historic Preservation included consideration of cultural landscapes, the interviews would have had a greater impact on recognition of Burrwood's considerable cultural and historic meaning, and the findings would likely have been different. Instead, the interviews were relegated to an easily overlooked appendix. The state cannot rely on the diligence of a few dedicated and underfunded ethnographers to reveal major cultural policy gaps for Plaquemines Parish. Better funding and greater institutional support is necessary to sustain these efforts.

Overall, the case of Plaquemines Parish raises the salient question of how cultural priorities are being established after Katrina. The *Louisiana Rebirth* plan is based on the conviction that Louisiana's cultural economy will resuscitate the state: "In the wake of Hurricane Katrina, we must make our Cultural Economy the engine of Louisiana's economic and social rebirth" (2005: 10). This $202 million cultural economy is defined as "the people, enterprises, and communities that transform cultural skills, knowledge, and ideas into economically productive goods, services, and places" (9). The lieutenant governor's lofty goals of rebuilding Louisiana's economy by mobilizing and expanding the state's culture industries are admirable, but the emphasis on culture as economic engine leaves Plaquemines Parish at a loss for support to preserve its cultural landscape and thus its cultural heritage. The state has prioritized those aspects of Louisiana culture that can feed tourism or produce commodities for national and global distribution. There is no will to conserve the cultural landscape of Plaquemines Parish because its main cultural contribution to Louisiana is the fact that this unique landscape exists and supports the livelihood and living culture of the people residing there. Plaquemines's cultural landscape is important to Louisiana because it nurtures cultural groups that enrich the state's overall cultural milieu and play important non-tourism-related economic roles. Emphasizing culture as an economic engine should not mean obscuring the importance of the cultural landscape to the people who value it most highly: Louisianans themselves.

The only way Plaquemines fits into the current Louisiana cultural policy is that the parish supports a small but lucrative sportfishing and hunting industry. In October 2004, Lieutenant Governor Mitch Landrieu set forth his agenda for the Louisiana Department of Recreation, Culture, and Tourism. According to this *Roadmap for Change*, Louisiana's natural habitat and ecology are very much a part of this culture industry; the department thus presented an ambitious plan to increase tourism and spur economic development by investing in Louisiana's cultural infrastructure. According to the report, "Information about what Louisiana has to offer, such as the history, natural beauty and culture, has not been marketed to the rest of the country or world," and "linking culture to Louisiana's ecosystem is viewed as matching up well with emerging trends and could give Louisiana, because of a most unique eco-cultural blend, a leg up on the competition" (2004: 6). Plaquemines's biodiversity has made it a haven for sportfishing and hunting, but this industry is very much at odds with the interests of local communities such as Grand Bayou that wish to restore and preserve their cultural landscapes.

The final chapter of the 2005 Mt. Auburn Associates report, *Louisiana: Where Culture Means Business*, concerns historic preservation. In the report,

Louisiana arts and culture advocate Jeanne Nathan, who is not a member of Mt. Auburn Associates, addresses the repair and maintenance of Louisiana's architecture and built environment, asserting, "Conservation of the natural environment is also relevant, since it involves the use and management of natural resources including water, land, forests, swamps, marshes, wildlife, each an integral part of the historic environment of the state" (161). Nathan's concerns and suggestions apply directly to Plaquemines Parish and can easily be formulated to factor in the importance of cultural landscapes, which in turn would spur the Division of Historic Preservation to begin accounting for and preserving cultural landscapes. But this is the report's only chapter that endorses historic preservation as important to Louisiana's cultural well-being. Moreover, the report's discussion of the cultural resources in southeastern Louisiana omits any discussion of Plaquemines Parish, which was harder hit by Katrina than any other parish except Orleans. Landrieu's *Louisiana Rebirth* plan is based largely on the conclusions and recommendations made in the Mt. Auburn report (*Louisiana Rebirth* 2005: 10). The report's discussion of historic preservation focuses primarily on the built environment rather than the cultural landscape and thus does not address Plaquemines's cultural needs, which are literally not on the agenda.

Dismissing Plaquemines Parish and its cultural needs has allowed Landrieu and Mt. Auburn Associates to ignore the serious threat to New Orleans's physical and cultural well-being posed by environmental degradation and the subsequent destruction of cultural landscapes in Plaquemines. Save America's Wetlands, a nonprofit advocacy group working to bring attention to the coastal crisis, has gathered some sobering statistics: Louisiana loses an average of twenty-four miles of coastal land per year: a land area the size of a football field is submerged every thirty-eight minutes ("Louisiana Coastal Facts" 2008). Estimates show that every 2.7 miles of wetlands reduces hurricane storm surge by one foot; Louisiana has lost more than 1,900 miles of wetlands since the 1930s. Wetlands act as speed bumps for hurricanes crossing Louisiana, and the loss of coastal wetlands is one of the major reasons that the storm surge overwhelmed the New Orleans levee system during Katrina (Heath 2007: 4A). And the wetlands in Plaquemines Parish serve as the primary natural barrier between New Orleans and the Gulf of Mexico. The environmental restoration of Plaquemines is necessary to preserve not only the parish's way of life and cultural landscape but also those of New Orleans. As the major state cultural policy agency, the Louisiana Department of Culture, Recreation, and Tourism occupies a position to forge partnerships that can address these cultural policy issues.

One possibility for partnership could come in the form of coalition lobbying efforts to gain federal interest in and funding for environmental restoration. Plaquemines-based restoration projects to restore the coastline and divert sedimentation from the Lower Mississippi into Louisiana's bayous have been under way in recent years, but government management of the levee system has jeopardized these efforts. In April 2007, President George W. Bush approved the $2.2 billion necessary to repair if not upgrade the New Orleans levee system but denied the $1.6 billion needed to extend and upgrade the levee protection for the southern half of Plaquemines Parish. These proposed upgrades would include incorporating freshwater diversion and siphon projects that would revitalize the marshland (Konigsmark 2006). Citing a simple cost-benefit analysis, the administration found levee repair in New Orleans to be justified because 98 percent of the affected population lives there; according to this rationale, the 2 percent who inhabit Plaquemines Parish are not significant enough to merit repairing the levees there. But refusing to rebuild Plaquemines's levees endangers not only the lives and cultures that flourish there but also the parish's coastal restoration projects. In the end, failing to repair Plaquemines's levee system endangers the physical safety and cultural well-being of New Orleans, reducing the value of efforts to protect the city.

The greatest threat to both New Orleans and Plaquemines Parish is not misguided cultural policy initiatives but coastal erosion. In fact, such erosion poses the single biggest threat to the survival of Louisiana and all the cultures it contains. As the situation in Plaquemines demonstrates, landscapes are cultural resources and should have a direct bearing on Louisiana's cultural policy. It is difficult to see how the plans set forth by the Louisiana Department of Culture, Recreation, and Tourism could be adapted to integrate cultural policy and environmental policy. Perhaps the best answer is the one with which the department began: emphasizing the state's diverse array of ecocultural offerings. Information campaigns and grant opportunities to restore damaged cultural sites could easily be combined with these environmental restoration efforts. Reintegrating cultural landscapes and environmental concerns into the *Louisiana Rebirth* plan will not only allow Louisiana policymakers to forge partnerships to protect both but also enable them to give a voice to the cultural concerns of Plaquemines Parish.

Cultural Landscapes in Plaquemines Parish

NOTES

1. Ware has undertaken extensive fieldwork among the Croatian oyster fishermen in the parish with the intent of publishing a monograph of her fieldwork and conclusions.
2. Ethnography comprises the second genre of cultural work in Plaquemines. While the ethnographers charged with completing the work have dealt specifically with lived culture and cultural landscape, state support for and the output of these efforts is dwarfed by the cultural resources investigations administered in accordance with the Division of Historic Preservation.
3. While the archaeologically determined historical merit of Fort Jackson has been recognized by the site's inclusion on the National Register of Historic Places and its subsequent renovation in the 1960s, the site has not yet reopened following Hurricane Katrina.
4. The information in this section comes from the fieldwork I conducted in May 2004 with Plaquemines Parish historian Rod Lincoln and in June 2004 with four members of the Grand Bayou community: Rachel Sylve, Carmelita Sullivan, Kim Sylve, and Paul Sylve Jr. Follow-up interviews were not performed because the interviewees had relocated and could not be reached for further comment.

REFERENCES

Alanen, Arnold R., and Robert Z. Melnick. 2000. *Preserving Cultural Landscapes in America.* Baltimore: Johns Hopkins University Press.

A Bayou Community's Cultural and Physical Survival before and after Katrina. Center for Biosecurity. 2006. http://www.upmc-biosecurity.org/website/events/2006_disease-disaster-democ/speakers/peterson/transcript.html. Accessed 19 July 2008.

Bring New Orleans Back Commission. 2006. *Report of the Cultural Committee.* 10 January. http://www.aeaconsulting.com/site/bnob/BNOB%20EXECUTIVE%20SUMMARY%20 20060202.pdf. Accessed 3 March 2006.

Burdeau, Cain. 2008. "Katrina Aftermath Erodes Bayou Culture." *ABC News Online.* 16 March. http://abcnews.go.com/US/wireStory?id=4460559. Accessed 21 July 2008.

"Defining Landscape Terminology." 2008. *National Parks Service: Guidelines for the Treatment of Cultural Landscapes.* http://www.nps.gov/history/hps/hli/landscape_guidelines/terminology.htm. Accessed 20 July 2008.

Gilmore, Kathleen, comp. 1983. *Archeological Testing at Fort St. Leon (16PL35), Plaquemines Parish, Louisiana.* May.

Goodman, Joan Elizabeth. 2001. *Despite All Obstacles: La Salle and the Conquest of the Mississippi.* New York: Mikaya.

Goodwin, R. Christopher. 1991. *Cultural Resources Investigations for the Westbank Hurricane Protection Project, Plaquemines and Jefferson Parishes, Louisiana: Final Report.* September.

Goodwin, R. Christopher, and Associates. 1985. *Evaluation of the National Register Eligibility of Burrwood, Plaquemines Parish, Louisiana.* Springfield, Va.: National Technical Information Service, U.S. Department of Commerce.

———. 1989. *Cultural Resources Investigations of Three Borrow Areas, New Orleans to Venice Hurricane Protection Project, Plaquemines Parish, Louisiana: Final Report.* November.

———. 1990. *Cultural Resources Investigations of the Citrus Lands Area: New Orleans to Venice Hurricane Protection Project, Plaquemines Parish, Louisiana*. Springfield, Va.: National Technical Information Service, U.S. Department of Commerce.

Hartman, Sandra. 2004. Interview. 23 May.

Heath, Brad. 2007. "Levees Not Enough on Louisiana's Vanishing Coast; Plans Try to Halt Damage from Loss of Marshes, Isles." *USA Today*, 21 February, 4A.

Hinks, Stephen, comp. *Cultural Resources Survey of Grand Prairie Second Lift Levee Enlargement Borrow and Linwood Revetment, Mississippi River M-69.7 to 68.0-L*.

Hunter, Donald G., comp. 1992. *Archaeological Surveys and Evaluations of Four Construction Areas in the Vicinity of Fort Jackson, Plaquemines Parish, Louisiana*. April.

Hunter, Donald G., and Sally K. Reeves. 1990a. *Cultural Resources Investigations in the Vicinity of Fort Jackson, Plaquemines Parish, Louisiana: The Proposed Homeplace and Tropical Bend Borrow Areas, Final Report*. Springfield, Va.: National Technical Information Service, U.S. Dept. of Commerce.

———. 1990b. *A Research Design for Cultural Resources Investigations in the Vicinity of Fort Jackson, Plaquemines Parish, Louisiana*.

Inon, Jack B., comp. 1993. *Phase II Cultural Resource Investigation of Submerged Anomalies, Breton Sound Disposal Area, Plaquemines Parish, Louisiana: Final Report*. September.

Jones, Dennis, comp. 1989. *Cultural Resources Investigations in the Vicinity of Fort Jackson, Plaquemines Parish, Louisiana: The Proposed Solari Borrow Area: Final Report*. 1 August.

Konigsmark, Anne Rochelle. 2006. "Louisiana Parish Wonders What's Next." *USA Today Online*, 1 May. http://www.usatoday.com/news/nation/2006-04-30-plaquemines-parish_x .htm. Accessed 19 July 2008.

"Laska, Shirley, Ph.D." *Social Science Research Council, Katrina Research Hub*. http://katrinaresearchhub.ssrc.org/person.2006-06-27.232302- 4/person_view. Accessed 19 July 2008.

Lincoln, Rod. 2004. Interview. 15 May.

"Louisiana Coastal Facts." 2008. *America's Wetland Online*. 6 February. http://www .americaswetland.com/files/NewCoastalFacts.pdf. Accessed 19 July 2008.

Louisiana Comprehensive Statewide Historic Preservation Plan. 2001. Baton Rouge: Louisiana Department of Culture, Recreation, and Tourism, Division of Historic Preservation.

Louisiana Rebirth: Restoring the Soul of America. 2005. Baton Rouge: Louisiana Department of Culture, Recreation and Tourism. http://www.crt.state.la.us/LouisianaRebirth/Plan/LouisianaRebirthplan.pdf. Accessed 2 November 2009.

Manning, Susan Camille. 2005. "Riding out the Risks: An Ethnographic Study of Risk Perceptions in a South Louisiana Bayou Community." Master's thesis. Louisiana State University.

Mt. Auburn Associates. 2005. *Louisiana: Where Culture Means Business*. Baton Rouge: State of Louisiana, Office of the Lieutenant Governor, Department of Culture, Recreation and Tourism, Office of Cultural Development, Louisiana Division of the Arts, 31 July.

Pearson, Charles E., comp. 2001. *Remote Sensing Survey of the Mississippi River Gulf Outlet, Ocean Dredged Material Disposal Site, Plaquemines Parish, Louisiana*. May.

Pelletier, Jean B., comp. 2001. *Phase I Remote Sensing Marine Archeological Survey of the Proposed West Bay Diversion Anchorage Area, Plaquemines Parish, Louisiana*. April.

Pine, John, and Myrtle Phillips. 2008. "Building Green For Health, Preparedness, and Health." *Earth and Life Sciences at the National Academies*. http://dels.nas.edu/dr/docs/dr17/pine .pdf. Accessed 17 July 2008.

Poplin, Eric C., Carol J. Poplin, and Paul C. Armstrong, comps. *Cultural Resources Survey of the Caernarvon Diversion Site, Mississippi Delta Region, Louisiana.* 8 July.

Roadmap for Change. 2004. Baton Rouge: Louisiana Department of Culture, Recreation, and Tourism.

Sullivan, Carmelita. 2004. Interview. 24 June.

Sylve, Rachel, Paul Sylve Jr., and Kim Sylve. 2004. Interview. 24 June.

U.S. Army Corps of Engineers, New Orleans District, comp. 2000. *Phase I Marine Archeological Remote Sensing Survey of Segments along the Southwest Pass of the Mississippi River, Plaquemines Parish, Louisiana.* October.

Ware, Carolyn. 1996. "Croatians in Southeastern Louisiana: An Overview." *Louisiana Folklore Miscellany.* http://www.louisianafolklife.org/LT/Articles_Essays/main_misc_croatians_s_la.html. Accessed 2 November 2009.

Wiggins, Melanie. 1995. *Torpedoes in the Gulf: Galveston and the U-Boats: 1942–1943.* College Station: Texas A & M University Press.

HURRICANE RITA AND THE NEW NORMAL
Modified Communication and New Traditions in Calcasieu and Cameron Parishes

KEAGAN LEJEUNE

"How's your house?"

"Okay. Yours?" Days, weeks, months after Hurricane Rita, this dialogue remained a familiar conversation starter in the areas of southwest Louisiana hardest hit by the storm. As they waited in line at the post office, gas station, or grocery store or returned to work or school, Calcasieu and Cameron Parish residents often encountered old friends, neighbors, schoolmates, or co-workers they had not seen since Hurricane Rita made landfall in late September 2005. Stuck in long, boring lines, people struck up conversations. When they did, they began them with this standardized greeting, a simple question about the status of a person's family or property. Expressing concern, this opening into the conversation immediately established a relationship. The response that followed usually downplayed the damage: "Nothing much." "My fence, some shingles." "Well, we had a tree that came through the kitchen, but everyone's safe." Next, the other person would return the question—"And yours?" or "How did you do?" Even though the phrasing in certain parts of the exchange undoubtedly changed from one conversation to the next, the structure of the communication event remained the same. Understanding the potential for discomfort in answering these questions, residents employed phatic communication (the small talk people use to establish a mood of sociability) as a safe way to discuss painful experiences and a polite way to reach out to other human beings without seeming too intrusive. With this talk, people could be neighborly without being nosy; if appropriate, these stock exchanges could build to deeper discussions concerning community members' lives. These brief conversations about homes exemplify people's desire to deal with confusing emotional issues through familiar practices, such as a normal phatic conversation. As such, phatic conversation stands as a powerful cultural tool (Malinowski 1994). Insiders demonstrate cultural knowledge and communal concern as they exchange patterned responses that convey a meaning much deeper than a literal one; as a result, a handful of words can address a host of complex social and psychological issues.

To communicate communal concern and feelings of solidarity and togetherness, many residents embraced other patterns of behavior, or traditions, and modified them to make public announcements about the peculiarity of their shared hurricane experience and the local culture's ability to withstand the chaos Rita brought. People turned to the past for a few reasons. Predictable and tangible, traditions proved reliable in this time of flux; personal and adaptable, they also proved capable of commenting on the incongruity of the "new normal" created after Rita.[1] Second, residents had previously faced and overcome adversity. When people settled southwest Louisiana, they called home a landscape others considered uninhabitable, made delicacies out of food others considered inedible, and expertly managed situations others considered impossible. People did so by relying on cultural traits of ingenuity and perseverance—traits many consider hallmarks of the region's current population (Edwards, Kniffen, and Pitre 1991). Finally, residents believed that their way of life could be maintained if they used ingenuity and perseverance to remake the old to fit the new. By employing and adapting traditions, often for ironic or humorous effect, residents coped with the anxiety and tension Hurricane Rita caused and made a concrete statement about the culture's ability to weather the storm. This embrace of tradition manifested in four primary forms: (1) signage occurring around the storm, (2) modified holiday decorations, (3) an arts and crafts movement, and (4) adaptations of certain key cultural events. Drawing from conversations with community members, personal observations, and field notes concerning larger communicative events, this chapter analyzes how visual presentations of these modified traditions existed as powerful statements of community spirit aimed at both community members and visitors to the area.[2]

Even though research concerning larger concepts discussed in this chapter exists, substantial research on residents' particular modifications to traditions after Hurricane Rita does not. Scholarly work on tradition, a large concept central to this chapter, dominates folkloristics. Traditions exist as complex, established connections to the past or perceptional interpretations of connections to the past in the present. Repetitive and laden with symbols, traditional rites symbolize a group's continuity and purpose over time and space.

Scholars have also thoroughly discussed another broad concept underlying this chapter's discussions, humor, which can relieve anxiety and serve other societal functions during times of tragedy or social crisis (Freud 2002; Dundes 1987a, b; Oring 1984, 2003). Freud praises humor's ability to relieve people's mounting anxiety as they interact with the incongruous and stressful world, and contemporary folklorists argue that humor plays an essential role in enabling humanity to cope with tragedy and disaster. Particularly relevant here are Elliott Oring's (1987) examination of the use of the joke after the 1986 Challenger explosion, Larisa Fialkova's (2001) analysis of jokes after the Chernobyl disaster, and Giselinde Kuipers's (2005) consideration of the function of laughter after the 11 September attacks asserting that humor offers people control, albeit subconscious, over irregularities and flawed futures, problems occurring in a dehumanizing world. These authors detail how people confronted an absurd world caused by disaster or tragedy and sought to understand this absurdity. They released pent-up fear and anger and reasserted themselves in this world by making jokes. Using humor that drew on cultural forms and known patterns to belittle the most horrible facts, people in these case studies regained control and reconciled the terrible events with their worldview.

A few works have discussed the particular traditions modified during Rita, though none of these authors focuses on the residents of southwest Louisiana or examines the connections among the various modifications to traditions after a natural disaster or societal crisis. For example, very little work considers signage occurring around hurricanes, the first form of tradition residents embraced.[3] Derek Alderman and Heather Ward (2008) address the practice of what the authors term "hurricane graffiti," a traditional form of community visual presentation. Alderman and Ward argue that these messages offer an "under-analyzed yet potentially useful indicator of the range of psychological needs, social tensions, and environmental attitudes circulating within coastal communities" (2). Furthermore, Alderman and Ward assert that analysis of hurricane graffiti would aid coastal managers in assessing "not only the feelings and expressions of individuals but also the broader currents of environmental and social thought within communities" (3). Finally, the authors posit that hurricane graffiti as discourse can be classified into seven main themes: history, defiance, desperation, territoriality, humor, prayer, and political commentary (5). Alderman and Ward define and detail these categories by describing pertinent examples, calling for further consideration of how hurricane graffiti fits into larger cultural contexts.

A bit more research exists about the modifications of holiday decorations, but these works do not center on modifications arising after natural disasters or on how these modifications communicate cultural desires. The best-known folkloric study of the usefulness of holiday decorations is probably Jack Santino's work, which contends that holidays "provide us with a national language" that we sometimes use to "communicate with strangers" (1994: 34). Santino develops the term *folk assemblage* to refer to an outdoor decorative display involving disparate images and objects that act as statements to these strangers. Such displays include not only the typical holiday fare but also objects, icons, and symbols from other aspects of an individual's life. Including parts of everyday life in holiday decorations enables people to make complex statements about how personal desires fit in with universal concerns. Manipulated decorations, then, express not only the holiday's sentiment but also deep-seated emotions of hope, sadness, or fear, all of which Hurricane Rita aroused. Despite the lack of research on this topic, many scholars recognize the importance of these adaptations and their communicative ability. These adaptations, if considered separately, highlight critical issues residents faced after the storm. Considered as a group, these transformations of established traditions provide an indication of how residents planned to make cultural changes to adapt to the new, often tragic or chaotic environment Rita created.

Hurricane Rita brought many residents of southwest Louisiana a quite different, more stressful environment, and many experienced anxiety and depression as they feared permanent changes to their way of life. When Rita hit, many residents were dealing with the aftermath of Hurricane Katrina, which had made landfall only weeks earlier. CNN, local television, and the local newspaper informed the Lake Charles population of Katrina's devastation. Moreover, homes in Lake Charles filled with relatives and friends who had fled New Orleans and its surrounding communities. The Lake Charles Civic Center held evacuees, and Lake Charles's Burton Coliseum sheltered pets and livestock. Local schools harbored students who needed to continue their studies despite Katrina's damage. Officials and relief organizations strived to serve the new population, while locals who had previously resided in New Orleans looked on with sadness and nostalgia for the city they had known. As Hurricane Rita formed in the Gulf of Mexico and set its course for Lake Charles, anxiety rose as people confronted an unknowable future that all surmised would be bleak. As Rita drew closer, people faced the stress of evacuating. After the evacuations, residents nervously waited for days and even weeks until the area was safe enough to enter. Before knowing what sort of damage their property suffered, many people feared the worst; returning to the area gave them firsthand knowledge of the damage. Roofs caved in under uprooted water oaks. Wind twisted walls and turned homes on their foundations, and water washed away everything but the slabs. Mobile homes cracked in half. The storm stripped siding, shingles, and whole boards off houses. Residents also saw damage to their core social institutions and daily routines, including the closing of schools.

Since the storm displaced many people and postponed activities, individuals often felt alone—adrift without daily conversations with neighbors, without weekly football games or family dinners, without seasonal celebrations put on by their communities. To make matters worse, during recovery, people were forced to interact with outsiders and to navigate unfamiliar governmental agencies and bureaucratic systems. Phone companies struggled to restore service; some newspapers halted delivery to certain areas; and fewer people were around to spread vital bits of news. As a result, the new environment denied folks their ordinary means of gathering information, sharing ideas, and even solving problems. Local officials, who now answered to federal agencies, no longer held all the answers. Moreover, residents contended with an emotion that was a combination of pity and frustration as the national focus on southwest Louisiana seemed to pale in comparison to the attention given to Katrina's damage to southeast Louisiana. Locals dubbed this problem "Rita amnesia" and felt dejected as the state and nation seemed to forget the troubles Calcasieu and Cameron Parishes faced. Some residents felt guilt about the damage they escaped; some felt exhaustion as they rebuilt their lives; and all residents felt stress as they worked on "getting back to normal," a phrase repeated often after Rita's destruction (Barry 2006; "Cameron Parish" 2006).

The first example of residents coping with anxiety by employing and modifying traditions and then displaying these adaptations to the community occurred as residents throughout the area began to prepare for Rita's arrival. People started packing, gathering keepsakes and important records. They filled cars with gasoline, boarded windows, stocked up on supplies, and prepared themselves for the storm. A mass exodus swept through Cameron Parish as residents, remembering the narratives of 1957's Hurricane Audrey,, evacuated; Calcasieu Parish residents followed. Unsure and anxious about the future, people wanted to exert some control over the unknowable, so they boarded their windows and storefronts with signs that would communicate statements to the outside world and to other residents. These signs, often homemade, contained many characteristics of graffiti, since residents employed them to communicate individual concerns and cultural messages (Tanzer 1939; Lindsay 1960; Stocker et al. 1972; Stein 1989). People yearned to offer hope to their neighbors, add a little cheer and humor to all those stressed by the approaching storm, or simply let out a little frustration. As graffiti has been used in times of natural disaster (Hagen et al. 1999), the popular tradition of making signs offered just such communicative opportunities.

Some may not consider the use of signs, plywood or otherwise, to be traditional. However, the use of signs is not new to residents of Louisiana. Many residents saw similar signs during the media's coverage of other hurricanes. Some had seen signs calling Ivan "the Terrible" or Katrina "a bitch," and in 2002, Cameron residents erected signs reading, "No Lili" or "Lili Go Away." When Rita came, Calcasieu and Cameron residents again painted messages on the boards covering their homes. Even though many observers have noticed this widespread practice and some even understand its communicative potential, others still question its ability to transcend individualism and thus exist as a patterned form of communication that expresses the community's feelings. Louisiana residents were obviously concerned for their families' safety and for the survival of their houses or possessions, but intensifying community solidarity and reassuring everyone that this unique culture would continue manifested as an equally strong desire. These same desires fueled those making signs in Alderman and Ward's study, and post-Rita signs easily fit into Alderman and Ward's seven categories.[4] Finally, regardless of an individual sign's classification, the hurricane sign exists as a complex text. It presents individual and communal concerns. It offers not only a spontaneous reaction to a storm but also a reaction that undoubtedly builds on signs or phrases residents have previously seen or heard about. As a result, these signs become dynamic interpretations of tradition. Adding to their complexity, the signs reflect deep-seated anxieties and deliver artful executions of humor. They locate themselves around a specific place and time but resonate with universal concerns and communicate easily through media and technology.

For example, one of my brothers living in Baton Rouge, Louisiana, who sheltered friends from New Orleans during Hurricane Katrina, opened his house to me a few weeks later when Hurricane Rita hit. By sheltering two different families and hearing their stories, he knew the stress brought on by these hurricanes. A few weeks after Rita, he forwarded me an e-mail from the first family he sheltered. The subject line read, "Something you can relate to." The accompanying image showed a house and a yard full of debris in the background and an old white refrigerator centered in the foreground. The refrigerator, leaning slightly, had obviously suffered water damage and no doubt had stood for days on end with its insides stuffed with spoiled and rancid food. The owner, like many others, brought the machine to the roadside for pickup. However, the owner had painted on the side of the fridge, "Do Not Open! Insurance Adjuster INSIDE."

My brother's message brought a smile to my face, changed my mood that day, and helped me remember that other people faced the same issues I did. People wanted to make a life again, and sharing experiences sometimes helped. The terse messages community members created on these signs reflect this phenomenon.

Acting in a way as spokespeople for the community and exemplifying the tenacity of the culture, some signs taunted, criticized, boasted, and argued with Hurricane Rita. One sign in bright red spray paint and propped in a well-manicured garden told Rita exactly where the community stood: "We're Ready Rita!!"[5] Many signs simply urged Rita to leave. Placing each word on a separate line and indenting each line a bit more than the one above it, one plywood sign said "Get LOST RITA"; another barked, "STAY AWAY." One person even painted "GO AWAY RITA" on the glass of a trailer's front screen door. Other signs communicated with even more personality. Before evacuating, the members of Theta Chi fraternity at McNeese State University sent a message on the boards covering the fraternity house's windows: "Bring It On RITA." After the storm, the fallen trees in the yard proved Rita's strength as the trunk of a toppled oak blocked most of the sign from view. Other signs called Rita a bitch, personifying the storm. Others turned from masculine bravado to humor to make a point, relying on familiar patterns and word association for their humorous effect. The plywood on bars made light of the storm by playing with the popular nickname of the margarita cocktail. A typical bar front, yellow siding covering one side and alcohol advertisements the other, stood as a rather wry community remark as its joke unfolded in spray paint on the plywood covering the front doors. "HEY BARTENDER," in green and placed on the top line, seemed tiny compared to the black second and third lines, "1 Rita" and "ON THE ROCKS," that dominated the middle of the sign. Smaller than the others, painted in black, and underlined in green, the final line added the punch line: "to go!" Other bars asked for the drink in the same fashion, and one bar displayed a sign saying, "NO Ritas Here." Early on, residents relied on humorous hurricane signage to diminish the taxing effects of the storm and lighten the tense situation.

The popularity of this hurricane signage or graffiti undoubtedly results in part from businesses that rely on the medium to communicate with customers. Marquees with simple messages such as "No Gas" or "We Have Generators" reflected people's pressing concerns, but some businesses added more to their signs. Experiencing the same feelings as residents, most

Modified Communication and New Traditions

Fig. 6.1. An example of a sign issuing warnings. Photo by author.

business proprietors opted for something beyond straightforward messages to perform multiple tasks simultaneously, to communicate the particulars of the business, and to make larger statements to the community. Lake Charles's Black Tie Cleaners simply printed out a message on computer paper, "CLOSED TILL RITA LEAVES," that effectively captured the community's anxious anticipation as the business owners, like other residents, put their lives on hold. Some businesses employed humor as well. The plastic letters on one marquee read "CLOSED TILL" on the first line and "MONDAY" on the second; the third line was blank, while the bottom line said, "RUNNING SCARED."

Even when employing humor, most of these signs attempted to exert some control over the situation. Feeling helpless, often without a voice, people saw these signs as opportunities to make themselves known or even to fight against the encroaching storm, impending and irrational. Especially after leaving their homes, residents used signs to protect themselves and their property.

Inundated with swirling, often exaggerated, reports of looting in New Orleans and with unfounded rumors about crime, many residents feared rampant looting after people evacuated. Even before Rita arrived, signs alerted passers-by: "WE KILL LOOTERS NO WARNING" in patchy maroon on plywood propped against a truck became a popular image during the time. Rikenjaks Brewing, located in a historic brick building in downtown Lake Charles, boarded up its large glass storefront windows: the plywood over the large windows west of the door announced, "ARMED & DRUNK!"⁶ The plywood over the doorway read "RIKENJAKS@BellSouth.Net."

As Hurricane Rita churned in the gulf, official agencies issued a mandatory evacuation. People holding close ties to the land were urged to leave it. At the same time, the environment shifted. Neighborhoods emptied, and many municipal operations ceased. In an atypical environment bereft of the normal means of communicating and maintaining property and rights, people did what they knew other hurricane evacuees had done and employed the tools of communication at their disposal. They made signs, which in some small way reduced people's anxiety. With little chuckles or half-grins, residents eased fears and nervousness as they posted these signs or saw posted signs in their neighborhoods or read them in newspapers or e-mails. These signs became emblems of the control residents could exert in this perplexing and chaotic time. With these signs, albeit sometimes vicariously, residents could stand against their fears, relieve their anxieties, and settle their nerves. Even if most people were not around, some people would stay to protect property. The looters had been warned. Residents could take care of themselves, and ordinary people, even facing something as disastrous as a hurricane, could manage with the limited resources available, especially if they were utilized ingeniously.

After the storm hit, some signs remained until the owners removed them, some lay in pieces, and some changed to adapt to the new situation. Ranging from simple announcements to more elaborate expressions of fear, anger, loss, hope, and togetherness, the signs became important communal messages in a time of distress. Since Rita destroyed the formal signs displayed by many businesses, these establishments again turned to handmade signs. With its large sign destroyed, Hong Kong Chinese Restaurant erected a small sign reassuring residents, "YES WE ARE OPEN." Some businesses, like Community Coffee, which displayed the message "Free Coffee," put up signs offering a little aid during a time when electricity, gas, and food were scarce. Businesses again turned to humor. The sign for Casa Olé, a Mexican restaurant on Ryan Street in Lake Charles, has a large brick ground piece with a lighted sign on its top and a marquee beneath it: the restaurant used its intact marquee to invite residents to "COME IN FOR A REAL RITA."

The use of humor in these signs extended beyond businesses. McNeese State University also suffered significant damage. Officials closed many buildings because of water and mold and postponed the start of the semester by more than a month. With the football field and field house flooded, the football team faced canceling its season. Debris covered the baseball field, and the dugouts had lost their walls and roofs. One dugout's damage was clearly visible to people driving by. Its roof, in crumbled sheets of metal, rested beside it. On its brick wall, painted a bright McNeese blue, someone used white paint to spray a message appropriate to a baseball dugout: "RITA-1 MSU-Coming Back Swinging." These sorts of signs rallied the community and inspired residents to persevere. One family whose house was completely destroyed put up a sign offering a clear message to other community members. The long banner on top read, "WE STILL HAVE GOD"; the one below proclaimed, "THATS MORE THAN ENOUGH." Faced with damage and despair, people made an effort to state their determination and belief, and these visual presentations became the community's sounding board.

While some signs sent messages of solidarity and community strength, other signs commented on the influx of outsiders. Some signs thanked these newcomers, while other messages expressed frustrations and criticism of external agencies. Settling a frontier, ancestors of Calcasieu and Cameron Parish residents practiced real self-reliance and employed a system of folk justice and governance. Community members, not a bureaucratic agency, established and enforced laws. Through this approach to survival, small pockets of closely knit groups persevered in a harsh, unforgiving landscape. When outsiders interacted with the local population, as during the timber boom of the 1900s or oil boom of the 1920s, locals often felt belittled, ignored, and even swindled. As a result, a degree of uneasiness about outside agencies still exists, and many residents consequently felt uneasy about outsiders' involvement after Hurricane Rita. In addition, many residents were unaccustomed to receiving aid from strangers, a new necessity that made the hurricane experience further disconcerting. Furthermore, local officials and news agencies warned of deceitful contractors flocking to the area to con residents, and residents told tales of insurance adjusters lowballing estimates and of federal officials shifting blame. Jokes circulated about the government's ineffectualness, and uneasiness spread about officials' apparent lack of concern. One sign prominently displayed on a busy highway running through a town a little north of Lake Charles conveyed a simple but forceful message: "FEMA SUCKS" in bold black letters on a white background. Other signs complained of the bureaucratic intrusion in residents' lives. During the last week of February, five months after the storm, a small sign was nailed onto an uprooted tree stump resting in a massive pile of debris: "TOO MANY LAWS" offered a succinct protest against governmental bodies preventing or delaying cleanup and construction as these offices ironed out details and finalized codes and budgets.

Still, the tradition of these signs is not limited to offering messages of exasperation about outside intrusion. Several residents used this traditional method of communicating during a storm to express gratitude to ordinary people volunteering and working to restore the community. Police officers, workers for electric companies, members of church organizations, and others traveled incredible distances to help the area recover. A store in DeRidder, Louisiana, put up two plywood signs to express gratitude: "Relief teams from all over the U.S.A.! Thank you for being here God Bless." The message was posted in the store's windows facing both the front street and the side street, indicating the owner's desire to reach the broadest possible audience and his reliance on the one available source of widespread communication. Churches put up signs of hope and faith in a divine plan, and schools displayed messages of community. The Cameron Parish Courthouse, one of the only buildings standing in the city of Cameron after the storm, draped a banner reading "CAMERON WILL RISE AGAIN" across its facade. These statements demonstrated residents' awareness of and desire to communicate with other struggling locals. Like the short and simple "How's your house?" these signs reached out to community members and connected residents. Since similar signs worked effectively during other storms in other locations, residents recognized these means as appropriate, useful tools of communication. They knew these signs, often employing satire or wit, as complex message boards easily adaptable to the current situation. Brief yet powerful, the signs communicated to insiders and outsiders and helped many residents confront rapid changes. As a means of communication, the signs facilitated residents' quest to add their voices to the narrative of the community's shared experience.[7]

People returned to their homes and began to modify other traditions. Perhaps even more obvious than the use of hurricane graffiti was the adaptation of holiday decorations to display the continuation of the prehurricane way of life and the new normal. Many people gauged the return of "normal" life by the degree to which they or the community upheld holiday traditions. This progress restored a sense of connection to the past and thus effectively communicated the culture's perseverance. Often seasonal and religious, holidays communicate a predictable yearly cycle and a supreme being's divine plan. Celebrating God and family, holidays provide an emotional center for participants as families meet, eat together, and exchange gifts. Holidays thus strengthen familial bonds, sometimes even those connecting living and deceased members. Passed down from one generation to the next, holiday decorations may seem trivial but become tangible reminders of those who have come before and stand as one example of a holiday's ability to provide emotional stability and feelings of connectedness.

Modified Communication and New Traditions

Many people who saw their roofs destroyed by Rita and lost their homes because of damage also said good-bye to their Halloween, Thanksgiving, Christmas, and Easter decorations. However, even without their standard decorations or their typical means of displaying them, residents still wanted to mark the progress of the year and of their lives by decorating for the season. Thus, residents combined their remaining holiday decorations with plywood signs, debris, and other items from the hurricane experience to make appropriate statements about their new lives. They improvised and modified decorations to reflect their life changes. Building on recognizable holiday decorations or customary yearly events, residents incorporated feelings about the hurricane and reconciled issues with which they continued to struggle. Readily accessible and immediate, connected to the past but adaptable to present needs, holiday decorations offered residents a broad, complex canvas. Objects could be arranged to convey intense emotions, and modified holiday decorations could communicate sophisticated messages, such as humorous or satiric expressions.

Examples of modified traditions occurred as early as Halloween, the first major holiday the community experienced after the hurricane. Since great amounts of debris (some of it quite dangerous) lined city streets and filled yards and since some residences remained vacant, officials in Lake Charles as well as surrounding towns decided to ban citywide trick-or-treating. Refusing to do without Halloween, residents looked for alternatives and began modifying their trick-or-treat rituals. Some organizations, like those sponsoring harvest festivals, had previously developed such alternatives, but October 2005 saw the creation of additional alternative Halloween celebrations. Many schools held Halloween carnivals that year. Immaculate Conception Catholic School organized its first Halloween carnival, which has subsequently become an annual event. Lake Charles's huge Trinity Baptist Church held a "trunk-or-treat" event. The church filled its parking lot with decorated cars, trucks, and even trailers that acted as "houses" from which owners distributed candy to children who moved from one vehicle to another. Trunk-or-treat events occur in other parts of the country, but the 2005 Lake Charles Trinity Baptist trunk-or-treat had at least two trucks decorated with the hurricane in mind. One owner lined the truck bed with blue tarps, draped the sides of the truck with blue paper, attached poster board with "FEMA" written on it, and even edged the trunk with FEMA streamers. Those distributing candy wore makeshift FEMA shirts. As one might expect, these displays evoked humor from parents escorting children; more important, however, these displays made a complex statement about the communal sharing that is symbolically communicated during Halloween and about the hurricane-related process of receiving aid, which many southwest Louisianans found uncomfortable. By adopting the persona of FEMA, the owners of these trucks lessened the anxiety residents felt about accepting aid, and by modifying this holiday tradition, they subconsciously—or maybe not so subconsciously—used Halloween to confront some of the community's uncomfortable feelings.

Many residents of Cameron Parish lamented the loss of trick- or-treating. One former resident of Grand Lake, Louisiana, who now lives in a Lake Charles apartment complex, remembered that her sons had roamed their old neighborhood, visiting friends and family, but "all that's gone now." She continued, "For birthdays, I would just let them out in the backyard at dark and all the kids would run around. I can't do that anymore" (Badeaux 2008). Adaptations of old traditions thus fail to replace residents' long-standing practices. Even though these modifications fit the moment, most people yearn to reconstruct their lives so that they can practice their familiar pre-Rita traditions.

As they did for Halloween, people altered their Thanksgiving and Christmas celebrations to account for new challenges. Thanksgiving 2005 found many families taxed by the burdens of being displaced or by having portions of their homes unusable, a state of affairs that in some cases continues, much to residents' displeasure. Area residents nevertheless wanted to celebrate the holidays and mark the progression of the year. News programs, local papers, and various experts counseled residents to take a low-key approach to the holidays. For Thanksgiving, many residents took this advice. People filled the few open restaurants and altered their typical travel plans. With many large family homes destroyed or with families separated, some people stayed home and had small family gatherings with simplified meals. Some even used the time off to help others in the area, and high school and college students often speak of a new appreciation of thankfulness as a consequence of their volunteer efforts in the wake of Hurricanes Rita and Katrina.

By Christmas, however, people were more reluctant to forgo all of their traditions, and residents sought to uphold even drastically modified versions of holiday traditions. Calcasieu and Cameron residents were not alone in such desires. The unique bonfires on the Mississippi River levee exist as perhaps the most popular examples of individuals altering holiday traditions to reflect Hurricane Katrina. People living along the Mississippi levee have traditionally built large wooden structures for Christmas Eve bonfires; in 2005, residents constructed a helicopter, seemingly a comment on the

Modified Communication and New Traditions

Fig. 6.2. Improvised holiday display in Lake Charles. Courtesy the *Lake Charles American Press*. Photo by Jamie Gates.

countless rescues during Katrina's flooding. In Lake Charles, many public statements were less obvious or well publicized. One jeweler advertised a rather large rectangular blue diamond, the "blue roof diamond," to mark the end of an unusual year and celebrate love that had endured this difficult time. Another idea present during the Christmas season involved using FEMA-issued Meals, Ready-to-Eat, Red Cross snack packs, or other small hurricane-related products as stocking stuffers, a humorous gift idea meant to alleviate some of the tension arising from a potentially stressful Christmas. One family sent Christmas cards featuring a local version of *American Gothic*: a man holding the iconic pitchfork stood with a woman, both wearing somber clothes and dark sunglasses, in front of their house and barn, which were covered in blue tarps. The blue tarp became the most powerful symbol for locals, the ubiquitous sign of damage, of outside aid and governmental and bureaucratic intrusion, and of the lingering effects of the storm. Recipients of this card received a joke, a nice bit of cheer during an odd holiday season. Such emotions helped to deflate the anxiety of trying to celebrate Christmas under these strained conditions.

Though presents and cards may offer commentary on the community's hurricane experience at the individual level, other visual presentations made broader, more overt statements about the community's desire to use modified traditions to get back to normal. Even though some homes and businesses could not decorate, others made extra efforts, and several residents

Fig. 6.3. Hurricane-themed gingerbread display. Courtesy of the *Lake Charles American Press*. Photo by Brad Puckett.

cleverly incorporated Rita into their Christmas decorations. One family placed its remaining decorations in the yard: an inflatable Coke polar bear, a penguin, and Tigger as a snowman and a Winnie the Pooh with a pot of "Hunny" flanked a towering inflated drumming nutcracker who held a small white sign reading, "I survived Hurricane Rita." Another person altered an inflatable version of Snoopy's doghouse so that it had a blue tarp on its roof.

Taking a step beyond altering purchased decorations, many residents used Christmas lights and tinsel to decorate debris, such as tree stumps and piles of trash. In one yard from which most debris had been removed, homeowners decorated the trunk of a fallen tree, draping the roots, now stuck up in the air, with green garland and hanging emerald, ruby, silver, sapphire, and gold Christmas ornament balls. A purchased sign spelled out "Happy Holidays" in elegant cursive.

Another holiday display seemed to make a more radical statement of participation in the Christmas season despite the damage caused by the hurricane. Because Rita forced many people to live in trailers adjacent to their homes or rendered some rooms uninhabitable, many people could not put up their Christmas trees in their usual locations. Some residents instead moved their trees to their front lawns or decorated shrubbery in the manner of a Christmas tree. One resident strung silver streamers on an oak stump and topped it with a star. Residents of another home spray-painted a smaller tree trunk silver and placed a small silver Christmas tree on top of it. Though the silver tree had no leaves, it had a string of lights ascending a wire cone frame and a large silver star at the top. Like regular Christmas trees, the new decorations infused the wintry world with color and light; unlike typical trees, these decorations altered a world of potential despair and tragedy into one of hope and comfort. Residents eventually came to see these decorations as statements of cultural pride, proof of an indomitable spirit and cultural ingenuity.

Another incorporation of the hurricane experience into the Christmas holiday involved altering not decorations but one of the season's community traditions. During a popular gingerbread house contest sponsored by the Southwest Louisiana Convention and Visitors Bureau, several entries featured gingerbread houses with blue-tarp roofs. One leaning house also had a blue roof; another entry had a roof covered mostly with white icing with a small patch of blue icing in one corner and pretzel sticks representing the boards used to secure the tarps. One entry had Santa's train on one side and a house with a fence on the other. The house's roof was covered with thick blue icing with "FEMA" stamped in black letters in a few places; around the house stood a few pretzel sticks, with others strewn on the ground, producing a perfect likeness of a blown-down fence, a bit of damage nearly everyone experienced. The cake decorator also bent the two trees in the yard. A sign between the train and the house had the words "Merry Christmas Anyway!" outlined in gumdrops.

Such alterations to Christmas displays and traditions enabled people to exert some control over the situation. "I remember seeing all the crates of decorations turned over and broken," a student from Hackberry said. "My mom bought a new tree from Lowe's and new decorations, but it was never the same" (Reed 2009). More significant than the loss of possessions and holiday decorations was the loss of family members—in particular, the elderly, who served as the center for many traditions. One student explained, "We used to gather at my grandfather's house, but he died in a hospital in Arkansas during the storm. He would decorate the whole house. We don't do that anymore" (S. Brown 2005).

By the time the Mardi Gras season arrived, displays involving aspects of the hurricane experience were well established. Since Louisiana's cultural tradition has often used Mardi Gras for social commentary, these events offered many residents a traditional and a very natural means of expressing ideas concerning the hurricane. In the Lake Charles area, changes affected two preexisting forms. First, residents altered existing Mardi Gras krewes and balls, establishing the "Krewe of DEBRIS," an appropriately French-sounding name that fits well with names of other Lake Charles krewes. Members of established krewes also scaled back typical celebrations or helped other krewe members who had suffered more extensive damage. Finally, participants modified their typical Mardi Gras practices. A few local balls involve costumed participants who organize into groups smaller than the entire krewe, adopt a certain theme, and dress accordingly. At one point in the evening, the costumed group then parades in front of the entire krewe. These themes often connect to popular culture or significant contemporary social events. For example, in 2004, many groups decided to celebrate Louisiana State University's football national championship by dressing in jerseys, cheerleading outfits, and general university merchandise. During Mardi Gras 2006, many of these small groups reflected the hurricane experience. For example, one group dressed as the New Orleans Saints, the National Football League franchise left homeless by Hurricane Katrina. Another group, led by the owner of a local contracting business, dressed as repairmen.

Second, displays on Mardi Gras parade floats and by parade-goers connected to the hurricane experience. Though Lake Charles's major parades lack the level of social commentary traditionally present in the Spanish Town Mardi Gras parade in Baton Rouge or various other Louisiana parades, a few striking visual presentations occurred during the 2006 parades. In the Lake Charles Merchants' Parade, which traditionally has the most social commentary, one truck was decorated in Mardi Gras colors with a sign in blue letters on its front grille: "WE SURVIVED RITA FEMA WAS WORSE." Finally, several new businesses, many of which were fencing or roofing companies, had moved into formerly vacant buildings along the parade route, and these new establishments made a concerted effort to create advertising displays that employed Mardi Gras decorations. As with the other holidays, these spectacles aligned traditional elements of Mardi Gras with specific aspects of the hurricane experience. While Christmas decorations infused beauty into yards full of debris, Mardi Gras poked fun at problems and appropriately made light of the worst of the situation. Throughout the holidays, these new traditions or alterations to standing traditions mocked FEMA, shrugged off damage, and lightheartedly accepted the inevitability of the long road to ridding housetops of blue tarps. In addition, even though individuals drove the adaptations of existing traditions and the formation of new traditions, these modified traditions, especially as they connected and built on each other, functioned at a level far beyond the individual. Any trunk-or-treater, any family member out to see Christmas lights, or any parade-goer witnessing these adaptations experienced a release of anxiety and gained a sense of pleasure or comfort from that release.

Residents also incorporated the hurricane experience into traditional activities through an arts and crafts movement. People created works of art and various other products in response to Rita. For example, as a method of expressing the hurricane experience and avoiding more waste, two residents began to use discarded blue tarps to make purses, some of which displayed the white FEMA letters imprinted on the tarp. Other residents made or bought birdhouses with blue roofs and hung them in trees left standing after the storm. The blue tarp soon became a potent symbol of the community's shared experience. During McNeese State University's 2005 football season and spring 2006 baseball season, the blue tarp became a rallying symbol, a sign of what the team and fans had experienced and conquered to play. Fans wrapped themselves in blue tarp sashes and attended games. They converted tarps into stadium signs: "COWBOYS BLUE TARP TOUR!" spread on the fences and bleachers spoke of the unusual season and the teams' perseverance. Several advertisements also adopted hurricane imagery, especially the blue tarp. Organizers of the university's Banners Series, a cultural series that marks the spring as powerfully as Easter does, designed their annual advertising poster with an image of a blue rectangular road sign reading "Cultural Evacuation Route" in front of a grainy beige backdrop that resembled a haggard environment. The blue color offered a message of connectedness that resonated with the entire community.

That people would reconnect to traditions while recovering from natural disasters, catastrophes, and other events inspiring confusion and despair does not come as a surprise. Equally unsurprising, news reports often cited the use of traditions as proof of progress or noted residents' habit of tapping into cultural identity as an important part of recovery. Six months after the storm, the *Lake Charles American Press*, the city's daily newspaper, included many signs residents made as evidence of the community's feelings about the storm. Six months later, officials again turned to a traditional practice to mark the one-year anniversary of the "Cameron Comeback."[8] Cameron Parish held a traditional trail ride with residents, local officials, state officials, and Lieutenant General Russel L. Honoré. A Louisiana native who took over command of the military's recovery force immediately before Hurricane Rita hit, Honoré became a sort of folk hero for his decisiveness during recovery efforts and his chastising of the media for being "stuck on stupid" as they were slow to recognize the damage caused by Rita.[9]

In 2008, the *American Press* again focused on an important part of Cameron's cultural landscape, the beach camp. Small camps formerly lined

Fig. 6.4. Humorous message on plywood covering windows. Photo by author.

Cameron Parish's beaches. Those small homes are now gone, and many people complain about the financial difficulty of rebuilding structures up to code. People who can afford to do so have rebuilt, but this progress has come with a price. "Everybody's new here," one resident of Cameron Parish said. "That's not how it used to be. I go to the store, and I barely see anyone I know." To make matters worse, September 2008's Hurricane Ike flooded all the homes in southern Cameron Parish, but some homes built after Rita remained standing, though mobile homes and temporary buildings did not. Talk of banning mobile homes in lower Cameron Parish has resurfaced. The changes to this traditional aspect of life in the small communities on the gulf prove difficult to measure. Cameron Parish held ninety-five hundred people before Rita, about seventy-seven hundred in 2006, and seventy-four hundred in 2007. The size of the future population remains in question, as does which cultural traditions this new population will embrace.

Prior to Hurricane Ike, Lake Charles and Cameron residents no longer needed "NEED POWER" or "Welcome Home" signs, and the blue tarps had for the most part disappeared. However, other signs have replaced them. Hurricane Rita now stands as a reference point in many people's minds. When Ike was bearing down on the area, people planned with Hurricane Rita in mind and compared the damage wrought by the two hurricanes. Rita thus replaced Hurricane Audrey as a benchmark. Signs posted during Ike mentioned Rita in them: one listed various storms that had hit the area, with all the names crossed out except Ike, the last on the list. One plywood sign for Hurricane Gustav, which hit Louisiana approximately one week before Ike, said, "RITA CHEATED ON GUSTAV NOW GUSTAV IS PISSED OFF," while the window on the other side of the porch read, "HAPPEY LABER DAY."

The people who have returned to Cameron Parish carry the memory of Rita with them. Owners named one newly built establishment the Hurricane Café. Other residents have constructed homes, continued their traditions, and rebuilt their lives. The sign on one large yellow home in Holly Beach tells the story of residents remaking a place their families have long called home: "'Le Phare' The Lighthouse 'La Lumière Après L'Orage' The Light after the Storm."

NOTES

1. When McNeese students, staff, and faculty returned to work after Rita, many wondered how people might adapt. In one conversation, an individual talked about the importance of getting back to normal. Martha Hoskins, a professor in the Department of History, astutely pointed out that we would not be able to get back to normal but that we could return to "our new normal." At the core of folkloristics, the concept of tradition has been examined thoroughly, especially the continuity and links to the past that traditions offer.
2. Personal emotions or biases might color these accounts and observations; however, this approach nevertheless seemed best suited for this chapter.
3. Some works (Varisco 2005; E. Brown and Baker 2006) have collected the signs and images created after Hurricane Katrina. However, these works offer little academic analysis.
4. In fact, humor and defiance pervade almost all of the Rita signs, and, as Alderman and Ward (2008) note, a piece of hurricane graffiti often contains more than one type of discourse.
5. This chapter cannot address every aspect of these signs' visual presentation. The visual portion of the humor of these signs is lost when one cannot see the image: line breaks, capitalization, text size and color, and other factors add texture to the message.
6. During Hurricane Ike, the same establishment put up a sign that read, "Still ARMED & DRUNK."
7. For a discussion on the important use of narrative after a disaster, see Bendix 1990.
8. A year after the storm, Cameron Parish also erected a monument to commemorate the caskets unearthed by Rita and the many possessions lost. Even though no Cameron residents were killed by the storm, they understood that the loss of possessions spawned disillusionment and symbolized an unknowable future. The trauma of this loss, they concluded, deserved a memorial.
9. I thank Marcia Gaudet for pointing out Honoré's importance as a folk hero. I thank Nick Spitzer for pointing out the importance of the trail ride as a cultural symbol and its use after Hurricane Rita.

REFERENCES

Alderman, Derek H., and Heather Ward. 2008. "Writing on the Plywood: Toward an Analysis of Hurricane Graffiti." *Coastal Management* 36.1 (January): 1–18.

Badeaux, Corliss. 2008. Interview. 27 August.
Barry, Don. 2006. "The Road Back: Battered Parish, Officials Bear the Brunt of Neighbors' Anguish." *New York Times*, June 20, A12.
Bendix, Regina. 1990. "Reflections on Earthquake Narratives." *Western Folklore* 49.4 (October): 331–47.
Blevins, Alison, and Jacob Blevins. 2005. Interview. 15 November.
Brown, Eric Harvey, and Lori Baker, eds. 2006. *Signs of Life: Surviving Katrina*. Jersey City: Brown and Baker.
Brown, Steven. 2005. Personal interview. 28 December.
"Cameron Parish: The Long Road Back." 2006. *Lagniappe*, January 5.
Dundes, Alan. 1987a. "At Ease, Disease: AIDS Jokes as Sick Humor." *American Behavioral Scientist* 30.1 (January–February): 72–81.
———. 1987b. *Cracking Jokes: Studies of Sick Humor Cycles and Stereotypes*. Berkeley, Calif.: Ten Speed.
Edwards, Jay, Fred Kniffen, and Glen Pitre. 1991. "Settlement and Society." In *Cajun Country*, eds. Barry Jean Ancelet, Jay Edwards, and Glen Pitre, 19–32. Jackson: University Press of Mississippi.
Fialkova, Larisa. 2001. "Chernobyl's Folklore: Vernacular Commentary on Nuclear Disaster." *Journal of Folklore Research* 38.3 (September–December): 181–204.
Freud, Sigmund. 2002. *Jokes and Their Relation to the Unconscious*. London: Penguin.
Hagen, Carol A., M. G. Ender, K. A. Tiemann, and C. O. Hagen. 1999. "Graffiti on the Great Plains: A Social Reaction to the Red River Valley Flood of 1997." *Applied Behavioral Science Review* 7.2:145–58.
Kuipers, Giselinde. 2005. "'Where Was King Kong When We Needed Him?' Public Discourse, Digital Disaster Jokes, and the Functions of Laughter after 9/11." *Journal of American Culture* 28.1 (March): 70–84.
Lindsay, Jack. 1960. *The Writing on the Wall: An Account of Pompeii in Its Last Days*. London: Muller.
Malinowski, Bronislaw. 1994. "The Problem of Meaning in Primitive Language." In *The Meaning of Meaning: A Study of the Influence of Language upon Thought and of the Science of Symbolism*, ed. C. K. Ogden and I. A. Richards, 296–336. London: Routledge.
Oring, Elliott, ed. 1984. *Humor and the Individual*. Los Angeles: California Folklore Society, 1984.
———. 1987. "Jokes and the Discourse on Disaster." *Journal of American Folklore* 100.397 (July–September): 276–86.
———. 2003. *Engaging Humor*. Urbana: University of Illinois Press.
Reed, Daniel. 2009. Personal interview. 18 January.
Santino, Jack. 1994. *All around the Year: Holidays and Celebrations in American Life*. Urbana: University of Illinois Press.
Stein, Mary Beth. 1989. "The Politics of Humor: The Berlin Wall in Jokes and Graffiti. *Western Folklore* 48.2 (April): 85–108.
Stocker, Terrance L., Linda W. Dutcher, Stephen M. Hargrove, and Edwin A. Cook. 1972. "Social Analysis of Graffiti." *Journal of American Folklore* 85.338 (October–December): 356–66.
Tanzer, Helen. 1939. *The Common People of Pompeii: A Study of the Graffiti*. Baltimore: Johns Hopkins University Press.
Varisco, Tom. 2005. *Spoiled: The Refrigerators of New Orleans*. New Orleans: Varisco Designs.

CONTRIBUTORS

Jay D. Edwards is a professor and the director of the Fred B. Kniffen Cultural Resources Lab in the Department of Geography and Anthropology at Louisiana State University. His research centers on folklore and vernacular architecture in the Caribbean and Louisiana. He is the coauthor (with Nicolas Kariouk) of *A Creole Lexicon: Architecture, Landscape, People* (2003) and the author of "Vernacular Vision: The Gallery and Our Africanized Architectural Landscape," in John Michael Vlach, ed., *Raised to the Trade: Creole Building Arts of New Orleans* (2002), and "Shotgun: The Most Contested House in America," *Buildings and Landscapes* (2009).

M. B. Hackler is Board of Regents Fellow at the University of Louisiana at Lafayette. He is a graduate of the Program in Arts Administration at Columbia University and is the editor of *On and Off the Page: Mapping Place in Text and Culture* (2009). He is currently completing "A Place Apart: British Travelers in the Antebellum American South."

Keagan LeJeune is an associate professor of folklore and English at McNeese State University. His interests include Louisiana folklore, Louisiana's neutral strip, outlaw legends, and hunting narratives. He has served as president of the Louisiana Folklore Society and is a member of the American Folklore Society. He has published several articles on Louisiana folklore. His book on an outlaw in Louisiana's neutral strip will be published by the University of North Texas Press and the Texas Folklore Society in 2010.

Benjamin Morris is currently a doctoral candidate in the Department of Archaeology at the University of Cambridge, where his research focuses on the relationship between culture and the environment. He is co-convenor of the Cultures of Climate Change Research Group at the Centre for Research in the Arts, Social Sciences and Humanities. His poetry and prose have been published widely in the United States and the United Kingdom.

CONTRIBUTORS

Jeffrey Schwartz is an urban planner and the director of a community development corporation in New Orleans. His interests include American pragmatism, *flaneurie*, street art, sustainable community development, land reclamation, critical geography, and web mashups.

Peter G. Stillman is a professor of political science at Vassar College. He has also taught in the Environmental Studies Program and the American Culture Program. His research examines issues of democracy, justice, the relation of the individual to the community, utopian thought, and environmental issues. He is the coauthor (with Adelaide Villmoare) of "Social Justice after Katrina: The Need for a Revitalized Public Sphere," in *Through the Eye of Katrina: Social Justice in the United States*, ed. Kristin A. Bates and Richelle S. Swan (2007).

Adelaide H. Villmoare is a professor of political science at Vassar College, where she has also taught in the American Culture Program. Her research addresses the politics of rights, feminism and rights, the death penalty, and public and private policing. She is the coauthor (with Peter G. Stillman) of "Social Justice after Katrina: The Need for a Revitalized Public Sphere," in *Through the Eye of Katrina: Social Justice in the United States*, ed. Kristin A. Bates and Richelle S. Swan (2007) and is the author of "Policing and the Politics of Public and Private in Post Katrina New Orleans," *Studies in Law, Politics, and Society* (2007).

W. D. Wilkerson is a doctoral candidate in English at the University of Louisiana at Lafayette. Her major focus is folklore, and her major research interests in this field are personal narratives, religion, and folklore in literature. She is currently completing "Italy as Palimpsest: Twenty-first Century American Women's Travel Writing on Tuscany."

INDEX

Page numbers appearing in *italics* indicate an illustration.

Absolut New Orleans, 101
Adorno, Theodor, 9
African Americans: food access and, 107, 119, 135; in New Orleans, 18, 19, 22, 36n4, 44, 45, 47, 48, 50, 55–56, 60, 83, 108, 119; post-Katrina, 44, 60, 107; shotgun houses and, 55–56, 57, 83
Airiess, Christopher A., 130–31
Alanen, Arnold R., 141
Alderman, Derek, 168, 171
Allen, Howard, 121
American Planning Association, 21
Anderson, Brett, 98
Anderson, Walter, 4
Angelo Brocato's Italian Ice Cream Parlor, 96
Antoine's, 97, 116
Army Corps of Engineers, 35, 144, 148
Arnaud's, 97
Arnold, Matthew, 13
Association of Cultural Economics and the Center for Urban Studies, 7
Atakapa-Ishak tribe, 153

Barthélémy Lafon survey, 65, 66
Baumgartner, Eric, 122–23
Beacon of Hope, 129
Beausoleil, 97
Begue's, 116
Bender, Harvey, 22, 23
Bereson, Ruth, 12
Beriss, David, 95, 96
Besh, John, 131

Bingler, Steven, 27
Blakeley, Edward, 124, 132, 133
Blanco, Kathleen, 25
Bohemia revetment site, 146
Boudreaux, Dwayne, 123
Boyer, Christine, 94
Briggs, Asa, 14
Bring New Orleans Back (BNOB), 18, 24, 33, 37n9, 140; Cultural Committee of, 11–12, 97; Urban Planning Committee of, 21–23
Broadmoor Improvement Association, 24, 26, 38n15
Broad Street Market, 130
Brookings Institution, 95
Brooks, Rick, 101
Brown Derby, 117
Bruno, Joe, 93
Buckner, Ed, 123
Burdeau, Cain, 156
Burrwood facility, 143, 148–51, 158, 159
Bush, George W., 17, 20–21, 162

Cable, George Washington, 114
Café du Monde, 116
Calcasieu Parish, 166, 170, 171, 175
Cameron Parish, 166, 170, 171, 175, 178, 184, 185
Campanella, Richard, 45, 49, 85n2
Canizaro, Joseph, 21, 22, 23, 37n10, 37n12
Caplin, Pat, 101
cast iron stoves, 78–80
Central Grocery Company, 116
Charles, Ray, 117
Chase, Leah, 95
Christovich, Mary Lou, 51

INDEX

Circle Food Store, 108, 122, 133
Citrus Lands project, 143, 144, 146, 158
Civitello, Linda, 95
Clawson, David L., 130–31
CNN, 169
Coalition Against Demolition, 31
Coates, Geoff, 133
Cochon, 100
Codrescu, Andrei, 14, 83, 96, 102
Commander's Palace, 97
Comprehensive Statewide Historic Preservation Plan, 148
Cook, Michael, 92, 93, 103
Cowen, Scott, 37n10
creative industries, 9
Creole cottage, *50*, *51*, *52*, *63*, *73*; gable-sided, 51–52; linear form, *54*; maisonette form, 52, *53*. *See also* shotgun houses
Crescent City Farmers Market, 133–34
cultural landscapes, 141–42
cultural policy: defined, 5, 6, 140; economics and, 7–12; Gulf Coast and, 5–6; history of, 6–7
culture, 12–13, 145–46

Dakin, Charles, *74*
Dakin, James, 55
Danzey, Sheila, 23–24
Danzey-Lambert Neighborhood Rebuilding Plan, 124
Davis, Mike, 17
Dixie Beer, 91–94, *92*
Dooky Chase, 95–96, 102, 103
double side-gallery cottage, *77*
Dr. John, 97
Duane Street Church, *74*
Duany, Andres, 37n9

Edwards, Jay D., 14–15
Elie, Lolis Eric, *Faubourg Tremé: The Untold Story of Black New Orleans*, 36n4
Eliot, T. S., 13
Empire Oil Field No. 1, 144
Erickson, Marie K., 121
erosion/subsidence, 47, 141, 142, 148, 149, 150, 151, 155, 162
ethnography, 151–52, 156–57

Farley, Tom, 27
Federal Emergency Management Agency (FEMA), 17
Festival New Orleans, 97
Fialkova, Larisa, 168
Fielkow, Arnie, 125
Fitzmorris, Tom, 97, 99
food access: African Americans and, 107, 119, 135; attempts to address, 121–26; automobiles and, 118–19; economics and race and, 119, 135; in emergencies, 126; government failures in, 132–34; post-Katrina, 120–21, 123–26, *125*; pre-Katrina, 119–26
Food Policy Advisory Committee (FPAC), 122–23, 125, 132
Fort Jackson Vicinity project, 143, 144, 146, 158
Fortune Magazine, 33
French Market, 113, 116, 123
Freret Market, *129*, 133
Freud, Sigmund, 168
Frey, William, 85n1
Friends of Cabildo, New Orleans Architecture Series, 48, 60

Gallier, James, 55
Gambit Weekly, 91
Gilligan, Johanna, 124
Gladney, Greta, 128, 130, 133
Grand Bayou, 141, 152; cultural landscape of, 157; cultural policy and, 159; economy of, 154–55; erosion/subsidence in, 155; ethnography in, 156–57; history of, 153–54; Native Americans in, 157; post-Katrina, 156; preservation in, 157–58
Grand Bayou Families United, 155
Green Charter School, 121
Gretna Market, *127*
Gulf Coast: cultural policy and, 5–6, 9, 11–12; culture of, 4, 14
gumbo, 99–100

Haitian refugees, 66, 67
Haitian Revolution, 57, 62
Haitian style cottage, *57*. *See also ti-kay* houses

190

INDEX

Hartman, Sandy, 155
Hastert, Dennis, 17–18
Heard, Malcolm, 51, 59
Heiner Brau Brewery, 91–92
Hesmondhough, David, 9
Historic American Buildings Survey (HABS), 61
holiday celebrations/decorations, modification of, 118, 169, 176–82, *179*, *180*
Hollywood, Louisiana, 148
"Holy Angels" Market, *128*
Holy Cross Neighborhood Association, 22
Honoré, Russel L., 183
Horkheimer, Max, 9
Horne, Jedidiah, 24
Houma tribe, 153, 157
Housing Authority of New Orleans (HANO), 29, 30–31, 32, 34, 35, 39n21
humor, 168
Hurricane Audrey, 170, 184
hurricane graffiti, 168
Hurricane Gustav, *184*, 184–85
Hurricane Ike, 184
Hurricane Isadore, 155
Hurricane Katrina: African Americans and, 44, 48, 60, 107; aftermath of, 5, 17, 18–19, 20–21, 25, 33–34, 139, 153, 155, 160, 169; culinary industry and, 92, 94, 96–97, 98–99, 100–1, 102; cultural policy and, 12; economy and, 83–84; food access and, 107, 108–9, 111, 112, 119, 120–21, 123–26, *125*, 131, 133, 134, 135–36; holiday traditions and, 118; public housing and, 29–31, 32; signage and, 171
Hurricane Lily, 155
Hurricane Rita: aftermath of, 4–5, 166, 169, 174–75; arts and crafts in response to, 183; as a benchmark, 184; legacy of, 3–4; modified holiday celebrations/decorations in, 169, 176–82, *179*, *180*; preparation for, 170; signage in response to, 170–76, *173*; stress related to, 169–70

J & M Recording Studio, 117
James Beard Foundation, 97, 98
Jean Lafitte National Park, 152

Katrina. *See* Hurricane Katrina
Katz, Cindi, 3–4
Kingsley, Karen, 51
K-Paul's, 100
Kuiper, Giselinde, 168
K-Ville, 99–100

Lafon, Barthélémy, 65
Lagasse, Emeril, 96
Lake Charles: Hurricane Katrina evacuation and, 169; Hurricane Rita aftermath in, 169–70; hurricane signage in, 173–74, *175*; modified holiday celebration/decorations in, 177, 179–81
Lake Charles American Press, 183–84
Lakeview Civic Improvement Association, 129
Lakeview Market, 129, *130*
Lambert, Paul, 23–24
Lambert Plan, 23–25, 31–32, 33
Landrieu, Mitch, 10, 11, 12, 160, 161
Laska, Shirley, 155
LeJeune, Keagan, 15
Les Cayes, *58*
Lewis, Jerry Lee, 117
Lewis, Pierce, 45
Lincoln, Rod, 153
linear cottages, *73*; Appentis Cottage, 62–63, *64*, *78*; Camelback, 78–82, *81*, *82*; defined, 61–62; double maisonette, 70–73, *71*, *72*; Gable-Fronted Single, 73–75; history of, 63–82; North Shore House, 77–78; Shanties and Cabanes, 65–69; single maisonette, 69–70. *See also* shotgun houses
Link, Donald, 100
Little Richard, 117
Logsdon, Dawn, *Faubourg Tremé: The Untold Story of Black New Orleans*, 36n4
Louisiana: Where Culture Means Business, 140, 160–61
Louisiana Cajun Prairie, 4
Louisiana Comprehensive Statewide Historic Preservation Plan, 143, 157
Louisiana Department of Culture, Recreation and Tourism, 10, 11, 97, 160, 161, 162

INDEX

Louisiana Division of Historic Preservation, 142, 143, 148, 150–51, 152, 158, 159
Louisiana Division of the Arts, *Louisiana: Where Culture Means Business*, 10–11
Louisiana Folklife Program, 153, 159
Louisiana Office of Cultural Development, 10
Louisiana Public Health Institute, 122
Louisiana Rebirth, 140, 161, 162
Louisiana Recovery Authority (LRA), 24, 25
Louisiana Regional Folklife Program, 152, 153
Lundgren, Justin, 101

Mandina's, 98
Mann, Charles C., 33
Mardi Gras Zone, 120–21
Marigny, Bernard de, 77
maroons, 59, 86n7
Marsalis, Wynton, 13
Martin Luther King Jr. Middle School (Berkeley, Calif.), 121
Matassa, Cosimo, 117
Matassa's Market, 117
Maylie's, 116
Mayo, James M., 118
McCarthy, Richard, 128
McGuigan, Jim, 8, 9
McNeese State University, 174–75, 183
McNulty, Ian, 91–92, 96, 98, 100
Meal, Ready to Eat (MRE), 100
Melnick, Robert Z., 141
Michel Fortier cottage, 69
Miller, Tony, 5
Molly's at the Market, 96
Morial, Mark, 23
Morris, Benjamin, 15
Mt. Auburn Associates, 10, 160–61
Myerscough, John, *Economic Importance of the Art in Britain*, 7–8

Naghi, Benny, 120
Nagin, Ray, 11, 17, 21, 24, 27–28, 34, 35, 133
Nathan, Jeanne, 161
National Association for the Advancement of Colored People, 23
National Endowment for the Arts (NEA), 6
National Endowment for the Humanities (NEH), 6

National Park Service, 157–58
National Public Radio, 120
National Register of Historic Places, 144
Nee, Brendan, 24
neighborhood/public markets: defined, 109–10; development of, *109*, *112*; economic effects of, 129; failures of, 131–32; history of, 113–16, 118; post-Katrina, 123–24; roles of, 111; societal effects of, 115, 127–28; symbolic aspects of, 130–31
New Orleans: African Americans in, 18, 19, 22, 36n4, 44, 45, 47, 48, 50, 55–56, 60, 83, 108, 119; Audubon neighborhood of, 50; brand identity of, 94; Broadmoor neighborhood of, 33, 37n9; Carrolton neighborhood of, 50; conflicting visions for, 19–20; culinary industry recovery in, 98, 99, 100; culinary tourism in, 94; cultural policy and, 11–12; culture of, 4; demographics of, 19; erosion/subsidence in, 162; Garden District of, 49, 50, 75; Gert Town neighborhood of, 50; Island District of, 49; Lafitte neighborhood of, 31–32; Lakeview neighborhood of, 22, 38n15, 120, 129; Lower Ninth Ward of, 22, 23, 27, 28, 38n15, *45*; Mid-City district of, 50; New Orleans East neighborhood of, 28; post-Katrina planning for, 21–22, 23; public housing in, 29–31, 32, 33; public participation in planning for, 19–20, 22–23, 24, 25, 26, 32, 34, 35; race in, 44, 45, 47–48, *47*, 60; rebuilding proposals for, 17; recovery and politics in, 84–85; recovery and race in, 85n1, 85n2, 85n5; recovery funding for, 26, 27, 34; restaurants and bars in recovery of, 96; right of return to, 18, 27–28, 29, 30, 36n1; "Shotgun Crescent" of, *46*; shotgun houses in, 50, 60; Sixth Ward of, 31–32; topography of, 46–47, *46*; Tremé neighborhood of, 31–32, 33, 108. *See also* Bring New Orleans Back; food access; Hurricane Katrina; Lambert Plan; linear cottages; Unified New Orleans Plan
New Orleans Community Support Foundation, 25
New Orleans Food and Farm Network, 124

New Orleans Office of Recovery and Development Administration (ORDA), 124, 133
New Orleans Rebirth, 11
New Orleans Times-Picayune, 23, 27, 37n9, 98, 102
Nossiter, Adam, 96, 102

Office of Recovery Management, 124
Oring, Elliott, 168
Otte, Marlene, 101

Parker, Carolyn, 22, 23
People's Hurricane Relief Fund, 36n1
phatic conversation, 167
Philadelphia Food Trust, 122
Phillippon cottage, *71*
Phillips Myrtle, 156
Piazza, Tom, *City of Refuge*, 101–2
Pierhead Wines, 92–93
Pine, John, 155
plaçage, 68–69
Plaquemines Parish: cultural landscapes in, 148; cultural policy and, 143, 158, 159–60; culture of, 140–41; environmental degradation of, 141, 161; environmental restoration of, 161; ethnography in, 152; historic preservation in, 147–48. *See also* Burrwood facility; Citrus Lands project; Empire Oil Field No. 1; Fort Jackson Vicinity project; Grand Bayou; Point Pleasant Camp
Point Pleasant Camp, 144
Policy Guide on Community and Regional Food Planning, 134–35
Preserving Cultural Landscapes in America, 141
private grocers, 114, 116–17, 118, 119
Professor Longhair, 117
Prudhomme, Paul, 100

quadroons, 68

Rebirth Brass Band, 97
Reeves, Sally K., 51, 59, 116
Renaissance Project, 128
Reyes, Dwight, Sr., 156

Rita. *See* Hurricane Rita
Road Home program, 20, 35, 37n5, 129
Roadmap for Change, 140, 160
Rockefeller Foundation, 21, 25
Rodrigue, George, 4
Rose, Chris, 99–100
Ruffins, Kermit, 97
Russell, Gordon, 23

Santino, Jack, 169
Save America's Wetlands, 161
Scarabin, Ida Mae, 152
Schwartz, Jeffery, 15
Second Harvest, 120
SeedCo, 121
shotgun houses, 54, 55, 56, 74, 75, 76, 79; African Americans and, 55–56, 57, 83; African Origins theory of, 55–59; Camelback, 80, 82; and Creole cottages, 55–56; database of, 61; defined, 51; density of in New Orleans, 60–61; double, 70; in the Garden District, 75; in New Orleans, 50; politics and, 59–61; standard history of, 51, 52, 55–56, 59–61. *See also* Creole cottage; linear cottages
Snow, John W., 17
Southern Food and Beverage Museum, 98–99
Stillman, Peter G., 14
Strom, Elizabeth, 7
Survivor's Village, 29–30
Sutton, David, 95, 96
Sylve, Kim, 155
Sylve, Paul, Jr., 153, 154, 156
Sylve, Rachel, 153, 154

Thomas, Oliver, 102
Thorsby, C. D., *Economics of the Performing Arts*, 7
ti-kay houses, 57, 58–59, *58*, 61, 70
Toledano, Roulhac, 51, 86n6; *National Trust Guide to New Orleans*, 48
Tropical Storm Bill, 155
Trudeau, Carlos, 65
Tujagues, 116
Tulane School of Public Health and Tropical Medicine, 122

INDEX

United New Orleans Plan (UNOP), 25–28, 31–32, 38n13, 38n15, 124
United States, cultural policy in, 6–7
United States Department of Housing and Urban Development, 29, 30–31, 34, 35, 38n17, 39n19, 39n21
Urban Conservancy, 133
Urban Land Institute, 21
Urban Planning Committee, 22–23

Valerie Boisdoré v. Le Negre Esprit, 66
Vietnamese market, 130, *131*
Vieux Carré Square, *67*
Villmoare, Adelaide H., 14
Vlach, John Michael, 57–59
Vogt, Loyd, 49

Ward, Heather, 168, 171
Ware, Carolyn, 142

Waters, Alice, 121
Waters, Maxine, 36n1
Weiss, Ellen, 51
White, Michael, 14
Wilkerson, W. D., 15
Williams, Raymond, 13, 14
Willie Mae's Scotch House, 102
Wilson, Sam, Jr., 51
Withers, G. A., *Economics of the Performing Arts*, 7
Woiseri, Bouqueto de, *57*, 66
Wood, A. Baldwin, 117
Woodland levee, 146
Works Progress Administration, 115
World War II, 148, 149, 150, 152, 159

Yúdice, George, 5

www.ingramcontent.com/pod-product-compliance
Lightning Source LLC
Chambersburg PA
CBHW030344240426
43661CB00052B/1736